Shadow Of the Great Depression

R. Otis Baker

This is the author's mémoire from his
first memory until 1961.

Cover design by Arlene Baker

First edition

Copyright (C) 2021 by R. Otis Baker
Library of Congress
Copyright TXu 2-276-795

ISBN   978-1-667808116

Dedicated to my wife Arlene,
and children,
Jeff, Yvonne, Cheryl and Renee'

Preface

I was born in a farmhouse in Southeastern Carroll County Maryland on March 7, 1936, in the shadow of the great depression.

The Depression was the gorilla in the room during all discussions from my first memories. You could not escape the influence of the Depression when discussing food, shopping, job hunting, searching for clothes or finding a roof to cover your head. This was a strong factor in the first 20 years of my life.

I was also born into the Communication Business. It took me a long time to realize this fact of life. My father was working as a traveling contract lineman for the telephone companies in Maryland, Pennsylvania, and Virginia. He continued in that line of work until late 1940 when the work started to diminish. My father, Harry Otis Baker's formal education was through the third grade. My father and his brothers worked the family farm from the first weather that allowed work in the fields until the last crop was harvested in the late fall. This left 2 or 2 and a half months for school. With the short time left for formal education it was surprising that he learned to read, write, and do mathematics. While he traveled, my mother lived with friends and different family members. My mother had been married at age 22 and had a son, GuyFred from that marriage. She was divorced from her first husband after a few years and was raising my older brother as a single mother when she started seeing my father. This was difficult during the depression. My father was in his mid-twenties, and 4 years younger than my mother. When they started going together, they could not get married because her mother Mignonette Hobbs did not approve of my father's background, he came from dirt poor farmers.

When my father passed away at age 86, my wife Arlene and I were left with the charge of sorting through a lifetime of boxes and mementos in my parents 'house as we prepared to move my mother to assisted living. Arlene and I could not take her in because we lived and worked in Chile at that time. My younger brother had a very sick in-law living with him and his wife was not well. My older brother was widowed and had recently remarried. With a new wife it would not have worked out to have our mother move in with them. They needed privacy to create a solid marriage. Assisted living was the best choice considering all our situations.

This was a very difficult decision for my brothers and me.

My mother took in many family members over the years. We always seemed to have an uncle, aunt, cousin, or grandparent living with us as we grew up. But circumstances and times change, and this was not possible for any of the three of us.

My parents never threw away anything that they received in the mail. We found electric bill receipts from the 1930s, service records for automobiles from 1935 going to recent dates. Canceled checks, property tax bills, every birthday card either of them received in 60 years. Many birthday and Christmas cards had money in them that my mother had not removed. 1-, 2- and 5-dollar bills. The most interesting documents we discovered were a pair of nearly identical marriage certificates. You had to read them carefully to discover the difference between them. The oldest was dated January 29, 1934. The certificate was from The Howard County clerk of the court in Ellicott City, Maryland. The certificate assured that on that day he had joined in holy matrimony Harry Otis Baker of Marriottsville Maryland to Sylvia Elizabeth Hayne of Baltimore Maryland.

One of my mother's four sisters, Audrey, everyone knew her as Mickey, had been a witness and another person I did not know was the second witness. Neatly rolled up with this document was the second marriage certificate. The only difference was that the second was dated January 29, 1935, and my aunt Mickey who signed in 1934 signed along with a different woman, unknown to me.

I went to my brother Guy and asked him to explain what this meant. Guy who was nine years old when I was born knew everything that went on but did not volunteer much of it to me unless I asked.

Guy said that the whole family was terrified of getting on the wrong side of my grandmother, Minnie. So, my parents were married without Minnie's knowledge and kept it from her for a year.

The War Years

In 1940 my parents were renting a house from my father's sister and her husband. The house was built on an acre of land that my grandfather had divided off his farm for them. The contract work was getting harder to find so my father got a job at the Rustless Steel Mill in Baltimore and in early 1941 we moved to Baltimore so my father could be closer to work. Commuting the 30 miles to Baltimore was not practical because of cost. We rented a house on North Payson Street in West Baltimore. Our block was the last full block in Payson Street. We lived in the end house on this block. The alley on the north side of our house was behind the western most end of Riggs Avenue. Across the street, behind the western side of Payson Street was a vacant lot that stretched 150 to 200 yards to the main line of the Pennsylvania Railroad. The railroad had 4 or 5 sets of tracks at that point. Donald, my younger brother, and I were under threat of death not to go near the tracks. We were sure that if we crossed the tracks and avoided dismemberment by train we would surely be beaten to death by my father. Trains ran in both directions day and night going under the city streets 2 blocks further northeast of our house. From there they went to Pennsylvania Station in downtown Baltimore. Most of the trains were powered by electricity that they picked up from a folding device that was on the top of the locomotives. That device slid along the overhead wires. Some engines pulling railcars for local industry located on rail sidings that lacked electrical overhead wires were still steam powered.

My mother's parents lived on the next street to the east of Payson, Appleton Street.

My grandmothers back yard was just across the alley and 2 yards down from our yard. I remember the family listening to the news's announcement about the Jap attack on Pearl Harbor on Sunday December 7th, 1941. We had a tall wooden Philco radio in the Parlor. I would listen to my weekday Serials on it every afternoon. There was "Jack Armstrong, All American Boy" and weekly radio shows like "The Shadow". News has never been the same since Lowell Thomas stopped reporting the news. I was so impressed with Lowell Thomas that we named our son, Jeffery Lowell Baker.

Catholic School in the 1940s

I started school in the first grade at St Gregory's Catholic school soon after we got settled. Saint Gregory's was 12 city blocks from our house. My brother Donald who is 3 years younger than me, started school a couple years later than I did. I walked to and from school every day. There were several boys in my class at St. Gregory's that lived within a block or two of our houses, we usually walked to school together. Sunshine, rain, snow, bitter cold there was no choice except to walk. But you learned, or else.

There was one Sister, (Teacher) per grade. That sister taught all subjects. First subject was always Catechism. The only way to get out of that was to be an Alter boy and be involved with a funeral or some event at the church next door. Next class was English, then Mathematics, then lunch. After lunch, was History, Geography and then Science. There was a 15-minute recess in the morning and another in the afternoon. Lunch was 30 minuets. There was no cafeteria, you carried a brown bag. You could buy a small container of milk for a couple cents. There was no candy or junk food in the school. But you learned. Children paid attention or got a smack on the hand with a ruler to direct their focus in the correct direction. Children knew that the Sisters opinion would always be accepted over your option by your parents. The playground was covered with the toughest fist sized stone and road tar known to man. When you fell on this surface you were sure to tear clothes and draw blood. When I tore my pants, I dreaded going home because I knew I would get a serious thrashing from my father to top off the despair I had to live within my mother's eyes as she tried to figure where she would get money for a new pair of long pants for me. But running is what boys do when let outside!

A Lesson In Morals

There is one episode that I remember vividly from those days. My mother kept a small jar in the kitchen closet with loose change in it. There were pennies, nickels, dimes but I don't remember seeing a quarter in the jar. There was a small corner grocery store at the north end of the alley behind our house. The store faced Riggs Avenue. The owners lived above the store, and they had a variety of canned goods, cereals, candy and such. No meats only a few vegetables. Of course, they sold cigarettes. They were sold by the pack and separately. You know, 2 cents for a cigarette. Occasionally my mother would ask me to run up to the store and get a box of something or a couple carrots. She would go to the jar and retrieve a few nickels and dimes and with them in hand I would go to the store. This activity imprinted on me that the money in the jar would get things from the store. I was home alone one day and decided that I wanted some candy. I was probably 6 years old at the time. I went to the cabinet and opened the jar and dug out some coins and went to the store. I walked into the store went to the candy display and selected several pieces of candy. The Store owner told me the price and I opened my hand to let him select the proper coins to cover the transaction. I went home and thought about how easy that had been to satisfy my desire for candy. A short time later I thought that I would go buy some more candy. On the third trip to the store the Owner asked me if my mother knew I was buying candy? I said no. I knew better than to lie to a adult. He told me he could not sell me anymore candy. I went home feeling sure that I would hear more about this activity when my mother came home. Sure enough, the store owner called my mother on the phone and explained what had transpired that afternoon. My mother waited until my father came home to review the complete story at the dinner table with my younger brother Donald there to watch how the Spanish Inquisition was administered in Otis Baker's Realm. My father explained that I had stolen mother's money and the punishment for stealing was just short of death. I was ordered to the basement and Otis followed me and after he found a suitable piece of scrap wood, I was given a good whipping of the behind. I made other trips to the basement over the years we lived in Baltimore, but in general Donald and I were good boys.

Streetcar Driver

My father changed jobs a year or so after we moved to Baltimore. He hired onto Baltimore Transit Company. The system was served by Streetcars that ran on steel tracks laid in the streets. They were powered by electricity that was collected by a sliding device that was attached to a spring-loaded arm mounted to the top of the car. The device picked up Electricity and carried it through wires to the controller operated by the streetcar operator then to the car's motor. The controller had a large heavy handle that set loosely on its top. The handle was rotated forward or backward to move the car in either direction on the tracks. When the Motorman left his seat for any reason, he lifted the heavy handle off the controller and took the handle with him so no one could operate the car while he was away from the driver's seat. Fares were collected in a fare box beside the door. Passenger dropped the nickels and dimes in the glass top box and the motorman could see that you paid the fare, he would periodically move a leaver and all the change would fall into the change box on the bottom of the collection box. The most trouble that motormen had when operating the car by themselves, without the aid of a Conductor was for kids to approach the stopped car and yank the spring-loaded rope that was used to pull the power pick up arm down off the catenary wires. The car could not get electricity to operate then. The object was to get the motorman to abandon the driving station to replace the trolly on the overhead wires. While the motorman was walking on the outside of the car to the back to reset the trolly, the young gangster would run to the front of the car and attempt to steal the fares from the fare box. This did not work when the motorman was Harry Otis Baker. He always grabbed the heavy handle off the controller as he started to the back of the car. When he returned to the door of the streetcar, he would meet the young punk trying to remove the fare box or leave the car usually without the fare box and the last thing that the punk would remember for the next 30 minutes was the 15-pound controller handle connecting with his skull. My father was very strong, having done manual labor most of his life. He did not like a Thief! He would usually be required to appear in court to face the young crook and describe the confrontation for the Judge. The results were always jail time for the would-be robber.

The newer transit lines were served by Electric buses. They did not use tracks, but drove like regular buses with internal combustion engines, except they were power by electric motors. The electricity was transmitted to the buses just like power to the street cars thru an overhead catenary and a trolly pole array. The main difference between the buses and the street cars was the need to provide a return path for the electricity. This was provided by having 2 wires in the trolly wire. The streetcars only needed one wire since the electricity could return to the generating source thru the grounded rails. The buses also were steered like cars but could not move farther from the overhead catenary than the trolly would allow or they were without power.

My mother worked at different stores in downtown Baltimore. She tried to get hours that let her get home about the time that Donald and I got home from school.

No One Wanted To Steal Kids

My mother trusted me to carry the rent money downtown every month. It was an hour's round trip, and she was busy. She gave me an envelope that contained the rent money in cash. I have no idea how much it was. I would not dare open the envelope to count the contents. With the envelope deep in my pocket I walked 3 blocks east to Fulton Avenue and waited for a # 1 streetcar. I had exact change and I may have asked for a return slip or something like that as I boarded the trolly. The # 1 went down to the intersection of Eutaw and Fayette streets where I got off the trolly. I crossed Fayette to the north side and entered the building on the corner, rode the elevator to the 4th floor and entered an office. I gave the envelope to the woman at the counter, and she gave me a receipt. I retraced my steps to the Streetcar and rode it back to Riggs Avenue and Fulton, got off the trolly and walked back to our house. I was 8 years old. Life was very different back then. Generally, people, including kids were safe on the streets of large cities. People were not influenced by terrible behavior they observed on TV (No TV) or the movies (They had a Code of Conduct they adhered to)

Kids learned from their parents and their parents behaved or went to Jail. Such novel ideas have been forgotten.

Crime Strikes Home

I remember a very unpleasant event that occurred while we were on one of our weekend trips to Carrol County. We arrived home in early evening and as soon as my father got to the front door, he stopped us and said someone has broken into our house. Go back and get in the car while I look through the house to see if they are still here. My father was all man, he did not fear anyone. After he had searched the house, we were allowed to enter. Whoever had robbed us probably had most of the day to do it. We called the police, and they took a report but there was little they could do. The crook had taken my father's shot gun and ammunition, a small amount of money my mother had saved in a tea pot in the kitchen cabinet, and some other small personal items. They always thought that a near-do-well teenager who lived down the block was the criminal, it could not be proven. We were very careful from then until we moved back to Carroll County when we left the house for any period of time. I personally felt violated and have always held thieves in very low esteem since then.

Television

Sometime in 1947 a person living on Riggs Avenue a block and a half from our house was reported to have bought a device that displayed moving pictures on the front of it. It was called a Television set or a TV. We had heard people talk about TV but none of us has seen a 'TV'. A couple of us boys walked up to the front of the house that we thought had the TV. It must have been the correct house because there were several people standing in front of the window and looking through the window. glass. They were looking in on these peoples living room and they were peeking around a crack at the end of the curtains where they could see a portion of the TV screen. I think the homeowners left a crack there to show off their new treasure to curious neighbors. Sure, enough you could see fussy people like images moving on the bright white screen. We could not hear any talk or music, but this was something to keep an eye on. A few weeks later my mother took Donald and I downtown and we saw a better demonstration of this TV thing at one of the Department Stores.

We did not get a TV for our house until 1953. But we survived.

Segregation

Life in the city was generally good. Baltimore was segregated at that time, but there was not much trouble between the races or the ethnic enclaves. There was a Little Italy, A Polish section, a German section. People wanted to live with groups they were comfortable with. When we moved to Baltimore the closest Black families were 10 blocks east of us. Saint Gregory's was on Gilmore St., and it was sort of the separation street between Black and White housing. The War and the jobs it offered to everyone put money in the black people's pockets and they wanted to get housing in the white neighborhoods. The move by the Blacks into blocks of houses previously owned by Whites was watched closely by everyone. The first white house owner to sell a house to a black family in a block that only had white owners was called a Block Buster and they were not well thought of. After the first house went the prices of the rest of the houses in that block fell and soon the block was all Black. My parents were not prejudice against blacks, but they longed to return to the country. My parents talked about going back to Carroll County often. My brother and I got along with the black kids that moved into our neighborhood.

I had a next-door black friend, Norman, who I played with every day. I would invite him to come home with me for lunch and my mother would fix us sandwiches.

I remember her kidding with Norman once while we were washing our hands in the kitchen before eating. She said, "Norman how can you tell if your hands are clean"? Norman laughed and turned his hands palm up to my mother and they were nearly white, and he said" Miss Baker, see my hands are clean." There was no resentment or anger in his demeanor, he was just giving a natural response.

Bike Trip

I remember when in 1946 I asked Norman if he would like to ride his bike with me to my grandfather's farm in Carroll County and spent a night, then ride home. This was to be the first long bike trip I undertook. The distance was maybe 25 miles. He agreed to go and I told my parents of our plan and they though that it would be fine if we rode on the side of the road. I had made the trip many times in my father's car, and I was sure I knew the way. We did not try to contact my grandparents because we did not believe it would be a problem. Norman and I went over our bikes and checked that all nuts were tight, and all bearings were lubricated and on the selected Saturday we set off early in the morning. The route was to follow Edmundson Avenue to Edmondson Heights. From the top of that hill, you could see Baltimore Harbor on a clear day. Edmondson avenue was US route 40 in the city and as we continued west the road became 4 lane divided highway. This was one of the first good highways in the country. We followed route 40 for about 15 miles to Marriottsville Road. We turned right on

Marriottsville Road and followed it to
Marriottsville, there we crossed the original
B & O tracks, still in service, after 100 years. It
was only another 10 miles to my grandparents '
farm. When we arrived, we rode up to the house.
I introduced Norman as my friend and neither of
my grandparents said anything out of the ordinary
but invited us both to join them for lunch. Lunch
was the big meal of the day back then on farms.
The reason for that seemed to be the need to feed
and water the horses at mid-day and because by
Supper time it was dark much of the year and
they had no electricity to illuminate the house and
stables. After Norman and I had lunch, I showed
him around the farm. We then had a light dinner
and were bedded down on two small sofa cots at
the end of the kitchen. The next day we got on
our bikes and retraced our route back to
Baltimore.

Subsistence Farming

My grandfather's farm had expanded from the 45-acre farm he had owned for a number of years to 95 acres since my uncle John, a lifelong bachelor, had bought the adjoining farm that had come up for sale and was letting my grandparents live in the house on the new farm and farm both places as one. My uncle was at that time in the Army and doing pole line construction on the Alcan hi-way in Canada and Alaska.

The front section of the house was a log cabin. You could only tell that it started life as a log cabin if you looked under the Clapboard sheathing and examined the log construction. The main house dated back to the 1840's or 50's. The first floor of the main house was one large room. There was a front door that opened onto a front porch that overlooked the front 10 acres of the farm. A stair way on one end of the room led up to a second story that contained two bedrooms. The other end from the stairway held a nice parlor stove that heated this end of the house. A doorway in the back of the room led into a large, 16 X 25-foot kitchen/dining room. Off the far end of the room was a small, 6 X 10 pantry. The back corner of the kitchen was occupied by a very large, very old, wood burning cook stove. The stove had 2 doors for stroking a fire. There was a water tank on one end to heat water and a large oven. The stove had 6 round lift out hot plates where you could set a pot directly in the top of these holes if the pot was sized to the stove holes. The holes were also for loading wood to burn. When a front and a rear stove plate were lifted out, the center separator for these 2 stove plates could be removed and a long oblong hole was available to place pieces of wood nearly 14" long on the fire. This stove burned 7 days a week year around. The fire would be 'banked 'at night by partially closing the chimney dampener. This would reduce the air flow and slow the fire for the night. There was a doorway at the Parlor end of the kitchen that led out on the same side as the pantry to a screened porch. The door to this porch was the everyday entrance to the house. There was a table on the porch that held a couple buckets of fresh water, which were carried up the hill from the spring. The distance was 200 feet, and the height of the rise from the spring to the house was 50 feet. This house had no running water, no electricity, until 1954 and no inside toilet plumbing. The outhouse was 150 feet behind the house. It was a nice solid 2 holer. I never could understand why they made 2-hole outhouses, I certainly did not want to share the use of one with anyone I knew, no matter how nice they were. There was a box open on the top in the corner of the outhouse that contained 30 or 40 corn cobs. These were left after you ran a ear of field corn through the hand cranked corn sheller. The shelled corn was fed to the chickens, and the cobs were dry and soft for post defecation cleanup. There usually was a Sears or Wards catalog hanging on the wall for cleanup, but I preferred to take a couple sheets of several day-old newspaper to the outhouse with me. The Baltimore Sun was delivered to the paper box beside the mailbox every day. My grandfather said he only went to the third grade in school. You would not know that when having a conversation with him. He was up to date on world events, politics, commodity pricing and anything else you would query him about. I remember going up to his bedroom at night after my grandmother passed away and he would be laying on the bed reading by the light of a kerosene lamp and the pages of the paper would be dropped on the floor as he finished them. He would say something like," Them Dammed Russians, they cannot be trusted". Shame no one in Washington listened to Westly Baker.

My grandfather farmed with horses. He never drove or owned a motor vehicle. The farm had 1 Guernsey cow, she must have been 12 or 14 years old, but she produced 5 gallons of milk a day. The cow, named "Souckie" could open the pasture gate with her horns unless the gate was double latched. The grass outside of the pasture looked a little greener to her. He raised pigs and chickens and planted a large garden every year. They were Hard Scrabble farmers. There was a wonderful spring under the tallest maple tree I have ever seen. There was a small spring house over the spring. Milk, butter and other food items that needed to be kept cool were put in large porcelain crocks and set in the water. I think the temperature of the water must have been around 38- 40 degrees F year around. When we drove from Baltimore to the farm every 2 weeks during the War my mother would usually return to the city with 1 or 2 pounds of fresh churned butter and a large container of fresh milk. My Grandfather's cash crops were sweet corn for the local cannery and wheat and barley for sale. Field corn was for his stock and chickens. Since they had no electricity, there was no refrigeration or freezer to keep beef. Pork was the long-term meat they lived on. During hunting season rabbits, squirrels and game birds augmented the protein diet.

Butchering

Every Fall when the weather got a frost bite in it my grandfather would butcher 2 or 3 hogs. This was always a big production. They would set up an "A" frame 20 foot long and 8 feet high. The hogs would be shot in the head one at a time. After the hog was killed, a horse was hitched to the hog, and it was pulled from the pen to the "A" frame. The hog was then hoisted by the hind legs with a block and falls pulley to the top of the "A" Frame. The front legs would almost touch the ground. Earlier that day a fire would have been started under the largest iron kettle you have ever seen. The kettle was under one end of the hanging frame. The man most skilled at butchering would gut the hog, saving all the inerts for later processing. These parts were made into sausages, scrapple and other parts of the hog that I avoided. The hanging hog was then maneuvered down so it was over the kettle. By now the head was gone and the hog was lowered into the kettle. Then the hard work of scraping the hair and bristles would begin. After all the hogs were hung and dressed, we were done for the day. A smoky fire was keep burning under the hanging hogs until the next day. This was to keep fly's and bugs off the hogs overnight.

The next day the meat was cut into loins, hams, shoulders and bacon belly and all the cuts of a pig. The meat was rubbed with salt, then carried to the smoke house behind the farmhouse. The smoke house had beams high in the building and the cuts were hung from the beams. There was a stove that had a fire started in it. Once the fire had a good set of coals under it, green apple wood was placed on a rack high enough above the fire that it would not ignite but would smolder and smoke heavily. When the fire was going at the correct heat the smoke would leak out of every crack in the sides and roof of the little building. This fire and the green logs were kept up for a couple weeks. When the meat was cured, it would stay preserved for months and months. Before freezing weather, the bacon and small cuts would be moved to tables in the dirt floored cellar under the main house. The hams were hung from the ceiling. There was a 'root ' cellar in the corner of the main cellar for rooted vegetables, such as potatoes, carrots, turnips, and more. This was also where all the vegetables and fruits canned during the summer and fall were stored. Flour, spices, coffee, tea were about the only items a Subsistence Farmer needed to buy in those days.

Summer In The City

Baltimore was very hot in the summer. No one had air-conditioned houses. I don't think that any of the downtown stores had A/C. We were fortunate to have purchased a new General Electric refrigerator in 1940, just before we moved to Baltimore. My parents had that refrigerator for 30 years. Some people still had Ice Boxes! Not electric refrigerators. The ice for ice boxes was bought every couple days from a black man that had a horse drawn wagon loaded with blocks of ice and covered with burlap bags to slow melting. He went slowly up and down the alleys behind our houses Shouting, "ICE, Get you cold ice". Other black men, they were all referred to as "Arabis" probably because they wore cloth draped over their heads to ward off the hot sun and cold winds, sold Watermelon and vegetables from horse drawn wagons. These fellows could be heard shouting the wares they were selling all day. There was a stable in downtown Baltimore near Lexington Market that rented the wagons and horses to these enterprising men.

Summer Escape

The way that many city dwellers dealt with the unbearable heat was to leave the city during the summer. The men had to stay and work, but the women and children abandoned the city   en-mass during June, July and August. My grandmother always had a shore place. Before the war they had a trailer on a rented lot in Southern Maryland on the Chesapeake Bay. The location was Solomon's Island.

The Patuxent River ran into the bay at that location. When the war started the government took control of much of the land in that area including my grandmother's lot. The water in the river and bay was very deep for bay waters at that location. The depth ranged up to 200 feet deep. The Navy wanted a protected location to test submarines, and this seemed to meet their needs. They also built a Naval Air Station that is there till this day, Patuxent River Naval Air Station. Also known as Pax River. When she lost her summer place at Solomon's Island, she found a place in the Bay Ridge area near Annapolis. The cabin was on Lake Ogelton, just across from the Annapolis Roads Club. You could row a boat into Annapolis from her place. Fishing and crabbing were good, and it was much closer to Baltimore than Solomon's. My mother had 4 sisters. Between them they had 12 children. All the sisters and their families lived in Baltimore or close surroundings. I did not go to the shore often; I was normally sent to my grandfather's farm in Carroll County. This was fine with me since I loved the farm.

My younger brother, Duckie, went to stay with our aunt Reccie, one of my mother's sisters, in Timonium, Maryland. She had 4 boys, the youngest Carroll, being Duckie's age.

By 1943 my older brother GuyFred joined the Navy and was off fighting the war. When I was at the farm, I did small jobs for my grandfather and found plenty of time to play. Play meant killing frogs, snakes, and anything else that moved with my BB gun as I patrolled the streams of the area. When summer ended, we went back to the city.

Young Enterprise

We kids were always looking for ways to earn money. Our parents had no extra money, so if you wanted money you had to earn it. We would find scrap lumber behind business's and build wagons to ride down hills and to haul groceries for women from the Acme market to their home. There was little taxi, or private car use during the war due to gasoline rationing, so kids with wagons of all description were found outside the larger stores on Saturdays offering to carry groceries home for the shoppers who were always women.

The standard method of building a wagon was to take the nice set of Roller Skates you received for Christmas and remove the adjustment screw that held the front and back of the skate together and nail or screw the back half of the skate to a 2 X 4 about 5 foot long. Do the same thing to the other skate back then nail the 2, 2 X 4 's together with a 2 foot long 2 X 4 at both ends. The front 2 X 4 was nailed to the bottom of the long stringers. You then got a 3-foot 2 X 4 and drilled a hole in the center of this board. The diameter was of whatever size bolt you could find that was 5 inches long. The hole also went through the forward cross beam. You would then attach the front sections of your skates to the ends of the longer, bottom forward beam, facing forward. The operator (Kid) could set on a section of plywood nailed to the side beams with his feet on each end of the lower front beam to steer the wagon. The final touch to this masterpiece of home engineering was a length of clothesline tied to both ends of the front steering beam that the operator could use to steady his steering by foot as he raced down one of Baltimore's many hills at breakneck speed. The piece of line also allowed the proud owner to pull the wagon loaded with a lady's grocery boxes from the Acme store to her home for 25 cents on Saturday mornings. The downside of these homemade wagons was the speed at which the steel surface of the skate wheels wore away. When that happened the sides of the wheels collapsed, and this could create a spectacular crash. But most of us lived thru these tribulations with no more than a few more scars to explain in later years.

Pickers

Walking to school presented a lot of time to examine the contents of the gutters and surrounding sidewalks areas. Even though people were poor, they still found enough money to buy alcoholic refreshments. It seemed that the people who populated our neighborhood had a strong taste for small quantities of decent liquor, as a result we found many "Miniature" liquor bottles. These "Miniatures" were 1/10 of a fifth of liquor. They were empty replicas of the larger bottles. I thought they were cute, and I started collecting them and taking them home, washing them out, and keeping them in a series of Cigar Boxes, these were also plentiful and well made, mostly of wood. My parents never complained about my collection since it did not cost money.

Post War

My father was hired by the Chesapeake and Potomac Telephone company of Maryland in 1945. This was made possible through the help of friends who worked for C & P and had known my father, Otis Baker for years. Nepotism, the hiring of friends and relatives, was rampant at C & P. I had uncles, aunts, cousins, and later brothers who worked for the "Company". After the war my parents wanted to move back to Carroll County. My Grandfather Baker decided to give my father and his brother, Arstelo, one acre of land each, adjoining an acre he had given their older sister Adele several years before.

My father labored for 2 years to build a house on that lot satisfactory to live in. We lived hand to mouth. We had very little savings. My parents went to the Sykesville Savings and Loan Association and asked for a building loan. The Association agreed to give My parents a building loan of $4000 after they had a well and electricity on the lot. The loan money would be paid to them in amounts necessary to buy certain materials and skilled labor services. There would be regular inspections to see that the money was being spent as required.

There were many memories of the Great Depression still in people's minds when it came to lending money. The drive from Baltimore to our lot was 25 miles. My father and older brother Guy would get off work at 5:00 and drive to the lot and dig on the hole for the foundation until 10:00 PM. Then drive home, get a night's sleep, then go to work as a lineman for C & P for 8 hours.

He did those 3 nights a week then worked on the house each weekend. My Dad had a well drilled for water for a couple hundred dollars which was a lot of money in those days. He topped the well with a hand pump and the water was sweet and good. Dad finished digging the 25'X 25' foundation about the same time. He had saved the money necessary to have the power company hook up a temporary electricity service beside the foundation hole. This meant that he could now get some money from the Savings & Loan to buy some materials and hire a carpenter.

Lumberjacks

A year or so before this time my father and I (I was 10 at that time) and my older brother, had cut several Poplar and Oak trees from my grandfather's wood lot. Those logs had been hauled to a sawmill, cut into dimensional sizes, and hauled back to our lot to be used on the house. The first use of that wood was to build forms for the footings for the foundation. Johnny Zepp and his brother-in-law Jerry Durr laid the block and built the house with help from my father and anyone else he could corral. The basement was built using concrete block up to the level of the first floor. We then placed the oak joists that had been cut from the wood lot logs.

These Oak beams were so hard that you had to file a sharp point on the nails in order to drive them into the beams. From there up to the square of the second floor on the front and back of the house and to the peak on the ends of the house, the house was built from Cinder blocks. Cinder blocks were cheaper and not as strong as concrete blocks but were fine for the above grade portion of the house. There was a cellar door that open to the outside on the driveway side of the house. Like most cellar doors this one was below grade as it opened from the cellar. It opened into a covered stairway that was constructed from concrete blocks up to about 4 foot above ground level. There was a roof on the stairway that was attached to the side of the house just beneath the kitchen window. The roof extended at an angle down to the block stairwell wall. A door that laid at an angle was hinged on the side of the house and was lifted and fasten open as it laid against the house wall. This stairway was cold in the winter and was often used as a storage place for leftovers when the outside temperature was in the 30th's. We would place a tight lid on containers and set them on the steps. With the outside door closed the food was safe and refrigerated.

This was a strong, durable, but small house. The square footage of both floors was 1,050 feet. The house was declared safe to live in by my father in summer of 1948. The county did not have building inspections back then, at least not to the extent that you had to be issued a COO (Certificate of Occupancy) If that were required, we would have been sleeping in the dog houses. There was no back door yet.

We hung a very heavy canvas tarp from the top of the door frame, and it hung down to the floor.

We pushed it out of the way to walk into the kitchen. The back door did not get purchased and hung until December.

We had bottled gas for the cook stove, we heated the house with kerosene space heaters. Very unsafe! but no central heat until a coal furnace was installed in the summer of 1949.

Temperatures in central Maryland drop to 0f several times in a winter, 20's and 30's are common. Dad installed an electric water pump for running water, but no indoor toilet., got that in late 1948.

Life Is What It Is

I describe the living conditions in detail, not because I'm looking for sympathy, but to demonstrate the way things were as recently as the middle of the last century. My brothers and I have often talked about our childhood, but we all agree that we did not consider ourselves as being poor. We always had food, we had clothes and a roof over our heads. That was all you needed. There were many other people living in basements that had a tar paper roof on it to make it waterproof. These were veterans who returned from military service with enough money to get a building lot and do the same thing my father and mother were doing. Building a life based on hard work and sacrifice.

School Days

I graduated from 6th grade at St Gregory's Catholic school in June of 1948. I started 7th grade at Sykesville High School in September of 1948.

Public school was a strange place for me. Sykesville High School was as different from Saint Gregory's as I would have felt if I were transported to the surface of the moon. For starters, we left the house and walked 200 yards to the bus stop.

Yes, we were going to ride a bus to and from school. When we got to school my brother Donald, we called him Duckie, this was 1948. Walt Disney had given the world Donald Duck, so every Donald was nicknamed Duckie, walked to the elementary school that was behind the 2 story High School building which housed the 7th through 11th grades. The first thing I realized at Sykesville school was that the Catholic schools in Baltimore were well ahead of the public schools in Carroll County. I was well ahead of what was being taught at Sykesville in every subject. This created a problem that I never got around. I was bored! I found a solution that did not sit well with most of my teachers. This school had a library! I had never been in a library.

I immediately found books on travel, history, science, and all I wanted to do was read. I would sit in class and read, and the teachers would get upset with me, but anytime they asked a question about the subject being studied I would be able to answer immediately.

I was listening to the discussions going on in the class, but it was like "Deja Vue, all over again". They could not put me ahead because in some subjects I was 2 years ahead of the class. Unfortunately, Foreign Language was not something I could master.

When I graduated from high school, I had the Math and Science grades for an Academic diploma but without a Language I received a General Diploma. A couple years after I started in the 7th grade the state of Maryland decided to increase High school to 12 years.

When I was in school only a few kids went on to college. Most of us went farming on our parents' farms or got a good paying job at one of the industries in Baltimore. Many joined the military. My graduating class from Sykesville had a total of 39 students. 19 boys, 20 girls. Most of them became successful in whatever line of work they chose. One became a very successful

Surgeon; another had a career in the Air-force that led to him flying B 52 Bombers over Hanoi in the Vietnam war.

College helped, but hard work and perseveration were just as good. As luck would have it, I would be in the first class that went 12 years.

Growing Up

My cousin, Otis Oursler was born in December of 1935, and he started school a year before me. Oatie as we called him graduated a year earlier than me. He was 3 months older than me. My aunt Adele and Uncle "Putts", (Charles), Oaties' mother and father had moved to their house 2 lots up the road from our house. They had built the house before the war but rented it out until the war was over because Putts worked in Baltimore for the C & P Telephone Company and like my father could not commute during the War. Oatie and I were inseparable until we were 16. At that time, we both discovered Girls and Cars and we went our separate ways socially. There was one thing in common with Oatie and I, we both wanted to earn money so we could buy the things that boys want, but our parents could not afford to give us. There was some work for 12-year-old boys, but it was scarce. We could help our grandfather, but he did not like to have us work together on his "Nickel". He told us, "One boy is a boy, 2 boys are 'half a boy, and 3 boys are not worth a damm." The third boy was a school mate of ours, Paul Smith. Paul lived 1/2 mile across the fields from us on the Farmland of Springfield

State Mental Hospital. His father worked for the
State and lived in one of the houses the state
owned as the result of buying a farm to add to the
Hospital property. One of the problems with
working for my grandfather was he did not have a
truck or tractor for us to drive. The way that he
did every job on his farm was under the harshest
conditions. We would rather find easier work if
we could. But that was not always possible, so
we worked for him when necessary. One of the
jobs that I disliked was "picking up stones" All of
the fields in this part of the county had been
farmed hard. The fields were not 'Contoured'.
That is a plan for laying out fields that the County
Farm Agent would help a farmer with. They
would use 'Contour maps of the farm developed
by the government, and they would take a field
that was square or rectangular and had been
farmed with the rows running up and down the
hills since the first day they were farmed. That
may have been for several hundred years. And
the agent would layout strips of land 100 to 150
feet wide that followed the elevation contours of
the land. Now when it rained the water would
not run down the crop rows in the fields and carry
away much of the topsoil. The rain would be
dammed by the level rows following the
contours. The older farmers objected to this

system because they said it required more work
to plow and cultivate the irregular fields but once
they understood that the new system would save
fertilizer and seed since so much of it was not
washed away, they bought in on the plan. But the
damage caused by years of topsoil loss left many
flint stones exposed in the fields. The answer to
this for my grandfather was to harness his team of
2 horses to a device called a "Drag" and pick up
the exposed stones and 'drag 'them out to the
county road which was not paved for another 7 or
8 years. We would fill the 'ruts 'with them. This
work was probably the same as the Egyptians did
to build the Pyramids. The Drag did not have
wheels. It was built by cutting 2 logs 6 or 8
inches in diameter to a length of 10 feet. Then
one end of each log was cut in a taper of 45
degrees. The logs were placed 4 feet apart with
the long side of the taper up. The logs were
joined with 2-inch planks nailed to the logs from
front to back. An edge was placed around the
ends and sides 2 inches wide and 2 inches high.
The front of the drag had a fitting in the center to
attach a Double Tree so 2 horses could be
harnessed to pull the drag. As you can see the
device was heavy before it was loaded with
stones that ranged in size from fist size to 20 or
30 pounds. The horses pulled the Drag thru the

field, and we loaded exposed stones on it until they were near to falling off, then pulled it to the closest section of road needing repair. This was hard work in hot summer weather for 10 cents an hour.

Trapping

Our uncle Arse, who built a house between our house and Oatie's house on his 1 acre of land, was a hardcore hunter and a good trapper. Arse said he would teach us to trap and that would allow us to make a few hundred dollars a year. You put a lot of work into trapping and waited up to 6 months to get your money out of the endeavor, but it was Character Building.

We had 2 rivers and a large stream near us. The animals we trapped were Muskrats, Mink and occasionally a raccoon. Muskrats were most prevalent and worth around $3 to $5 a hide. Mink was highly desirable at $25 to $35 a hide.

You were not supposed to trap Raccoons but if they stepped into a drown trap they would drown. When I caught 'Coons I would make a hat out of the hide. You had to wait until there had been a couple of good cold weeks to trap acceptable hides. The cold weather 'set 'the fur in the hide and the hide trader could tell if the hides were trapped after the fur was 'set 'by cold weather. The biggest river near us was the North Branch of the Patapsco. The river started in northern Carroll and Baltimore counties and collected streams as it flowed southeast toward the

Chesapeake Bay. East of our homes it merged with the South branch that started in western Carroll and Howard counties. The 2 branches met near Woodstock Maryland. When we were kids, around 1947, the City of Baltimore started construction on the Liberty Dam on the North Branch of the Patapsco River. The Dam site was in the area we trapped just south of the intersection of Snowdens Creek and the North branch of the Patapsco River. We trapped this area for several winters while the dam construction was underway. The trees had been removed from the river basin and it was cleaned up very well. We caught Mink and Muskrats in this area. The last winter we trapped the basin was the winter before the dam was closed to back up water. I remember collecting our traps at the end of the season. Water was due to be backing up soon and we wanted to recover the traps that were on the east side of the river. We walked into the basin on the west side from the road that extended from Day's corner past Earl Capps farm and ran up thru the woods to the Oursler's farm. At the top of the hill in that woods was a road cut by the city that ran east to the top of the dam. You could walk down that road and watch the construction if no one chased you off. The river was not frozen, but it was very cold the day that

Oatie and I walked the west side of the river. We had 8 or 10 traps on the other side. The water was swift and cold, but I took all my clothes off and waded the river naked. I left my clothes piled on the ground and Oatie built a fire to warm me when I came back. I walked the riverbank and gathered up our traps and the Muskrats that were in them and waded back. I was freezing! I dried off with a rag we carried and redressed. As I put clothes on, I started to feel warmer, and by the time I was fully dressed I was ready to walk out of that basin for the last time. The concrete pour for the dam was continuous, and we were there checking traps at dawn many days and watched the work going on under the bright lights in the middle of all this quite

Hunting

Everyone we knew hunted back then. First day of Squirrel and Rabbit season might as well be declared a school holiday. You hunted from sunup until time to catch the school bus. Many of the kids would take their hunting clothes and shotgun to school with them on the bus. This was so you could go home with a friend and hunt with them in the woods near their homes. Your shells were in your hunting coat pockets and the gun was empty of ammunition. You would stand your gun in the corner of the coat closet in the back of your Home Room and hang your coat on a hanger in the same closet. There might be 2 or 3 other guns in the closet. No one gave any of this a second thought. Why should anyone care, we did not have a TV showing us killing and murder on and on, or movies encouraging people to kill everyone on the street.

Bounty Hunters

There were no deer in our part of Maryland in that time period. They had all been eaten during the depression. The hunters blamed the lack of rabbits, quail and pheasant on too many hawks and owls. The state of Maryland listened to hunters back then and they offered a bounty of 50 cents to be paid for every hawk and owl killed. The local barber, Happy, sold hunting and fishing licenses, so he was commissioned to pay the bounty for every hawk and owl presented to him. Now before I go any farther, I must say that in retrospect this was a very uninformed program. But when Oatie and I heard about it we were quite interested. We had explored every acre of land on the 4 farms that bordered my grandfather's farm. And more importantly we had permission to hunt and trap on those farms if we did not shoot guns near the cows, horses and farm buildings. We knew how both birds of prey hunted. They would land on any high point in a field and watch for mice, small birds and rabbits, they would then pounce on the animal and eat it. We decided that the best way to catch hawks and owls was not to go after them with a gun and waste ammunition and time, but to give them what they wanted most.

A high hunting point. We cut some 8-foot-long posts from small trees in the wood lot. The posts were about 3 inches in diameter. We nailed the chain that is attached to a # 1 steel trap to the post about 18 inches from the large end of the post. We then took the post with attached trap to a high enough spot in a nearby field that we could observe with binoculars from our houses. Some of these posts were a 1/4 to 3/8s of a mile from our houses. We dug a hole 2 foot deep with a shovel and set the pole in it. We then set the trap and placed it on the top of the post. We checked the traps from our houses with binoculars. When we caught a hawk or owl they would be hanging on the side of the post. We would take a burlap bag and a club and go to the trap and kill the bird and bag it to take to Happy. When we took the first Owl to Happy, he said that if we brought the Owls to him alive, he would give us $5 for them. We did not catch as many Owls as Hawks but that was a lot of money. We asked him what he wanted the Owls for. He said there were a lot of Crow hunters who would use an Owl staked by one leg to the ground as bait to draw crows for them to shoot. He said that Crows hate Owls because the Owls attack the Crows when they are flying.

We said we wanted the Owl returned to Happy after the Crow hunters were done with it. We wanted the bounty on the Owl. Remember we were 2, 12-year-old boys looking for money. This was a Bad program paid for by the State of Maryland. Since then, much has changed because of enlightenment. It is now against the law to kill Hawks, Owls and Crows. The Biologists found that there were many reasons for the decline in rabbits and game birds in cycles, and Hawks and Owls had very little impact on the decline.

Scrap Men

Oatie and I found out that there was a good market for scrap metal at that time. Having traipsed over several thousand acres of farmland as we trapped, hunted and just plain explored the surrounding farms we knew where there were Treasure Troves of metal. Farmers did not take their "Junk" to dumps. That would have taken time and cost money. Farmers loaded Junk on to a wagon and hauled it to a secluded corner of their farm and dumped it into a ravine. I guess they thought that it would rust away, or they would die before its presence caused a problem. We analyzed the situation and investigated the logistics of selling scrap.

The result of this study was that there was a local trucker, Harry Wampler, who we were directed to talk with.

We called Harry who lived 5 miles away, and he said he would be down our way to pick up a couple of steers he was taking to market and could we meet with him to discuss our project. This might seem strange, 2, 12-year-old boys having a business meeting with a grown man, but there were young men barely older than we were supporting their mothers and siblings.

Harry stopped by and told us that iron and steel were bringing around $ 1.00 to $ 1.10 per 100 pounds.

He said if we came across copper, it was worth $3.00 sometimes more. Harry told us that he could haul 1.5 to 2 tons of metal in one load to the scrap yard in Baltimore and sell it for us, if we would load it on his truck. His charge to do this would be $40. He recommended that we get a place to collect the scrap close to our house where we could keep an eye on it and close to the road where we could load it on his truck without getting too far off the county road. He did not want to get stuck in a muddy field. We got permission from my grandfather to collect our scrap on the edge of the field that bordered my father's lot, and it faced the road. The next thing we needed was a good wheelbarrow. Later in life I heard New Yorker's and other workers refer to an item that came to their use as having, "Fell off a Truck". In our case we knew that my uncle had a world class M5 Wheelbarrow. We never asked him where it came from, but it looked like ones I had seen around the stone quarry where he worked. The M5 had a robust single wheel with a pneumatic tire. The tire must have been 6 or 8 plies. This was when an inexpensive tire had 2 or 4 plies. The tire could be safely inflated to 60 pounds if you had a compressor that would provide that kind of pressure.

The M5 was built of heavy gauge steel and equipped with large oak handles. We told Unc that we would take good care of his 'barrow and he could have it anytime he needed it.

Over the next 2 years that M5 carried nearly 10 tons of scrap metal as we cleaned up every junk pile in a 1.5-mile circle of our houses. We found discarded plow shears, the digging blade of a plow. They were in the corners of fields, right beside where the shear was replaced do to being bent on a large rock or just too dull to turn hard ground.

A full shear off a horse drawn plow would weight 8 to 10 pounds. We found farm equipment that was as much as 50 years old in the corners of wood lots. We cut them up with hack saws. Slow and tiring work but we reduced them to a size that we could load on the M5.

When we had as much metal on the M5 as we thought we could move, we started for home. This was very difficult work. Most of the route was thru dirt and grass fields. We keep a length of lumber with us that we could place on the ground to roll the wheel on. We never knew how much our load weighed until we arrived at the pile of scrap building up in our yard. We had an old scale there hanging from an A frame with a hook on the bottom. Every piece of metal was weighed as we unloaded the 'barrow. The heaviest load we moved in all our time gathering and selling junk was over 1400 pounds. We were like ants. Sometimes we would lift the handles of the M5 off the ground with Oatie on one side and me on the other. We would push the 'barrow 5 feet then set it down and get our breath. Then 5 feet more. Time was not the driving factor, moving the metal was the challenge. We found several old automobiles in our quest. I mean Old. Like model "T" Fords from the teens. They were not salvageable, or someone would have made off with them. They were junk. The only way to move them was to cut them up. Cars of that age were built with a lot of wood. Most of the wood was rotted away, the rest we ripped off and got to the rusted metal.

The motor, transmission and rear end were the treasure of the find. But they were also quite heavy. We moved them to the scrap pile on the M5. We called Harry when we had 2000 pounds. He said he would let us know when he could arrange to take it too Baltimore. We kept adding to the pile, when Harry got there a couple weeks later, we told him we had over 2500 pounds of scrap. He doubted our figures but said load the truck. We got all the pile of scrap on the truck, and we were done. Harry called us the next evening and said that the load weighed 3200 pounds. He said the price of scrap that day was $1.05/100. Total was $ 336. After Harry's fee of $45, We had $291. Our split was $145 each. That was the most money either of us had ever seen. We collected scrap metal until there was not a piece of scrap left within miles of our houses. There were other things going on in my life that brought opportunities to earn money and learn things you could not learn in school. One lesson I learned from my brother Guy was to look for money from sources other than the family. Don't ask to be paid for something you did for mom or dad. Bring money into the family don't take it from the family.

New Lines of Work

The local Catholic Church at which I was an altar boy, was St Joseph in Sykesville. Sykesville was about 4 miles from where we lived. I walked that road hundreds of times. Back then drivers would pick walkers up almost all the time. Without the walker even having to put their thumb out to signal that they wanted a ride. Hell, we all wanted a ride, but some drivers were afraid to pick up hitch hikers. The difference here was that almost everyone driving on that road knew everyone that would be walking on the road! After a few weeks of attendance at St Joe's I got to know most of our neighbors who were Catholic, and I would call one or another of them and ask if they would pick me up on their way to church, this arrangement led to some of the parishioners asking me to baby sit their small children. That was good for 25 cents an hour on Friday or Saturday nights.

The Brighoffs

One of the families was the Brighoffs, Bill and Ann. They had 4 kids that ranged from 5 to 9 years old. They lived about 10 miles from Sykesville, and about 5 miles from me. I think that I only baby sat for them about one time before Bill asked me if I wanted to help him some on his farm. Bill and Ann were like a lot of people who bought small, 100 acre or so farms and planned on working the farm into a productive farm while working full time at a regular job. Bills regular job was as a carpenter. Bill was a good carpenter, and he had some good ideas as to how he wanted to move his farm forward.

Bill had a brother-in-law who owned a farm much closer to my grandfather's farm than Bill Brighoffs farm. His brother-in-law, Bill Miller, had a farm that was just separated from my grandfather's farm by one small farm and a small river, The Piney Falls. The road in front of our house, Brangle Road, was dirt and flint stone. This road continued past my grandfather's farm, another small farm, a couple houses on building lots and then crossed the Piney Falls on an old concrete bridge.

As soon as you crossed the bridge the farm on the left side of the road for more than a half mile was Bill Millers place.

The farm on the right stretching for a mile or so was the Sothern's place, a farm of close to 250 or 300 acres. Bill Millers farm was 100 acres or so. He had a dairy herd of 30 Holstein's. I had not met Bill Miller yet. I told Bill Brighoff that I would like to work for him, but I did not want to walk all the way to his place and back when he wanted me to work. He said he would give me rides, but the first time I came over to his place which was the following Saturday he wanted me to pick up a mule from Bill Millers farm.

He said the mule, Jack was a very smart mule and would do a nice job of plowing his garden and other small jobs around his place. Bill Brighoff did not have a tractor at that time.

He said Bill Miller would hang a halter and reins on his gate post because the farmhouse, barn and stable was over a half mile from the main gate. He said that Jack would probably be eating grass with the dairy herd in the lower pasture near the main road. He said just put the halter on Jack and jump up on his back and ride him over to Bill Brighoffs. He said be sure to lock the gate securely because Jack could open gates. I found the halter and I found Jack.

And there started a couple year relationship between Ralph Baker and Mr. Jack, the 22-year-old mule. Now Jack thought he was retired to a life of leisure hanging out with the girls of the herd and controlling the growth of some fine pasture.

Jack let me put the halter on him and after I let him out of the pasture and locked the gate behind us, I jumped onto his back without a saddle and lightly flipped the reins and Jack started up the road. Well, I thought this will be fine but after 100 feet Jack decided that this was not going to work, and he stopped. I climbed down and tried every move and command I knew to get Jack to proceed.

Finely I got in front of him and pulled him easy and he walked. That was how we made the 6 miles to Bill Brighoffs.

When I arrived and explained the reason for my delay Bill Brighoff said he was not surprised. Bill said that Jack would probably be O.K. and he would keep Jack at his place if he needed him. I learned that day why Bill wanted Jack. We hooked Jack to a single row double throw tilling plow and Jack walked down the narrow path between 2 rows of strawberries planted on raised mounds with the care and finesse of a ballerina. He did not step on a single berry plant or cause the plow to veer into either row of berries. Jack was great! I worked with Jack on many gardening jobs, and he was always easy and careful. The next Friday night Bill called me and asked if I could work for him on Saturday. I said yes and then he asked me if I would mind picking up Jack and bringing him with me from Bill Millers. I was surprised that Jack was not still at Bill Brighoffs. Bill said Jack had opened the gate to the pasture that Bill Brighoff had him in and had walked home to Bill Millers one night during the week. He said that Bill Miller had come home after dark and found Jack standing at the gate waiting to be let in with his girlfriends.

Bill Miller

Bill Miller was a successful farmer. He shipped milk from his herd of Holstein cows to Baltimore, he also raised pigs, hay, corn and wheat.

Bill asked me to work for him the summer of 1949. Bill Miller had a 5-foot cut combine (Thrasher) pulled behind his Farmall H tractor and used it to harvest wheat, barley and oats while it was standing in the fields. He had a baler that was also pulled behind a tractor and baled hay or straw on the move. This was modern equipment that hardly any other farmers owned. Hay had traditionally been harvested by cutting it, then after it dried in the sun for a few days it was racked into windrows with a rake that made piles of hay the length of the rake, about 12 feet. These piles were 15 or 20 feet apart depending on the denseness of the hay crop, and then were loaded by hand with pitch forks onto a wagon pulled with horses or a tractor and hauled to a barn or piled up in a hay rick (stack) for future animal feed. The new method of harvesting hay was to cut it, let it dry, then rake it into continuous windrows created with a side delivery rake.

The hay raked in continuous rows is easy to pick up with a baler and you can have a wagon hooked to the back of the baler and someone on the wagon can stack the bales until the wagon is loaded. I know there are newer and better methods of processing hay in today's farming, but this method worked well with the equipment then available.

Since very few farmers had this expensive equipment Bill was able to do what at that time was called "Custom Work" for other farmers. He would bale their hay after it was cut, cured and raked. We would sometimes haul it to their barns for them. Getting hay in was always a time critical activity. Once the hay was cut you needed to get it dried, baled and stored inside before it was rained on. Wet hay would mold in short order. Sometimes wet hay and wet straw would create a situation that led to "Spontaneous Combustion" and a fire would develop that would destroy the barn where it was stored. I can remember Bill and I working until 2 AM on a few clear dry nights in order to get hay out of a field because rain was predicted for the following day. Grains such as wheat, oats and barley, were raised for horse and cattle feed and for sale.

Old Methods Live On

The way my grandfather raised, and harvested grains was 100 years old. Wheat and other grains would be ready to cut sometime in June of each year. You hoped to be able to cut it before you got a high wind and rainstorm that beat the grains down in the field. When they were beat down or "wallowed" as they referred to it, it was difficult to salvage the crop for harvest. But, if all went well the grain was cut with a binder, either horse or tractor drawn. The binder cut the grain 3 or 4 inches above the ground and wrapped and tied a string around a large armful of the straw below the grain head. Workers would walk behind the binder and gather up 10- 12 of these sheaths and lean them together to form a shock of grain. Two or three sheaths were then bent in the middle and placed across the top of the shock in different directions to shed rain off the shock. This kept the grain reasonably dry for a week or two until it could be thrashed.

Thrashing

Grain thrashing was a cooperative project between a few neighboring farmers. There were a limited number of grain thrashing people in a county or group of counties.

The only thrasher I knew owned a large farm in Howard County. The next county south of Carroll County Maryland. He scheduled his work well in advance and everyone knew where he was working for weeks before he got to us. I was only eleven the first summer I was involved in thrashing. There were small jobs that a 11-year-old could do. Bagging grain as it came out of a chute on the thrashing machine was one job a strong young boy could handle. There was a chute that brought the grain down from the thrasher and it split into 2 pipes that bags would be tied on too. There was a diverter in the pipe at the split that directed the grain from one bagging spout to the other.

You would tie a bag to one spout and open the delivery to that bag while you removed the full bag from the other spout. You would place a new bag on that spout, tie up the 100-pound bag of grain and place it in a pile away from the work area. By then the other bag was full and you would change the diverter handle to the spout with the empty bag and continue the process. This was steady hard work for a 11-year-old boy. There were much worse jobs on the thrashing machine. When I was 12, I was asked by a good friend of my grandfather and a close farmer to rick straw that was blown out of the thrashing machine into a barn where it was stored in a loose state. This was the worst job I think I ever had.

The temperature outside was 95 f. inside the barn with no ventilation and the warm stream of straw and chafe blowing on me from the large tube from the thrasher it had to be 110 f or higher. The only protection against inhaling the dust and chafe while breathing was a damp handkerchief. I did that for 4 hours, then asked to be relieved by someone.

Elliott Carthorn

There were not many Negros in the area, but this farmer, Elliott Carthoun, a transplanted English Gentleman, had a negro working for him full time, Petey Louis. Elick asked Petey to relieve me. Petey said to me, as he took the fork and climbed into the barn to take my job,

"I wondered how long you would last at that job" and laughed.

Petey was great fun to be around and us boys kidded and tormented him, and he gave it right back to us. Petey hated snakes and we knew how to get a rise from him. He was up on one of the wagons stacking sheaves of wheat on one occasion. One of us boys pitched half a wheat shock up onto the wagon and when we looked at the ground where the shock had been standing there was a 5-foot black snake. One of us immediately slipped a pitchfork under the snake and threw it up on the wagon in front of Petey. Petey was off that wagon like he had been fired from a canon, headed straight for the snake thrower. I was glade it was not me, because I could just stand and laugh as Petey chased the kid around the wagon until someone hollered at him to get back on the wagon so we could get the wheat to the thrasher.

The Thrasher's Coming!

The Magnificent Rumley Oil Pull tractor pulled the Thrasher with the large stationary baler hooked to the back of the Thrasher from farm to farm. The complete rig on the road had to be over 60 feet long. When the rig was set up to thrash, the tractor was turned to face the thrashing machine and a long endless belt at least 12 inches wide was draped over a 4-foot pulley on the side of the tractor. The belt led back to a pulley at least 18 inches in diameter on the front side of the thrasher. The thrasher was chocked so it remained stationary, and the Rumley was backed until the belt was tight. When the power take off pulley on the Rumley was engaged the 2 monster cylinders on the Rumley barked and the belt moved, and the thrashing machine looked like a carnival ride as it came to life.

There were pulleys on the sides of the thrasher that began to turn as they drove the sifting belts, there were levers that articulated up and down to shake screen tables inside of the machine. There was an open end up high on the front of the thrasher with a belt 5 feet wide that protruded several feet in front of the opening and disappeared into the maul of the machine. The belt started to move endlessly into the maul. This was where the grain sheaths would be carefully placed off the end of pitch forks with the grain end facing the maul. God help anyone who let a pitchfork slip as they feed the monster. The stalks of grain were beaten mercilessly which separated the grain from the heads on the stalks. The hulls that had covered the grain became part of the chafe that was blown out a pipe with the straw to a pile on the ground. This created a large straw pile that the farmer used to bed cattle and horses with. If the straw was to be baled, the large stationary baler was driven by a belt connected to a pulley on the back of the thrasher. The compressed straw bales were 125 pounds each and wire tied. These were piled up 50 feet or so behind the baler and covered with a large tarp to keep them dry until a truck could come to take them to a buyer. When the baler was being used, the chafe was separated by the thrasher and blown out the straw pipe into a chafe pile by itself.

Good straw was valuable. With the baler placed behind the thrasher, the chute that delivered straw to be ricked would have just chaff directed to it and it could be pointed off to an area were the farmer wanted to pile the chafe. Chafe could be used for gardening or such and the clean straw directed to a chute leading to the baler input. If you were not baling the straw, you blew the straw out the chute to a straw rick. Another method off handling grain was to load it into a high sided truck and take it directly to the local grain buyer, Southern States, in Sykesville. This was what many farmers did with a portion of their crop. Grain was a good cash crop. When I say, "Grain" I usually mean wheat, but many farmers, including my grandfather also raised a crop of barley. Some may have raised Rye, but I never knew of any Rye produced in our area. When 2 different grains were thrashed, you first ran the thrasher until it was clean of the first grain, then you could start thrashing the second grain. This took care so as not to get them mixed in bagging. A small farmer like my grandfather did not have cattle to feed grain to, his 2 horses ate corn and hay. The cow ate the same things.

So, his crop of grain usually went directly to Southern States.

When I visited Greece in 1980, I was surprised to see that they were still harvesting grain using the same methods we used in 1948.

Co-oping Labor and Equipment

There were about 3 farms including my grandfathers that co-op-ed every year for thrashing grain. My grandfather farmed with 2 horses and one hired man. Some of his neighbors farmed with tractors, Elliott Carthoun had at least 8 fine work horses and another 4 or 5 English riding horses. If Elick, as he was known, came to visit my grandfather he did not drive his car, a nice Studebaker. Elick rode one of his beautiful horses. When the Carthoun's arrived to help thrash Elick and Petey drove 2, 4 horse teams pulling 2 big wooden farm wagons to haul grain from the fields with. The Arrington's brought a 1937 Ford 1.5-ton flatbed truck and a Farmall H with a rubber-tired farm wagon and drivers and field help.

First Time at The Wheel

That '37 Ford was the first motor vehicle I ever drove. I was allowed to drive it in the fields. I was 12 years old. The principal farmers traded labor and equipment, but the hired hands like me and my cousin were free to hire on with any farmer who wanted us after my grandfather's work and commitments were met. As a result, we worked for as many as 5 or 6 farmers in the surrounding area during harvest time.

Give Us Our Daily Feast!

Another great tradition of Thrashing was the meals. Women from the Co-Op ing farms worked together and prepared some of very finest meals for the workers that I have ever had the pleasure to partake of. A typical meal at my grandfathers on thrashing day served Ham, Sausages, Lima Beans, Peas, Sugar Corn, Sauerkraut, Potatoes, Tomatoes, Lettuce, Cucumber and Onion slices marinated in vinegar, Fresh baked bread, Rolls, coffee, tea, milk & Pies of several types depending on what fresh fruits were available topped off with homemade Ice Cream.

Meals of this caliber were served every day at each Farm. We started early and worked late, until dark. The big meal was midday. We had to take a 2-hour lunch (It was called Dinner) to feed and care for the horses. Oatie and I would follow the thrashing operation as far as we were needed. This was usually not more than 4 or 5 miles. I worked more and more for Bill Miller because he had work for me and could afford to pay me.

Bad Things Happen to Good People

Bill Miller had a terrible run of luck that started in late 1949.

First the city of Baltimore changed several rules pertaining to milk shippers. Bill's farm failed on several major changes to the rules. The first one would have been hard to comply with. They said that your spring had to be located at a higher level than the milking parlor. Bill's spring which had a great flow of clean cold water was probably 15 feet lower than the barn that housed his milking parlor.

It did not matter that the spring was 1500 feet away from the barn or that he did not keep milk in the springhouse. Water from the spring was pumped by a Hydraulic Ram to a water tower in his farmyard. The major problem though, was that his milking parlor was under his barn. The barn was a 2-level barn with storage for hay, straw and grain on the upper level that you accessed via a long slopping driveway on the front side of the barn. The back of the barn provided access to the lower level by doors that opened into the barnyard. The milking parlor was on the lower level and their new rules said that you could not have any building over a milking parlor. The only answer to continue shipping milk was to build a completely new milking parlor away from the barn and lower than the spring. Bills milking operation of 30 couple cows did not warrant that kind of expenditure. I don't remember how much time he had to get in compliance with these rule changes but while he was thinking about it he was struck by a much greater tragedy.

Bill and his wife had a daughter who was 4 or 5 and his wife was pregnant with a second child. The disease of Polio was rampant during the 1940's and 1950's until Dr. Sauk developed a vaccine. Bill's wife contracted Polio and she and the unborn baby perished. It was a terrible thing. I don't know how Bill got through it. His mother took his daughter to live with her and Bill decided to give up farming. He told me he was going carpentering with Bill Brighoff. He asked me if I would be able to do a lot of the day-to-day jobs around the farm until he was able to sell it. Bill just did not want to be on the farm without his wife. I agreed to do all I could.

Pig Man

Bill sold the dairy herd first. Until he sold the
herd He would milk before he went to work with
Bill Brighoff and put the milk in ten-gallon milk
cans in the large water filled cooling cabinets in
his garage which was under the house. Needless
to say, we ate a lot of homemade Ice cream
before the herd was gone. Bill had a 5-acre hog
lot with a nice bunch of hogs penned there. He
had a large self-feeder in the middle of the lot.
This feeder was at least 10 feet long and had
troughs on both sides of the bottom. There were
2 hinged tops, one on each side. You could dump
300 pounds of feed in each side at a time.

The feed flowed down for the hogs until it was
empty. He also had some big open troughs away
from the feeder. These we used to feed milk
from. The hogs loved it. There were 2 boar hogs
in the pen that had to weigh 800 or 900 pounds.
They had big tusks and Bill said they would gore
you to death in a heartbeat then eat you if you
were careless around them. We had a 2-wheel
dump cart that we pulled behind the 1938 John
Deere B. This tractor was built with steel cleated
wheels. Sometime since birth the spokes had
been cut near the steel rims and pneumatic rims

were welded to the original spokes. We were now on rubber! The B was hand start, no electric starter, you locked the foot brakes, set the throttle, opened the compression valves on the 2 cylinders, then turned the 20" flywheel on the side of the engine.

This was connected to the engine crankshaft that was on the back of the engine positioned across the width of the tractor. The other end of the crankshaft on the opposite side of the tractor mounted the clutch assembly which was operated by a long handle. To start the engine, you rotated the flywheel and when one of the cylinders hit, you quickly reached down and closed the compression valve on this side of the engine then rushed to the other side of the tractor to close that valve. The distinctive sound of a John Deere was known by everyone, sort of like todays Harley's. An easier way to start the B was to back it up the sloped driveway to the barn and set the brake and leave it in gear until the next time you needed it. Then you just jumped on, pulled the clutch leaver back to disengage it, put it in gear and let the brakes off. When it was rolling at a good pace you pushed the clutch lever in and Bang, Bang, Bang you were in business. When feeding the hogs about 4 times a week, I would hook up to the cart, go to the building where we keep the

100-pound bags of feed, and I would throw 6 of them in the cart and drive down to the garage door that led to the cellar of the farmhouse. There I would load 3 or 4 10-gallon cans of milk in the cart and pull down to the hog lot. If I was lucky the pigs were far enough away from the gate that I could jump off the tractor and open the gate, then get back on the tractor and pull into the lot and jump off and close the gate before their curiosity drew them to the gate. Sometimes I would just jump up on the back of the cart and walk thru the cart and up the tongue to the tractor. Next, I would back up so the cart was at one side of the feeder then I would go over the tongue to the cart and reach from the cart and open one side of the feeder, fill it with feed, close that side and open the other side and fill it. When I left the feeder all the hogs would be there eating so I could drive to the milk troughs and standing on the cart I could dump the mike into the troughs. That would always bring some of the hogs running to the milk. From there it was easy to escape the hog lot because of the hog's preoccupation with their guts. During the winter we put the pigs in part of the space under the barn where the milk parlor used to be. That made it easier to feed the pigs, but there was no more milk for them, and I had to shovel all that stinking crap they created onto a manure spreader and spread it on the fields. That job was a close call on worst job ever. Eventually Bill sold the farm and built a nice home in Eldersburg about 6 miles away.

Woodsmen

Oatie and I continued to trap during the winter.
The fall that I was 14, Oatie and I took on a
project for another farmer, a carpenter who
owned a farm near Bill Brighoff's farm. He
knew both Bill Miller and Bill Brighoff as he
carpentered with them. His name was Earl
Clapp. His Farm was the original Miller Farm
that bill had lived on in his youth. Earl and his
wife Madeleine had 2 boys that were pre-teens
and Oatie and I took turns babysitting for them on
weekend nights so the Clapps could go out.

Earl heated his house with wood that he cut
from his large wood lot. In late summer he asked
Oatie, and I if we could get wood in for him for
the winter. Of course, we said yes. We were
making .35 cents an hour by now and this looked
like work for many weekends. We went out into
the woods with Earl on a Saturday morning, and
he marked 5 or 6 large, beautiful Red Oaks of 3
to 3.5 foot in diameter. All these trees were 70
feet or higher.

I had never seen a gasoline powered chainsaw
at that time. The first time I got my hands on a
gas chainsaw was 15 years later! Earl had an 8-
foot 2 man crosscut saw with him and a sharp

double-bladed axe. He also brought a 10-pound sledgehammer and 3 or 4 different size wedges. We were set.

Earl said, "I need to see what you boys know and determine if you plan on cutting wood or killing yourselves or somebody else".

He said, "Explain to me how you are going to drop this tree, where will it fall and if I'm satisfied with that explanation, I'll let you cut the tree down. If I think you are doing something stupid, I'll fire you". With that sound vote of confidence, we looked at the tree, which stood straight as an arrow and had what appeared to be a very even distribution of large limbs. This was important in felling a tree because imbalance on one side or another could affect where you planned on dropping the tree. We told Earl that we would drop the tree down between two of the other standing trees in a space about 20 foot wide. We said that this would place the wood in a good position for loading onto the tractor drawn wood cart. Earl was satisfied with our logic and plan, so he told us to get on with it. We started with a low cut with the 8 foot saw on the side we wanted to drop the tree on. After we were a little less than 1\3 of the way thru the tree we removed the saw and placed it 10 inches above the lower cut and sawed down to intersect the lower cut.

When we joined the lower cut, we removed the saw and knocked the wedge of wood from the cut. On the opposite side of the tree, we made a cut at an angle down toward the cut on the other side. The downward cut was continued until the saw blade was completely inside of the cut with a couple inches of space behind it. We then set a wedge in the cut behind the saw. We drove the wedge into the cut with a sledgehammer to keep the tree from setting back on the saw and pinching it in the cut. If you let this happen then you had to use the ax to cut a wedge of wood out to tree to free the saw. You really wanted to prevent this from happening.

If the tree was setting back to the side away from your notch you had a real problem, because the tree wanted to fall in the direction opposite of your intended plan! Other factors, somewhat out of your control that can affect your planned drop were wind and miscalculation of the limb balance on the tree. We did these operations as we had done on many trees and our first tree for Earl fell where we planned.

Earl went back to his farming and Oatie and I cut the Oak into 4-foot lengths. This tree was on its way to firewood. Many farmers heated their homes with wood that they cut from their own woodlot. This was labor intensive, but much cheaper than buying coal or converting their heating systems to oil. Before we could move the wood to the wood lot we needed to split the logs into fire wood size. This meant splitting the 4-foot-long tree sections first in half, then each of the half's into at least 3 more pieces each. This was done with wedges and a 10 or even a 15-pound sledgehammer. Oak would split clean. Some woods were difficult, to impossible to split. To split a log for cord wood the wedge was held in the center of the log at one end. Then driven in with the sledge. After it was driven in about half the wedge length the log should start to split. The next step was to place a wider wedge in the split beside the first wedge. This would likely split the log in half. Some time it required that you use the axe to cut some pieces of wood down in the split that were still holding the halves together. This process was continued on each halve until the log was in 6 or 8 pieces. These were piled up and could be left to dry in the wood lot or loaded on a cart and hauled to the wood pile close to the house. There it would be stacked until the day that you set up the stationary saw and cut the 4-foot lengths into 3, 16-inch sections ready for the stove.

Some people paid wood cutters by the cord for cutting wood. A cord was a stack of 4-foot split logs 4 foot high and 8 foot long. Oatie and I always worked by the hour and all our employers were happy with this arrangement. Hauling the wood from the woods to the household wood pile was a separate work function. Usually done as fill-in work. Cutting wood to stove length was a project the required setting up the farmer's stationary saw.

Earl had a front mount saw for his tractor that was belt driven from the power take off pulley on the side of the tractor.

The tractor was set up near where you wanted the stove cut wood stored. The tractor was chocked so it was immobile. The Saw had a blade 4 foot in diameter on the side of the tractor opposite of the power take off side. The saw had a hinged table with a secure back side toward the front of the tractor. The blade was beyond the end of the table and had a protective cover over the top half of the saw blade. When the power takeoff was engaged the blade rotated and the hinged table was pulled toward the saw operator and away for the front of the tractor. A section of wood 4 foot long was laid on the table with about 16 inches protruding beyond the blade end of the table. The table was then pivoted back toward the front of the tractor and the piece of wood would lift the shield up off the blade as the wood was forced forward into the downward spinning blade. When the table reached the end of its travel, the end of wood was cut off and fell to the ground. The table was pulled back to the forward end of its travel.

The remainder of the section of Cord wood was slid under the path of the saw, to the desired finished cut length and the table was pivoted back for the next cut. After two cuts on the 4-foot section the remaining piece of firewood was pushed off the table onto the ground and a new section was placed on the table. This was dangerous work for any grown man. Oatie and I started cutting wood at 14 and did it anytime we could get the work. We both stopped doing this type of farm work when we were 16 because we had driver licenses and a new world was opened to us.

A Boy Needs Wheels

Our working to earn money did not keep us from doing many of the things that we thought were proper for boys our age to do. I remember we were always interested in motorized machines and vehicles. One of the first motor vehicles we got our hands on was a Cushman Motor Scooter when we were 13. Oatie,'s father was one of 17 siblings, girls and boys. When we were in our early teens this family, The Oursler's, which had grown up on a farm just 3 miles from Earl Clapps farm was scattered to the 4 winds. But 2 of the brothers, who still lived on the family farm, had never married, and were 2 of the nicest gentlemen I ever met.

They were probably in their 60's at that time. They were Jim and Herb Oursler. From time-to-time Oatie and I would drift over to the Oursler place as we called it, and just mess around. The primary attraction of the Oursler place was the 1946 or so Cushman Motor Scooter setting in one of the sheds.

The Brothers had said that we could mess with the Scooter and see if we could get it running but could not drive it further than the length of their driveway. The driveway was about a half a mile long and dirt and flint stones. We were satisfied with that constraint until we got the scooter running then we would see if we could get permission on that range of travel. The scooter belonged to Taft Oursler who lived 200 miles away near Deep Creek Lake in far western Maryland. We took the carburetor of the 1-cylinder engine apart and cleaned it good, put fresh clean gas in the tank, cleaned and gaped the spark plug, and after a lot of jumping up and down on the kick starter and some priming with raw gas, we got the engine running. After driving the scooter up and down the stone and dirt driveway for a few trips we decided to see if we could get permission from Uncle Taft to drive the scooter farther up and down the dirt road that led out to Earl's place.

This required several phone calls over a couple of week period to contact Taft. Taft reluctantly gave us permission with a promise from us that we would be careful and not get hurt or hurt someone else. From then on, we were on the lookout for ways to become mobile.

There was a regular stream of older farm owners who were giving up farming because of advancing age or death. Nearly every Saturday there was a farm equipment and livestock sale complete with auctioneer. When we could hitch a ride to a sale we would try to go. This was particularly true if there was something of real interest in the Sale Flyers. I went to a sale with my uncle one Saturday and there was a small 2-cylinder gas engine amongst the junk piled on a table ready to be auctioned. I kept my eye on the engine and when it was auctioned, I bid on it, and had high bid at 3 dollars. That was a little high, not knowing if it ran or not. But I wanted it. The engine was 2 cylinders, flat, opposed, with one cylinder on each side of the crankshaft. The engine was 2 cycle air cooled, with a kick starter in the front that you stepped down on to turn the engine over and start it. There was a centrifugal clutch assembly on one end of the crankshaft. I had seen this type of clutch on the Cushman Scooter we used to play with at the Oursler farm. There was a 1/2" "V" pulley attached to the outer side of the clutch. This Was a Maytag washing machine engine. This pulley drove a "V" belt on the washer's transmission. The little engine had a gas tank on the top with a sign that said several things. First of importance was the mixture ratio of gas to oil since the engine was 2 cycles. This meant that all its lubrication came from the fuel mixture. No oil in the gas, no engine after a few minutes of operation. 16/1, was 1 part of oil to 16 parts of gasoline. This meant 1 ounce of oil to

1 pint of gas. Since most people mixed a gallon at a time you would put 1/2 pint of oil in a gallon of gas. The other interesting label on the engine was MAYTAG. This was a washing machine motor. Many farms in rural America in the 1930's and 1940's were still without electricity. The Lady of the house would have been very happy to have this motor on her new MAYTAG washer. When mounted under the washer the motor would start with a kick or two with the throttle set in the start position, with a bit of choke, as soon as the starter was kicked down the motor would fire up. She would turn off the choke and the engine would run at a fast idle, then clothes, water and soap were added, and the function leaver was moved to Wash, and the engine speed would advance, and the centrifugal clutch engage as it spun faster, and her clothes were washing. The washing machine had to be located out of doors because of the exhaust. Preferably on a porch or a well-ventilated location because the exhaust would kill you. When washing was done, the motor was shifted to start {Idle} and the soapy water was drained by dropping the hose that was hung on the side of the tank and connected to the bottom of the tank. The wastewater could be drained to the ground or collected in a large tub to be used with the next

load of clothes. If you washed the lightly soiled clothes first, you could wash the men's clothes next. After the water was drained the wringer leaver could be engaged and the clothes fed into the wringer rollers and that water would drain to the ground and her clothes were ready to hang on the line. Well, I did not plan on using this motor on a washing machine. Oatie and I were going to build our first powered ride. We built a wagon using some of the design principles I had used in building roller skate wagons in Baltimore. The side rails were 2X4's. A 2X4 was bolted to the back end of the 2 parallel side rails. Then a second 2X4 was bolted to the front of the side rails. A third 2X4 that was 1 foot longer than the front cross beam was bolted with a large single bolt in the center to the top beam. We then made a trip To DeVries Herring Hardware store in Sykesville and bought 2 axels, 4, 12 "semi "pneumatic tired wheels that fit on the axels, and a 10-inch X 1/2" "V" belt pulley. We purchased a 2" X 1/2" "V" belt pulley and a 20" X 1/2 " "V" belt. We were set. When we got back to work on the Go Cart, we strapped the axels securely to the front and back beam. We mounted the motor just in front of the rear axle on a traverse platform. We bolted the 10" inch pulley to one of the back wheels. The smaller

pulley was bolted to the clutch. Then the motor
was adjusted so that the pulley on the clutch
aligned with the pulley on the rear wheel. The
motor slid forward until the belt was drawn tight
between the 2 pulleys. The motor was bolted
down tightly in that position. The front beam /
axel was steered by the drivers 'feet. The throttle
was controlled by a line that pulled the throttle
open and a spring that closed it when the pressure
was released on the line. The first test was on
the dirt road in front of our houses.

The rear wheel spun a lot on the dirt, but we
were able to drive it carefully up to the junction
with the macadam, or "Tar and Chip" road that
led to Sykesville.

We both took a number of trips up and down
the road, being careful of the very few cars on the
road. You might go 10 minuets between cars,
and you could hear them coming well before they
came around the last corner and into view of us.
The only Police in our area were the Maryland
State Police. There was 1 Trooper who covered
the whole south end of the county. If he came
down to our dead-end road more than once a
month it was a lot. I say dead end because they
would usually do a U turn at the end of the paved
road and return to civilization. We ran this
machine up and down the road and overrode the

governor on the motor to get faster speeds. After a couple weeks we blew up the motor. Maytag did not build these motors for our kind of use! We were always searching for new playthings.

Things That Go 'BOOM'

Boys like things that Go Boom! We found different types of Go Boom devices. One was to place a lump of Carbide in a quart jar, tape a flat rock to the jar, and punch a number of holes in the lid, then toss the jar in a deep section of our local creek. The water would leak into the jar and the carbide would rapidly turn to gas and the jar would explode. The shock of the exploding jar would usually stun or kill a few fish that were near the jar when it blew up. This was not the normal use of carbide at that time. Carbide was used in the 1900-to-1920-time frame for headlights on automobiles. Electricity replaced carbide in the teens and 20's but it was still used for lanterns when I was a kid. The fish would float to the surface, and we would salvage any that were eating size. I think this was not a legal activity, but we only attempted it a few times. Dynamite was easier to get hold of and made a much larger explosion. Dynamite was used on every farm to remove stumps and large rocks. My grandfather had a few sticks and some caps and fuse that my uncle brought home from work. He kept it in a shed behind the house. We would help ourselves occasionally to a half stick and a couple caps and 6 foot of fuse and go to the woods and see what we could blow up. 1/4 stick taped to a piece of heavy metal, with a cap and 3 feet of fuse would drop 6 foot down in the river before it went off. You would see a lot of fish from that explosion if they were there. These activities were diversions. What we really were interested in was things that earned money.

Back in the 1940's you could write to the U S government, I think it was the Department of Agriculture, and they would send you pamphlets on a great number of things you needed information on. I got a Pamphlet on how to tan an animal hide. I used those instructions to tan a raccoon hide and then I made a Cap from the hide. I think that I pushed the curing process a little, because the cap had a smell that was not attractive to young girls. I threw it away after a couple weeks.

Another pamphlet we sent for described how to make Black Powder, as in Gun powder. We tried that several times and got some good results without losing any fingers or body parts. There were 3 ingredients, all of which could be purchased in any drug store at that time. Charcoal was sold in tablets, this had to be ground into fine powder. We used a Bowl and round glass device with a large end on it. The two of these together are known as a "Pistol and Mortar".

The second material was sulfur. It was also sold in tablets that required powdering. I'm not going to name the third ingredient because I don't want the all-knowing G'vment to lock me up in Leavenworth for fostering sedition. I will say that after we had purchased these ingredients on several occasions the Druggist, who knew us boys well, would not sell them to us. He figured out what we were making.

We did not dare grind all these ingredients in the same mixture. We felt there was too much of a chance that the mixture would explode in our face. We mixed the finely ground ingredients carefully and tested the flash point by spreading a teaspoon of the powder on a rock and placing a short piece of dynamite fuse in the powder. NO CAP. Then lit the fuse. We found that our mixture of Gunpowder was not good enough to flash off on every attempt. So we devised a satisfactory solution to that problem so all of our rockets and fireworks would ignite reliably every time. I will not describe our solution since I am very sure that in 2020 most 13-year-olds or 30-year-olds for that matter would kill themselves doing the things that boys of my age did.

Our Cabin in The Woods

Another project that we started around age 12 and continued to work on until we were 16 years old was what we called "Our Cabin". This cabin was built on a corner of woods that belonged to the State Hospital but was secluded from the main campus and at the edge of their farmed fields. The Hospital had hundreds of acres of farm fields.

Many of the patients who were in good physical condition and not climbing the walls with mental illness enjoyed farm work. These patients grew fields full of beans, sweet corn, potatoes, beets, cabbage, lettuce and tomatoes. The vegetables were used by the kitchen that prepared meals for all the 1500 patients and for the attendants and employees. The employees of the hospital paid for their meals at a very reasonable rate. We started our cabin with some scrap boards and tin roofing we found on a barrack that had fallen on State property due to lack of maintenance. A barrack was a building like a barn. Barracks were built to store hay, straw and machinery in, not animals. A barn was used to house animals as well as those items stored in a barrack. We moved the materials we needed from the barrack site across the fields to our Cabin location in the woods. No one questioned what we were doing if they even saw us. Paul was, Paul Smith senior's son, Paul senior held a very responsible job with the state, and no one would question what his kid was doing!

Unless there was a need for laborers in the fields, they were always empty of people.

We bought nails and what bolts we needed and built a 3 room 2 level cabin. We found a couple of windows from dilapidated shacks; a door was built from scrap wood. We found a small "Brooder house stove" in our travels. A Brooder house was a chicken house used to raise chickens in from eggs until they were ready to lay. We would go to our cabin on rainy or cold days and build a fire and be comfortable. We often spent nights there year around. Oatie's father would bring us used dry cell batteries that still had enough charge left in them to light small 6-volt bulbs. We ran wire and connected bulbs all over the acre of woods we had laid claim to. We also had light in the cabin from the same little bulbs. We never got to show our magnificent cabin to any of the girls that came into our lives after 'Drivers Licenses'.

Zip Line

When we were removing material from the barrack site, we had noticed that there was a "Hay Fork" inside the full length of the barracks peak. Hay forks were used to unload hay or straw from wagons and lift it up to the top of the barrack or barn and move it the length of the building to deposit the hay or straw anywhere in the building you wanted to store it. There was a door at the very top of one end of the building and the Hay fork track stuck out 5 or 6 feet through a slot in the top of the door.

When the two sides of the door were swung open to the outside of the building a trolly with a large pair of pointed tongs could be maneuvered to the end of the track, and the forks could be lowered onto a load of hay or straw, then pulled close with another line, and the tongs would grab a large bundle of hay or straw. When the tongs were closed on the hay/straw they would lock. The tongs would now be raised by the cable that lowered them with the help of a horse or a tractor. The tongs and the grabbed load would be lifted to the height of the track. Then a line that controlled the movement of the trolly from one end of the track to the other would be pulled on to place the trolly and load over the location where the load was to be dropped for storage. At that point the trip line was given a good tug and the tongs were unlocked and sprung open and the load would fall into the building.

What attracted us to the 1800's contraption was the fact that it was 125 feet of track with a trolly rolling on it. What a great ride that would make if it was hung from a few trees on a gentle grade! Well, we took the parts we needed for our project and slepped them to our cabin site and found a couple of trees leading down to our spring. The distance was maybe 150 feet. We had removed the tongs, believing that sooner or later one of us would be run through by them. That left just the wheels and cart frame. We built a swing seat and attached it to the trolly cart.

The track was hung from brackets on the designated support trees, giving the necessary side clearance to let the cart run from the top to the bottom of the incline. I should say, miraculously, the first manned flight went true to planning. The stop was abrupt, and you could be thrown from the seat, but this ride was carnival ready. As with many of our projects the challenge and enjoyment were in the planning and building stages. We soon got bored with riding down a 125-foot track and pulling the cart back up just to ride back down. Maybe that is why I do not care much for amusement parks.

I went to Disney Land in 1977 and have no intention of ever going back.

My Romance with Boating

We were in one of the wooded lots on my grandfather's farm one day and came across a Popular tree that had been struck by lightning and felled. The tree had burned for a while and as luck would have it the heart wood had burned out of a section of the trunk for over 10 feet. What this left to the eyes of 2 adventurist boys was the start of a dugout canoe. We found an Adze in my grandfather's tool shed and went to work on enlarging the cavity in the log while we thought about how we were going to close the 2 ends of the log so it would float. We used an 8-foot crosscut saw to cut the log ends off leaving us a finished canoe of about 10 feet.

We then got some scrap particle board and made 2 flat ends for our canoe. Not very hydrodynamic but it seemed to look like it would keep the water out. The next problem was how to keep the log from rolling over as soon as we launched it in the nearby creek. This was solved by getting 2 empty 2.5-gallon oil cans from the tool shed and tying them too 2 pieces of wood that we nailed to the sides of the top of the canoe. In the South Pacific they would call them Outriggers.

We dragged the very heavy canoe to the creek and armed with a couple pieces of scrap wood that we called oars we set out on our maiden voyage. Well, we found out quickly that the boat needed deeper water to float than our little creek possessed. We were able to move the canoe to a small pond in the creek that floated it, but just barely. We had a lot to learn about displacing your weight in water in order to float and other nautical stuff like that. But the log canoe kept us out of more serious trouble for a couple weeks and added to our desire to find a boat.

Continuing Ventures in Boating

Oatie and I were always thinking about things to build including boats. So, it was not surprising that when our good friend Paul (Chubby) Smith told us that his dad could get us some coffins to play with, that we thought Boats! As I have mentioned before, Paul's father worked at the state mental hospital, Springfield. He was involved with all the maintenance work for the hospital. He drove the small diesel railroad engine that pulled cars full of supplies from the main line of the B & O Railroad to the hospital on their feeder siding track, he worked in all the shops that repaired and built things for the hospital. He had a hand in everything that happened on the property.

It seems that they had a surplus of coffins that they had made to bury patients in. These coffins were built for burying the poor in pauper's field. They were pine wood, nailed together and simple. They wanted to get rid of a few coffins to clear out some space. We said we would like to have 3 of them. Chubby's dad brought 3 coffins home and we took them to my house to work on them. My grandmother, Minnie Hobbs was living with us at that time, and she had her nose in everything that went on at my house. We had one of the coffins sitting in the back yard and were trying to figure out what we were going to do to turn it into a seaworthy vessel. Minnie looked out the door and saw me sitting in the coffin and she had a hemorrhage! She screamed at me and said that I would bring down the wrath of God on me and my friends for playing with something as serious as a coffin. I was not sure how or why this would bother God, but I figured that by the time my father got home from work she would have cooked up a good enough story to get him on her side and have him whip the hell out of me. We got rid of the coffins before we even had time for one voyage in them.

First Love

Life continued. I rode everywhere on my bike.
I thought about girls, but I did not know what you
were supposed to do with them or how or when
to do it. I would ride my bike to visit a girl and
we would set in the parlor and talk, but not get
close. We would set in the yard and talk, but not
get close. There would be dances at school with
music from a record player and the girls would
dance with another girl and the guys would set on
the side of the auditorium and talk. We were
probably wishing we were playing basketball in
the auditorium instead of watching girls 'dance.
But when I was 14 and in the 9th grade, I noticed
a 7th grade girl that was different. She had poise,
the way she walked was different, she was very
pretty. She seemed to have several girlfriends,
but I did not see her around boys. I was very
smitten by this girl and again I did not know what
to do. I found out that she walked to school and
only lived a half a mile from the school. About
the only place to run into kids from school, away
from school, was to see them in downtown
Sykesville on a Friday or Saturday night. But
that was iffy. I could not just walk up to her and
say" Hello, my name is Ralph Baker and I think

you are the greatest girl I have ever seen, and I want to be your Boyfriend forever". That would have got me laughed into the next week and it would be the end of any chance I might have with this perfect creature. My big break came at a Sadie Hawkins Day dance in the fall of 1951. I started 10 Th. grade in September and was 15 years old. Sadie Hawkins was a caricature created by Al Capp, a popular cartoonist at that time. Remember, most people did not have TVs at that time, so comics in the newspapers were followed closely. Capp's hit cartoon was called 'Little Abner 'and was about a bunch of country bumpkins living in Appalachia. Sadie Hawkins was the oldest spinster living in the town. Every year the town elders would declare a day as Sadie Hawkins day and any unmarried male that unattached girls could run down were bound to marry them. So, in the time of my youth girls were not forward as they are today. It would have been very unusual for a girl to ask a guy for a date or do anything in a forward manner. The Sadie Hawkins Dance was meant to turn the tables on this kind of female shyness. Girls were encouraged to invite guys to the dance. I'm sure that some did, but no one invited me. Uninvited guys were not only welcome to attend the dance but were needed, otherwise the dance would be sparsely attended.

Girls that lacked the fortitude to ask a guy to the dance usually came alone or in the small groups of girls that they hung out with. I, like most of my friends and male classmates came alone. One thing I should mention is the size of the school I attended. The year I graduated, 1954 the 4 grades in high school numbered 275 students. The senior class had 39 students. 19 boys and 20 girls. You can see by these numbers that everyone in high school knew most of the other kids in school! The numbers also dictated that a dance like this one would not have more than 80 or 90 kids in attendance. The entertainment for the dance was a Phonograph record player. A teacher would play the records and other teachers would act as chaperons to maintain order.

Cake Walk

We were not a rowdy group, but caution was a good idea. Sometime during the event a teacher announced that they were going to hold a cake walk. A cake walk consisted of all the participating girls gathering into a ring holding hands and facing outward while all the participating boys would hold hands and create a ring facing inward toward the girls. A designated teacher would stand outside of the boys 'ring and would have a cane in her hand and hold it up in the air and the 2 rings would start walking in opposite directions as the music was played on the record player. As each pair of students passed in front of the cane holder, she would lower the cane in front of them then lift the cane up as the next pair of counterrotating students approached her. This went on for a minute or more, then abruptly on a down swing of the cane the music would stop! The couple, walking to opposite directions that had the cane in front of them won the cake. That night as all the stars were aligned and the Angels trumpeted, the cane dropped, and the music stopped in front of the lovely Miss Alice Arlene Burdette and Farm Boy Ralph Otis Baker. I could not believe my luck!

Of course, this meant that Miss Burdette had to acknowledge my existence. I think that it was the first time I had heard her speak. I do not remember how the first conversation went, but I do remember me offering the cake to her and she suggested we share it with our friends, which we did. For the rest of the evening, I spent as much time in her company as I possibly could and I asked her if I could walk her home, accompanied by her friends who lived nearly next door to her. This was the beginning of a relationship that has lasted over 70 years.

A Real Job

With the summer of 1951 approaching I was looking for a full-time summer job. I was 15 so I did not have a driver's license yet, so I needed a job close to home. I asked Ed Arrington if he could give me a summer job on one of his Line Crews. Ed and his brother Tom supervised the crews for the family utility line construction company, M F Arrington and Sons. The M was for their mother Mrs. Maggie. I think the F was for their deceased father Frank. M F Arrington and Sons had been doing contract pole line construction for Baltimore Gas and Electric company and some contract work for C & P Telephone Company for many years. The Arrington's had a large farm that bordered my grandfather's farm on the better part of 3 sides. I had worked at farm work for Ed many times over the last 3 years. They kept some of their line trucks on the farm so it would be great to be able to walk to the farm and get on a truck in the mornings to start the workday. Mr. Edward Arrington was scary serious to me. When I would ask him a question, he would always look at me like I was a fly on the wall about to annoy him. Once when I was 10 years old, I did some farm work for him and at the end of the job I went to his house to pick up my pay.

Ed met me at the door and invited me into his office. He had a big check book laying on his desk. He never asked me if I would mind taking a check for my work, he just pulled his ink pen out of the ink well in his desktop and started writing a check to me as he discussed the number of hours and rate per hour we had agreed upon earlier. I really wanted cash, but I was terrified to tell him that I did not know what to do with a check. When he finished signing the check, blotted it and he tore the check from the book, handed it to me and thanked me for doing the work. There was no way I was going to tell ED ARRINGTON that I did not know what to do with a check. I said thanks and folded the check several times and shoved it into my pocket. The weather was hot, and I was sweating and by the time I got home I was wet all over. I told my mother about the check, and she thought nothing about it. Ed Arrington did not bother my mother; she had known the Arrington boys since they were young men. She said, give me the check and I will stop into the Bank later in the week and get it cashed for you. I pulled the crumpled piece of paper from my pocket, unfolded it and nearly broke into tears. The check was soaking wet with sweat and the ink, (no ball point pens back then), was illegible. My mother scolded me and said Ralph you must be more careful with important papers like checks. You will have to ask Mr. Arrington to write you another check. This was turning into the worst day of my life; I did not want to face Ed Arrington again and admit how stupid I was and beg him to write another check for me. Checks cost 10 cents back then. I only made 35 cents an hour. Would Mr. Arrington deduct 10 cents from the check amount. How cross would he be with me? I was terrified! Well, there was nothing to do but walk back to the Arrington place hope he was still there and face the music. When I showed the check to Mr. Arrington, he looked at me with a gruff look then smiled and said, Boy checks cost 10 cents, be more careful with them. I promised him that I would be very careful in the future, and he gave me a new check. I held the check in my hands until I got home to give it to my mother. So, this is the Ed Arrington who I was asking for a summer job. This would be the first job that I had for an extended period of time, going in every day with the same people. What was he going to say to me? The first thing Ed asked was how old was I now. I told him 15 and he said there were some work functions that I could not do until I was 16. He said you will not be allowed to drive the truck; you cannot climb any poles that have wires on them Hot or Cold.

He meant it did not matter if the wire had electricity in them or not, I could not be on that pole. But he said what I wanted to hear; you can have a job as a Grunt. That meant a ground hand. I would dig holes for poles and anchors, I would send tools and material up to the linemen on hand lines, keep the truck clean and neat, load supplies on the truck either after we came back to the farm or in the morning before starting time. And of course, do anything that the foreman or the linemen asked me to do. For this I would earn 50 cents an hour! Work on the Line Crew was very rewarding. I was working with grown men who had to work to earn a living. There was kidding around but work was serious. Baltimore was growing after World War 2 and new housing developments were moving to the west of the city. Utilities went in right after the land was graded and we were one of the first on the scene. The streets and alleys were laid out and we had job plans drawn by Baltimore Gas and Electric Co. that showed where we were to set poles and the poles length and girth. The locations of anchors to hold the end of the pole lines and other necessary information to do the Electric Plant work. We did not have pole hole digger trucks then, so all holes were dug by hand.

Low person on the totem pole to dig holes was me. I took a digging set, which consisted of a set of long handled tools, a spade, a scoop and a 9-foot digging bar as well as a 5-foot shovel and dragged them to the first hole location and went to work. Pole hole digging was not bad work as long as the ground was not rocky. If when digging you encountered a massive rock, you could usually get the engineers to let you move the hole a couple of feet. If not, then they would have to find a way to crack the rock or reroute part of the line. Once the holes were dug, we set the poles and anchors then the linemen installed the arms and hardware including transformers on the poles and we pulled in the wire. When everything was connected, we left the job. This section would not be cut into the hot part of the electric system until houses were built and the service loops connected to them. The work was hard but the guys on the crew were great. I enjoyed that summers work very much.

The Open Road

My brother GuyFred was 9 years older than me. My mother had been married to Guy's father for a couple years then they were divorced. Guy is my 'Big Brother 'and I have never thought of him in any other way. Guy joined the Navy in 1943 when he was still 16. Like many young men at that time, they lied to join the service rather than run off to Canada to avoid the service as they did in the 1960's. He was a Seabee and was in until 1946 when the war was over, and the servicemen were released. Guy was married to Jo who he met while working at the State hospital. Jo was an RN there. In 1951 they were living in a small house in Eldersburg, which was no more than a crossroad junction at US highway 26 and State route 32 about 10 miles from Sykesville. I would spend nights with them from time to time. They were a lot of fun and it got me out of the house. It turned out that there was a family that lived next door to them that provided some interest to me. Melvin Crites, his wife and 3 children lived there. One of Melvin's children was Donna Jean. She was in Arlene Burdette's class, and I thought I might like to get to know her better. That never happened though. But I did become friends with her father. Melvin drove a Tractor Trailer truck for East Coast Trucking. He had a regular route from Baltimore to Philadelphia. He invited me to ride with him on one of his round trips and I was eager to go. We road in his car to a warehouse district in Baltimore. There he checked out a big Mack tractor and we hooked up to a long trailer and we were off to Philly on US highway 1. It must have taken us 4 hours to get to the Philly terminal. Then we disconnected the trailer and connected to another trailer and drove back to Baltimore. It may not sound like much of an adventure but to a 15-year-old it was!

I was hooked on traveling. The call of the Road and Travel in general has never left my soul.

One Foot in School, One in Manhood

When I started back to school in September of 1951, I was 15 years old. I noticed that a couple of the high school students wore white pants to school every day. When I asked someone about them, I was told, "Oh, they work at Springfield". Further inquiry led to the realization that a limited number of students, who's family might need extra income were allowed to work at the State Mental Hospital, Springfield that was immediately beside the school property. I started to research the prospects of me getting a job there. I went to the counselor and stated my case that we were certainly in the "Working Poor" category, and I would like to apply for a job there. The counselor said that I would have to be 16 to work at the Hospital. I told her that I would be 16 in early March. She said that it would take time to get it approved. With my parents ' approval we could start the paperwork and contact the employment staff at Springfield. She said the work hours were 2:30 to 11:00 PM. She said that working students, a maximum of 3 each year, were released from school at 2:00 PM. Since you missed the last class every day you would have to make the class up on your own.

My last class was History, and I was a voracious reader, so I did not plan on having a problem with that subject. All I would have to do was take periodic tests in History. She said that the work week at the hospital was 44 hours a week. This meant that you worked 6 days one week and 5 days the next week. Payday was every 2 weeks. My parents gave their approval for me to work there. I met with the Supervisor who I would work for if I was hired, and he knew some adults that knew me, and they spoke well of me so he said he would approve my application to go to work as soon as I was 16! I would need a car. I asked my mother to sign on a loan for a used car and she agreed. The week I was 16 I received my Maryland driver's license.

Mom and I went to look at cars. I found a 1949 Plymouth Convertible, Black with a White top. I think it cost $ 995.00. I financed it for 2 years. I was Styling! The care of citizens with mental affections was similar in most of the States until the early 1960's. Maryland had a large hospital in Sykesville, Springfield Mental Hospital, which cared for patients who were suffering from mental incapacities but were not considered dangerous to themselves or the general public. There was a separate care group at Springfield named the Epileptic Colony that housed Epileptic patients. Criminal Mental Patients in Maryland were lodged at Spring Grove Mental Hospital in Catonsville near Baltimore. All these hospitals were segregated during that time period. Colored patients, as the Blacks were called at that time, were committed to the State Mental Hospital at Crownsville near Annapolis, Maryland. Springfield was the largest mental facility in Maryland. The campus covered over 1400 acres. Springfield was a beautiful facility. The buildings were well built, most were brick, a few were stone. They were laid out in several groupings. The two largest groups were the Men's Group, where I would work and the Women's Group, which had only female Attendants. There was a large administrative building, The Hubbner Building, and surrounding grounds. The Epileptic colony was a separate group of buildings. The hospital had its own Power Plant that generated electricity and steam (piped to the buildings for heat.) There was a railroad track that ran from the Power Plant to the B & O Railroad main track 5 miles away. The hospital owned a small diesel engine that ran down to the siding off the Main track and picked up rail cars loaded with coal for the power plant and many types of supplies for the hospital. In addition to the main grouping of buildings there was a building with rooms for unmarried female employees, another for unmarried male employees, and a building for married couples. There was a nurses building, all nurses were female at that time. Accommodations in these buildings were rented from the hospital at very reasonable rates. There was a large kitchen building in the Men's group that prepared food for all of the male patients in the hospital. The ambulatory men patients who were not suffering severe lack of mental control walked to the kitchen / dinning building for all 3 meals. The wards that housed severely affected patients were served by delivering the food to the wards in Steam Carts on large trucks with power lift gates on the rear. The carts were rolled into the wards by the attendants and patients who could help. They were set up in the kitchens and the food was served by the attendants and helper patients on trays of dishes and bowls to the tables where they were seated. After the meal the dishes were cleared of food, washed and dried and stored for the next meal. The truck picked up the carts later and returned them to the kitchen. The women's group had its own dedicated kitchen and food service arrangement. The total number of patients in the hospital ranged between 2500 and as high as 4000 at one time. White shirts were part of the uniform I had worn to Catholic school. I also had white shirts for altar boy service, so a few more white shirts to meet the Hospital dress code and the State provided 5 or 6 pairs of white pants was all I needed. I would put my soiled pants in a laundry cart weekly and pick up my washed and folded pants at the administrative office when they were returned from the central laundry. Your pants were marked so you got yours back without a problem. My other clothes were still laundered at home. Black shoes and white socks and I was set. Another service available to the employees was the privilege to eat in the employee's cafeteria. The food was wholesome and inexpensive. You paid for food with tear out coupons that had a cash value in dollars or cents that could be used instead of cash. Employees got the coupon books in the office and the book value was deducted from your pay. It was sort of like the old company store arrangement of business that owned everything in a community associated with the business, like a coal mine or a southern mill town. I would drive to school in my convertible and park in front of the school. Only 3 or 4 students drove to school. I was Hot Stuff! I would leave school at 2:00pm and drive to the administrative building at the Men's Group and park. When I checked into the office, I would see my name on a ward assignment chart. I was normally assigned to "I" ward, The Infirmary. This ward housed the patients who were convalescing from surgery or were physically sick with anything from a broken bone to a doctor treated illness. One of the Staff doctors made rounds every day to examine patients and write medication to be administered. The head attendant on "I" ward for all 3 tours was always an LPN, Licensed Practical Nurse. Attendants could apply for LPN training after they had worked at the hospital for a reasonable period of time. It could be a good career path for a High School graduate. We had diabetic patients from wards with ambulatory patients that would walk the few hundred yards to "I" ward for their insulin shots once or twice a day. We had a posted list of these patients that we checked off as they showed up and we would check their ward for them if they didn't show up. Everything was run in an organized manner and the patients were well cared for. There were around 25 beds in the large room where patients requiring bed care were placed. Many of these older men were in what today would be referred to as Hospice Care. We fed them, changed their bed clothes often, especially if they soiled them, provided bedpans and service to them. We changed their positions in bed often to help prevent bed sores. This was difficult because many of them were propped up in bed to facilitate breathing. We were also in many cases the last people to see some of them alive. It was not uncommon to do a bed check, there were no call signals that the patients could summons help with, and fine a patient deceased. There were not many times, other than when we were serving meals to the ambulatory patients, that at least one attendant was in the bed care center. The vision of death was a maturing experience for a 16-year-old. I was not adversely affected by the experience though, because I had been hunting and doing farm work for 5 or 6 years and had seem more death involving animals, not humans, than many 16-year-olds. The most sobering job that I had to help with was the preparation of the deceased for pick up by the crew that removed the body to the hospital morgue. When a person dies all their muscles relax and if appropriate action is not taken quickly the body will discharge fluids and feces. Packings were inserted in all orifices and a length of gauze was tied around the penis to control discharges.

The body was then wrapped up in a clean sheet to await pickup by the attendants from the hospital morgue. I liked "I" Ward more than any of the other Wards because there was always something going on there. The dayroom/dining room was where most of the patients with reasonable cognizance spent their time. There was a black/white TV that they watched. Some just sat and stared at the walls or ceiling or. maybe out of the windows during the day. The 2 or 3 attendants were busy with bed ridden patients and administrating medicines. The Shift Supervisor, J B, would often spend some time on our ward talking to Noel, the In Charge LPN about the patients and determining if we needed anything. There were strict rules forbidding employees from eating patients 'food. Since "I" ward was an Infirmary, we had a small kitchen. The other wards did not have kitchens. We needed to keep some food in the refrigerator in case a patient missed a meal because of some problem or needed juice or food with a medication. Sometimes the supervisor would ask if we had any orange juice in the kitchen. He knew we had juice to drink with medicines and he might say I think I need a glass of orange juice to take an aspirin. He would go into the fridge and reach behind the various bottles and containers of food and come up with a small jar of crystal-clear liquid. Nothing would be said by anyone as he poured 1 or 2 fingers of the liquid into a glass and follow that with a few ounces of orange juice. This would wash his aspirin down nicely.

There were many young men and women working at Springfield who were from Appalachia. There were people from West Virginia, North Carolina, Kentucky, Tennessee and Ohio to mention a few states. This was 1952 and we were in a non-war, war in Korea. Some of the attendants were CO's or Consciences Objectors. That meant they had been given Deferments by their Draft Boards because their Religion did not allow them to fight in wars. There was a stipulation with these deferments though, that they must find employment in a job that was necessary work during the time the Nation was at War. Employment at a mental institution was acceptable. When they went to work at Springfield the employment office had to send a letter to the employees 'draft board assuring the board the person was employed there and that Springfield would notify the Board if the employment was terminated. They were all good people who were raised in strict religious environments. Some were Brethren, some Quakers and several other Sects spread throughout the Midwest. There were other mountaineers not so much driven by religion as by the fact that there was work in Maryland and not so much work in their native states. Now some of the members of the latter group would return from a trip home with some corn carried in a most portable form, Moon Shine. Sometimes a small jar of this liquid would end up in our refrigerator. Certainly, I did not let any of that Vile stuff cross my young lips.

Surgeries on patients were performed at the Hubbner building. One exception that I was aware of was "Electro-Shock Treatment" This was a treatment that many today compared to the "Blood Letting" of the 1700's and 1600's. On Saturday mornings "Shock Therapy" was conducted on the Sun Porch, as we called it.

It was just off the bed care room. I was not part of the team that administered this treatment, but I did see the results. Under a doctor's supervision the patient was strapped to a table and electrodes, metal discs connected to heavy wires were placed on the front sides of the patient's head. The idea was to send electrical current thru the patient's head and frontal lobes of the brain.

I saw several patients treated this way but none of them seemed to be in any way improved by the treatment.

Displaced Persons

One interesting thing at that time was the number of doctors we had who were "DP" s. A DP was a Displaced Person. They were allowed to enter the United States from Europe after World War 2. Remember the war just ended 6 years before the time I'm writing about. During that 6-year period Europe was being rebuilt under the Marshall Plan. When the war ended most of the cities and the housing in those cities was destroyed. The US started a program that let professional Europeans migrate to the USA to start new lives. When a doctor migrated to the USA, they had to spend time learning to speak English and learning the rules that were required to obtain a certificate to practice medicine in the State of Maryland. Springfield and other mental hospitals allowed these Doctors who had Medical Licenses issued by countries in Europe to practice limited medicine during the period they were establishing themselves in America. The biggest problem we had with them was understanding their English with a strong European accent. The few that I dealt with seemed to be knowledgeable and interested in the work they were doing.

Springfield had close to a thousand acres of fields that they farmed for vegetables to feed the patients and feed for the Award-Winning Dairy Herd they maintained and milked. Some of the patients worked with the dairy herd and many more worked in the fields raising the vegetables. Several of the wards had only patients there that worked in these endeavors. "J" ward which was directly under "I" ward was one of the wards that had mostly farm workers. I was occasionally assigned to 'cover" 'J" ward. This was mainly seeing that everything was going along trouble free. The patients were well behaved and like most people's adult relatives. I got the feeling that many of these patients were considered an inconvenience or minor burden on these relatives and for that reason the relatives convinced someone to commit the person to Springfield.

I guess after the mental hospitals were shut down in most states in the 1960's and later that these types of people ended back living with relatives or under Interstate bridges. Every ward had a little different type of patient. "K" ward was very much like "J". "A" , "B" and "C" were right behind the Men's group administrative building and housed men who were older and needed closer supervision from the attendants. They were the wards where you would find some patients that were showing some signs of dementia.

The Cuckoo's Nest

The "F" ward was one I dreaded being assigned to. It was right out of "One flew Over the Cuckoo's Nest". I say that, although I never saw the movie. Every time someone mentioned the movie, I reminded them that I had seen the Stage show and did not think I would like the movie. When I went to "F" ward I forgot about eating. No matter how hard you worked at cleaning it was never enough. Catatonic patients sat huddled against a wall and reached under their gown which was all the clothing you could keep on them and they dug feces from their rectum and smeared it on the walls. Just Lovely! There was no communicating with them. They were in another world. All you could do was strip them, shower them, put a gown on them and deal with another pleasant situation before you came back to clean them up again. Some of the other patients were memorable. I remember a patient that helped quite a bit at "I" ward. His Name was Roland Berggruen. When I would come in to work, I would greet Roland and almost always his response would be, "How did you recognize me Ralph, I'm traveling Incognito today". I had to look up Incognito to find out what Roland meant. When we got off at eleven o'clock, 2 or 3 of the older Attendant's would ask me if I wanted to go to a bar with them. Carroll county was dry, so you had to drive 10 miles into Howard County to find a bar that was a little higher class than the two "Catch them as they cross the river" bars just beyond Sykesville. I went along occasionally even though I did not drink alcohol at that age. Usually, I went home and got some sleep to start school the next day. Arlene Burdette and I started seeing more of each other now that I had a car. Some mornings I would pick her up at home and drive her to school. On Sundays we would take drives for 30 or 40 miles. When summer came, I found a morning job at a Jewish Day Camp in Marriottsville. They had a large swimming pool, and they needed a lifeguard. I had taken a Red Cross Water Safety course earlier in the year and they awarded me a Senior Life Saving Certificate. This was although I was not quite 16 at the time, I took the test. I was a very good swimmer and nearly 16 so they made an exception and gave me the Card. The job consisted of servicing the pool filter system first thing in the morning, cleaning flotsam from the pool and making everything ready for the first swimming activities at 10: a m. I Life Guarded until 2:00 then left for work at Springfield, unless

I had a day off in the middle of the week. If I could stay later, I did.

That job lasted about 2 months. Then Day Camp season was over. School was about to open, and I would start my Junior class in September. High school for me during the 11th and 12th grades was very much like that of the other kids in my class except I led a sort of Dr Jeckel and Mr. Hyde life. I attended basketball games on Friday nights for important games. I would trade a Saturday night for a Friday night off with a coworker. But I had 2 different sets of friends and they never met each other. It was a little like living in two worlds.

Road Trip

A good example was a trip I took with a fellow I worked with. His name was Mosley, his first name was Bill, but no one used their first name. I was Baker, he was Mosley other guys were Barnes etc. Mosley was from Far Western North Carolina. I say Far Western because you could not get to his house without going through Tennessee! Mosley was 19 or 20 years old, and he worked at the men's Group with me. We were listening to Country Music on the radio one night and Mosley said, "You know it's not far of a drive from my home to Nashville." That got us to talking about making a short trip to his home with a visit to Nashville. Now this was not the conversation I would have had earlier in the day with a school mate. That discussion might have involved a drive to Howard County for something. The time of year was late fall and Mosley and I talked about doing a trip to Tennessee on several occasions. We soon decided that we would make it a long weekend of 4 days. We would take off a Friday, Saturday, Sunday, and Monday in mid-November. When you worked for the state of Maryland your vacation time and your sick time accumulated at the rate of 1 day a month each or something close to that. So, I had some vacation time I could request and so did Mosley. I told my mother what we planned to do, and she had met Bill when he came home with me a few times, so she told us to be careful. That was the way I was allowed to grow up and I am so thankful for that trust from my parents. They must have felt I deserved it. I told Arlene what I was going to do and asked her not to make a big deal of it at school since I would be missing a couple days attendance. Bill and I threw some clothes in our suitcases, filled my Plymouth with gas and left early Friday morning. I had less than $200 in cash with me. There were no credit cards back then, so it was cash or nothing. Gas was 18 to 20 cents a gallon and I got 20 miles per gallon on the Plymouth. I never asked Bill how much money he had with him, but I was sure he had more than I did. We drove west to Fredrick Maryland on route U S 40 then South-West on US 340 to Harpers Ferry. We continued south to Front Royal Va. We decided to drive southwest on the Skyline Drive rather than on US route 11 which was the main road going southwest to Bristol which was on the Tennessee boarder. As it turned out this was the wrong time of the year to drive the Skyline Drive. Arlene and I had taken several Sunday drives along the Skyline Drive since I had got my car. Those drives were all during the summer. The Drive was not closed to traffic when we approached the entrance, so we drove on up the mountain. The drive was twisting and turning and as we got higher up in the mountains, we encountered some fog. The road had patches of ice on it, but this is not a road on which you drive fast so it was safe. As we reached the higher elevations the world turned into a picture book wonderland. The trees were draped in whore frost. This is formed on anything that stands still for a few minutes in the fog when the air temperature was near or below 32 F. Whore frost was built up on the tree limbs, trunks and on the foliage of trees, fence posts, rocks and grass. The light sparkles on the ice. This looked like a scene from Dr Zhivago, even though the movie was not made until 1965, 12 years after my trip over the Skyline drive in the fall of 1953. But there is no better description of the scene. The drive was long and slow, but it was one of the most memorable sights I have ever experienced. We drove to the exit at Route 211 then went west to US route 11. This was well before the Interstate Highway System was built. The US highway System dated back to the 1920's and 30's. These roads were mostly good 2 lane

roads, occasionally they were 4 lanes with a
double yellow line separating the 2 directions of
traffic. All the roads were dangerous. Cars were
dangerous! Brake systems were single, meaning
all the brakes were connected to one master
cylinder. If any part of the brake system failed,
you had no brakes! The emergency brake might
stop you in a half a mile if you pulled on it hard
and long enough. We used a lot of time on the
trip over the Drive, but it was unforgettable. We
drove late into the evening, crossed into
Tennessee then drove narrow one lane roads
along the North Carolina / Tennessee border. We
eventually entered a dirt road that went up a
hollow to a cabin. We parked in the yard, got out
and walked through the couple inches of snow on
the ground and went up to the door. Bill's
mother greeted us and was very surprised to see
Bill. He had not advised her of his visit because
he was not sure of when we would get there, and
he did not want her worrying about him.

  She greeted me warmly as I looked around the
house. There was a bedroom off the right side of
the living room we had entered. There was a
large wood stove in one corner of the room, and it
was very comfortable there. I could see a
doorway to the kitchen and what appeared to be
the doorway to another bedroom. Bill told me

when we were in the car that there was no inside plumbing at his house. I told him I had grown up with outhouses so that was not a problem for me. What turned out to be of some concern was when Bill showed me "Our" bedroom with only one large bed. I had never slept in the same bed with a man in my life! There was no problem since the bed was made up with 2 sets of sheets and quilts. There was a large "Thunder Jug" in the corner of the bedroom that Bill said we could use if the need arose in the middle of the night. I was fortunate not to need to use the Jug or outhouse after we bedded down for the night.

Since the next day was Saturday, we were leaving early to drive the 300 miles to Nashville to see the Grand Old Opry. We left after a nice breakfast and drove the 300 miles in about 8 hours. Although the speed limit in Tennessee at that time on open highway was "Safe and Reasonable", the first state that I had driven in that had a speed limit over 50 or 60 mph. You could drive 70 or 80 in Tennessee back then, with 2 lane roads and small towns we averaged 40 mph. I will forever remember the old Ryman Auditorium. I only remember a few of the performers from that night. One was Roy Acuff, the master of ceremonies, Also, Hank Snow and Minnie Pearl were on stage. We enjoyed the show then started the long drive back to Bill's home.

Speed Trap

We had one sour event on the drive. I was driving and we came to Crossville. I slowed down but not slow enough for the midnight sheriff who was on collection duty. I might have been speeding, the only intersection in town had a flashing yellow light. We got stopped and I was as polite as could be, but he wrote a ticket for $50. I gave the cop the $50 which really cut me close on money. The cop said that Out of State drivers had to pay or spend the night in jail until the Justice of the Peace came in at 9AM. I paid and we crept out of Crossville, Tennessee. We arrived at Bill's home late and slept late. The next day was Sunday and we declined the offer to attend church. After lunch we drove to a few of Bill's friends 'homes to visit. We then went to a hangout, but there was no liquor sold on Sunday so not many people were there. We just messed around in general as two young men would do, then went back to spend some time with his family. After a good night's sleep, we drove back to Sykesville. We went straight up U S 11 with no detours into the Mountains!

School Boy

School life went on as usual. There were dances, basketball games when I could get off work to attend and drives on weekend days that I might get off from work. Basketball was the only sport in our school other than Track. We did not have enough kids to field a football team. The only school in our county that had a Football team was Westminster High. Westminster was the county seat of Carroll County Maryland. Westminster was in the center of the county and had a large enough number of students to be graded by the state as a class "A" school for sports competition. Sykesville was a class "B" school as were 5 of the other high schools in the county. I did not play basketball, but we had a very good team when I was in high school. Sykesville won the State Class "B" title at least 2 of my high school years. Needless to say, there was strong attendance at the "Away Games" as well as the home games.

Long Lonesome Road trip

Early in the summer of 1953 I took several days off from work and included them with a weekend to get a 5-day break to drive to New Bern, North Carolina to visit my Aunt Mickey and her daughter, my cousin Kay. Kay and I were born 1 month apart. Mickey's husband, Joe Sprague, was a "Lifer" in the Marines. Joe was in Korea fighting the war at this time since the Korean "Peace Keeping Mission" was not over yet. Aunt Mickey and Kay were living in Dependents Housing at Havelock N. C. near Cherry Point Marine Air Station. Ft Lejeune was just down the road from there and the home of the 2nd Marine Division which Joe was attached to. I think my aunt told me the quarters in Havelock served both bases at that time. I had spent some time with them during summer breaks on a few previous times. I had ridden the Greyhound bus on those occasions. This would be my first long trip in my car by myself. The distance was about 400 miles from Sykesville to Havelock N C. I remember the drive on Highway US 1 from Washington DC down to Richmond, then you pick up US 17 and followed it down closer to the coast than US 1 into New Bern and then on to

Havelock N C. One thing that I remember
vividly about this trip is an encounter I had with a
hitchhiker. I was a very trusting soul at age 17, I
had not met any unsavory characters in my short
life, so even though I had heard bad things about
hitchhikers I had never ran into a bad one.
Somewhere in Virginia I saw a young guy on the
side of the road "thumbing" as we called it back
then. It was not unusual to see a hitchhiker, but it
was threatening to rain, and I thought It should be
OK to give him a ride for a while and maybe
keep him dry. The speed limit was never higher
that 50 mph on those roads and as low as 35 quite
often. This gave you time to think about your
actions before you had to commit to stopping or
not. At times I miss the slower speeds when I
remember the lost items I found alongside the
roads or even in the road in days gone by.
Wrenches, Hammers, Ladders, Suitcases, the
beauty of driving slowly was that you had time to
assess the traffic behind you to determine if it
was safe to make a quick stop, the total amount of
traffic, and was it safe. Anyway, I stop a few
hundred feet past him and watched him as he ran
up the road to get in the car. When he reached
the car, all the windows were down for
ventilation, so he leaned in the passenger window
and asked how far I was going. I said down into

Carolina a way. He said he would like to ride with me, and he would try to pick up a ride going farther south from wherever I was leaving 17. I invited him to toss his duffel in the back seat and get in. He seemed to be about 20 or so and clean cut. I introduced myself and said that we should be in New Bern in about 2 or 3 hours and that was as far as I was going. He said that would be a big help. We carried on a conversation in small talk. I did not want to discuss anything of importance with him. I think he felt the same way. After an hour he looked at his watch mentioned the time and said he was going to miss his watch. I asked why he thought he would be missing the watch and he said I must sell it to get enough money to get to Florida. I sort of shook my head to acknowledge that I heard him but did not comment. After we rode 10 or 15 miles the fellow asked me if I would like to buy his watch. He described it to me, and I glanced over as he removed it from his wrist. It was a beautiful gold Wittnauer. The Longlines - Wittnauer company made some of the best watches in the world. They still sell high price time pieces today I was impressed with the watch but told the guy politely that I could not afford a watch. I said I just have enough money for gas to get to New Bern. I did not want him to think that I had any

amount of Real Money on me. He then said I
will let you have it for $20. I knew this watch
was worth a couple hundred dollars, but I could
not spare any money. I said thanks but I could
not do it. When the first road sign for New Bern
appeared, the fellow looked at me again and said
he would let me have the watch for $10. I was
embarrassed to refuse him again, but I said I just
don't have the money. When we got to the New
Bern area where I had to turn to go to Havelock I
pulled to the side of the road and he reached in
the back and retrieved his bag, opened the door
and got out of the car. Before he closed the door,
he thanked me for the ride and then he said I
really need some money, you can have this watch
for $5 if you want it. I told him I wanted it from
the first time I saw it, but I just am very short of
money. But since I'm close to my aunts I will
take a chance on giving up $5. I got $5 from my
pocket, and he handed me the watch. We said
goodbye and I never saw him again. The watch
was a Wittnauer automatic wind with a lovely
stainless steel stretch band. I wore that watch for
10 years. It was admired by everyone who saw it.
I don't think it was stolen, because you could tell
he was torn about selling it, but he needed the
money. I was torn because I really wanted to
give him more money, but I did not have it. I

always hoped he remembers me fondly as someone who helped him in a tough situation, not as someone who took advantage of him. When I arrived at my aunt's home I was greeted warmly, and we got caught up on the comings and goings in our lives. The Marines own a long stretch of Atlantic beach at Onslow. Most of it is used for military maneuvers such as to practice amphibious landings, but a small portion is reserved for Marine Corps Dependents use, at lease that was the case in 1953. So, we went over to Onslow and swam and had a good time. I remember their quarters had a small coal/wood burning stove in the vestibule by the entrance door. This stove was solely for the heating of domestic water for the house. So, if you wanted to take a shower, you had to build a fire 30 minutes before the shower. I think we took in a movie while I was there. I told them about the watch and their first thought was that the watch was stolen. I told them why I thought he owned the watch, but either way I was now the owner, and I would treasure it. After a couple days visiting, I filled up with gas and headed home.

More Growing Up

When I got back to Maryland it was more of the same, school, work, trying to spend as much time with the lovely Arlene Burdette as I could manage. The regular drill back then was that Juniors would buy their Class Rings in the spring before school closed for the summer. When Guys got their rings, they would immediately give them to the girl they were going steady with. She would wrap the inner part of the ring band with string, tape or what have you, then paint that glob with nail polish to reduce the ring to a size that would stay on their finger. She would now flash that ring finger in front of all her girlfriends to show that she now had a ring in her boyfriend's nose.

So not to break tradition I gave Arlene Burdette my class ring and I have not seen it since, except on her finger. The Auditorium of our school was also the basketball court, assembly hall and theater. It was not large and as the classes became larger there was a need for a larger forum for many activities. The County did not spend much money in the south part of the county. My grandfather said that the only time you would see a County Commissioner was right before election time. Because of the obvious need for a larger forum, we would ask the administration at Springfield for permission to use the large, nice auditorium they had at the Women's Group. They would usually let us use their facility possibly for a small contribution to the activities fund or something just to keep it business like. Of this I'm not sure because that kind of stuff was well above my Pay Grade.

We felt like Grown Ups when we attended a dance at the Hospital. The auditorium had good acoustics and a rotating glass Disco ball with many little reflectors on it. You would see these decretive balls on television and in the movies, but never at a high school dance. They were not called "Disco" balls back then because Disco did not come on the scene until the 60's or 70's.

Arlene's mother was a world class seamstress. She made all of Arlene's dresses and gowns. The Gowns she made for Arlene were envied by everyone. I was very proud to escort Arlene to dances or to any affair. She had Class and still does 70 years later. Mixing school and work was never a problem for me. What I looked forward to, though, was graduating and going to work. The Guidance Counselor encouraged me to consider going to college. Not many kids in our school went to college. Most of them went to work on their parents 'farms or in whatever business their family was involved with. No one in my family had ever gone to college and they were all earning a good living. That happened to be the thinking of many kids including me. So, my plan always was to graduate, get a job, marry Arlene when she graduated and get on with life.

Class Trip

During the spring of 1954 the senior class took a class trip to New York City. Only about 25 of the 39 kids made the trip. We rode a bus to Baltimore and boarded a train bound for Grand Central Station in NYC. The trip was for a long week end I think we went up on a Thursday and returned on the following Monday. We were booked into a nice, but reasonably priced hotel. We were heavily chaperoned. The boys had rooms on a different floor than the girls. There were 4 people to a room if memory serves me right. What I remember most was seeing somethings for the first time. New York was unlike the couple big cities near us. We rode on the subway, no subways in Baltimore or Washington in 1954. We went to the top of the Empire State Building. Wow, you could see halfway across New Jersey. We could not get over Times Square, the people, the lights at night. The smaller things like Horn and Hardart cafeteria, where the food was behind little doors on the wall, and you could see what was for sale behind a glass window. The price was on the window. It was even change, like 25 cents or 50 cents. You put the correct amount in the coin slot and the door opened. Lunch was served. We attended a Broadway show, maybe it was off Broadway, but the only time I had been to a live show was at Ford's Theater in Baltimore. Of course, that does not count the time that an older friend took me to the Gayety Burlesque Theater on East Baltimore Street when I was 14. We jammed a lot into 4 days and nights and most of us stayed out of trouble with the chaperones.

California Or Bust

During the spring of 1954 I was talking with a good friend who was graduating with me in June. Bob Bruce lived at a Home for Boys in Eldersburg, a nearby town. The home was run by a church, I think it was the Methodist church. Bob and his brother Bill who had graduated 2 years earlier had been at the home, Strawbridge, since I had started school at Sykesville. There were several boys from Strawbridge going to Sykesville. They were all good kids. Bob asked me what I was going to do after graduation, and I told him I was thinking about taking a trip to California in my car. Arlene would not get out of school until 1956, so I thought I might look at California in that time. Bob could not stay at Strawbridge after graduation, his brother had joined the Army when he graduated, but Bob did not want to do that so he asked if I would mind if he went with me to California. I thought it would be a good idea. Two of us could split expenses and it would be cheaper for each of us. We started planning along those lines. Then I ran into Terry Deering at one of the Saturday night dances held every week in the local Firehouse.

These dances were legendary, a country band played until 12 midnight.

All the local boys and girls attended these dances. There were fights out back on occasion, some hidden hard drink might be found in presence and much intermingling of the sexes happened. Defiantly a step up from Chaperoned school dances. Terry had completed a "Kiddie Cruise" in the Navy. The Navy had them for several years. Regular enlistments were 4 years, but a young man could join at 18 and stay in the Navy until he was 21. He then could take a discharge or reenlist. Terry was 21 and out. While talking to Terry I related my plans for a trip to California. The first thing out of TD's mouth was my car or yours! Terry had a nice 1952 Chevy 2 door hard top, and I liked it. But when he found out that I had a convertible he said we should take the Plymouth. That was fine with me. Bob knew Terry and the three of us spent a lot of time leading up to June graduation for Bob and I planning the trip. We thought that we would keep an eye out for work opportunities and if one turned up to provide short term work for at least 2 of us we would try to make that happen. There was much to do to get the Plymouth in top shape for a long trip. The mechanic we all used lived 1/2 mile down Brangle Road, the dirt road

that ran in front of our house. He was Billy
Freezer. I remember when he came back from
the war. He had an acre of land down beside the
Piney Falls, a river about 20 feet wide and
normally only 3 feet deep. His lot was waterfront
but up a grade of 10 feet or so from high water.
Billy was a very fine diesel mechanic, but he
worked on all systems of cars and trucks. He had
a day job in Baltimore working for a large truck
dealership. Billy went over the engine and said
all the rest of the Plymouth was good to go. The
last consideration was tires. I ran tires until you
could barely see the treads before I replaced or
recapped them. I was working on my car one day
when my older brother GuyFred stopped by and
looked at my tires. He said" I fornicate on thicker
rubber than you drive on" I replied "Was that a
statement insinuating that I need new tires? "We
both laughed. Tires only lasted 15,000 miles at
the most on the roads we had in our area. Car
front ends were crude by present standards, tire
materials were not as good as they now are.
Also, I probably drove like a Mad Man. Many
people would have their tires recapped with a
new cap of rubber that reached down the side of
the tire an inch or so. This new cap and your tire
were heated in a special "vulcanizing" mold and
pressure was applied to force the tire and cap to

bond as one. When the process was done properly the tire would last nearly as long as a new tire. The cost was about half that of a new tire. I knew a company in Pennsylvania just across the state line from Carroll County Maryland that did reputable recapping.

The problem was you had to dedicate a day to the trip and the process. If a tire had a problem, you then had to drive up there for resolution of the problem. Tires needed to be balanced after the recapping. The only balancing devices that any service station we knew of had was a Static device. The device had a rim that pivoted on a point in the center. There was a bubble level in the very center of the device that you looked down on. The wheel and tire would be removed from the car and placed on the balancing device. The heavy side would go down and the air bubble in the center of the device would move with the imbalance. The objective of the "Game" was to place weights that later could be fasten to the wheel's edges on the right side of the wheel and with finesse get the bubble of air in the center of a black ring painted on the face of the level. When this was accomplished the wheel/tire was thought to be a balanced assembly. Being a frugal and enterprising farm boy, I used a different balancing method. I would jack up one side of the front of the car with the extremely dangerous bumper jack. Then place a cement block or a large wooden block under the body of the car so that when the car fell off the bumper jack no one would be injured. There were stories in the paper every week about someone injured or killed when a car on a bumper jack fell and crushed the dummy who was working under it. With the wheel off the ground, you would use your brake adjusting tool and back the 2 brake shoes away from the brake drum. Now the wheel should turn easily. To make it very easy you would remove the grease cover from the nut that held the front wheel on the spindle. Then remove the cotter pin that locked the nut, then back the nut off a half a turn. Now the wheel would spin rather easily. You would find at this time that there was a heavy side to the wheel / tire / brake drum assembly. When the wheel stopped turning the heaviest point should be at the bottom. I would them move the wheel 1/4 turn in either direction then stop. This should leave the heaviest point facing front or back. When you released the assembly, the heavy point would return to the bottom. With experience you would get a feel for the Wheel Weight you needed to attach to the light side of the wheel. I got wheel weights from filling stations that threw them away when they removed them from a wheel they were balancing. They always wanted to sell new weights to their customers. Weights came in 1/4-ounce increments. If I did not have the precise weight, I needed I would cut a larger weight down to size with a hacksaw. When you could position the wheel at any position on a clock face and it would stay, not drift to the heavy side I was done, there was no heavy side! The wheel was in balance. And I guarantee you the wheel was in better balance than any done in a service facility until the new class of Dynamic balancers came on the scene. The clean-up work was to readjust the brake shoes, lubricate the bearings with grease, tighten the spindle nut to the proper tension replace the cotter pin and grease cover, take the car up a step or 2 on the jack so you could remove the block, then let the car down. You could only balance wheels on the front of the car with this method. The back wheel had the resistance of the rear end assembly and had to be moved to a front wheel spindle for balancing. To do the back wheels you would have to remove a rear wheel, put the spare on where the rear wheel came from then remove a front wheel, and place the back wheel on a front axle for balance or leave it there. This work like most work done on my car was performed in the yard because not many of us had garages. That's why we were called "Shade Tree Mechanics". When I told Chubby Smith about my planned trip, he suggested that I needed a sign to place on the rear bumper of the car. There were no bumper stickers in 1954 so a sign required imagination. Chubby said that there was a patient that worked at the power plant with his father who was a great picture painter. Chubby said he would get him to paint a small piece of wood with our trip intention on it to hook to the rear bumper. A few days later he gave me a sign that was about 3 inches by 12 inches with a picture of a covered wagon pulled by horses with a desert background and the caption painted over the picture "California or Bust". During the "Dust Bowl" times of the 1930's, the Okie's migrating from their drought destroyed farms of Oklahoma and the Midwest often had signs like this on their 1920's and 1930's Ford's and Chevrolet's.

I drilled a hole in each end of the piece of wood and attached it to the bumper the day that I turned in my resignation to my boss at Springfield. The last couple weeks of school were filled with many activities. I had accumulated some money in the State retirement fund that I needed for the trip. They suggested that I might want to leave the money in the fund in case I wanted to rehire into a state job. With ignorance and confidence in my decision-making ability I suggested that I would not return from California.

Westward Ho!

When school was over and graduation complete, I swore to Arlene that I would come to get her and take her to California to live with me when she graduated. The three Musketeers left Maryland in June and headed Southwest to the Shenandoah Valley of Virginia and down to Tennessee. We stopped in Nashville for a night to see the sights then continued west to cross the Mississippi at Memphis. We crossed thru Arkansas and the only thing I remember about Arkansas was a race we got into with a local guy after we came out of liquor store. He had what he thought was a bad 48 Chevy and he pulled out the same time we did heading west. I jumped on it and pulled away from him and we raced about 1 mile and came to a 2-lane bridge over a river, and he was out in the left lane but not overtaking us, but we were both running at over 90 maybe 100 and a car was coming toward us in the East bound lane so the Chevy let up and must have retired to the East. When we got into the car Terry had climbed up on the top of the folded top and stretched out across the back of the car. Not a safe place to be at 90 MPH! Fortunately, he did not get thrown off

We crossed into Oklahoma. We saw a sign pointing to Ten Killer Lake and thought that it would be a good place to wash up and to scrub the car. The lake was new, the dam having only been completed in 1952 according to local information. We found a dead end on a road that must have crossed the newly flooded area and did a little swimming and wiped the car down with wet rags. There was not much built up on the lake shore at that time After spending the night there we went back to the HI way and continued toward Oklahoma City. When we drove thru Oklahoma City, we saw a strange sight. There was a live, pumping, oil well on the State House lawn! We were looking for any type of work but did not find any until we talked to someone in a gas station who told us that we could find work if we headed north in Oklahoma and on into Kansas. They said the Wheat harvest was under way and there would be work associated with the harvest. We turned North. We slept along the road.

Roadside Mechanics

Somewhere in north central Oklahoma we approached a rig on the side of the road. There was a straight bed Dodge truck with a large Massy Harris combine strapped to the bed. The cutting head looked to be 14 feet. It must have protruded 3 feet on each side of the truck. Towed behind the truck with just the rear wheels on the ground and the front of the machine up on the very back of the truck bed was another combine with its cutting head hanging out over each side of the truck. There was an older Dodge pickup stopped behind the rig.

We pulled to a stop and got out and walked back to the Dodge truck that had its hood open and a man hanging inside the engine compartment. I said "Hi! Are you having a problem?" The fellow straightens up looked at us and said, "A little bit". I said we might be able to help you. We are heading North and looking for work. He said Well, I just lost my helper. When the truck stopped running, he said he was going to hitch on ahead and look for work. Sort of left me on my own. He said my name is Cliff Davis. We introduced ourselves and I said I know a little about Chrysler engines, maybe I can help. The engine in the truck was pretty much the same as the engine in my convertible. I had a meager collection of tools in my car. I got the small toolbox out of the car, and we looked under the engine hood, and I could smell gas so I thought that the problem might be ignition related. I removed the center wire from the distributor and using a pair of pliers with rubber coated handles I held the wire close to a bolt head on the top of the engine. I asked Cliff to try to start the engine. When he cranked the engine there was no spark coming from the wire which went directly back to the coil. I had a test light made up of a 6-volt bulb in a socket with 2 wires connected to the socket.

When you placed one of the wire ends on an engine ground and the other wire end on the hot Battery terminal the light lit. I touched the wire on the coil that led back to the ignition switch and the other test led to ground and asked Cliff to turn the switch on. The light lit. I told him to leave the switch on and I connected the test light between the other terminal on the coil and to ground and I saw no indication of continuity in the coil primary, but it was a poor test without a voltmeter. I asked Cliff what make of engine was in the combines and he said he thought they were Chrysler industrial engines. I climbed up and looked at the engine on the combine on the truck and it looked like a Dodge flathead 6 cylinder. With Cliffs permission we removed the ignition coil from the combine engine and installed it on the truck. The truck started up on the first try. Cliff was noticeably relived, and he said I have work for at least 2 of you. He said that when we got to combining, he could employe all 3 of us. Cliff was concerned about letting any of us drive the truck with the combines. So, he said, I'il drive the truck, and one of you can drive the Pick-up and we'll go about 30 miles up the road to my next job. He said, I'll go first, and you need to follow me close with the pickup because it has the Wide Load sign on it. He said that there was a store on the way that might have a coil and we would stop there. The store was part food, part gas, part auto repair and some parts. They had a coil that would work.

Farming Again

We continued to the farm that Cliff had agreed to combine for earlier in the year. It seems he had made a trip thru all the country he normally worked during the spring. He had gotten agreements with several farmers that he would be at their place on or about a certain date to harvest their crops. We pulled onto the farm, and everyone shook hands and discussed the weather and the work to be done. The farmer told Cliff that he was selling all his harvest to the grain elevator company. Cliff said he could standup the 5-foot-high truck sides and back section, that I hadn't noticed, folded on the bed of the truck. He said that he thought that the Elevator was close enough that he could take a full load of grain to the elevator and return before we filled the hoppers on the combines. This would allow us to keep cutting all day without delay. Cliff said that Bob and I could run the combines and Terry could drive the grain truck. He would supervise and assist with the offloading of grain from the combines into the truck. He planned on making the first trip to the elevator with Terry to get the procedure nailed down. Everyone was satisfied that we had a plan.

There was some afternoon left so we unloaded the machines and ran the engines, lubricated them and Cliff gave the three of us a quick demonstration on the operation of the combines. One thing that amazed me was the sparse quality of the wheat crop. I did not want to upset anyone, but I said that the wheat looked like it might produce 10 bushel per acre. What did they think? The farmer said he would be happy to get 10 bushel an acre. He knew we had farmed in Maryland, and he asked us what kind of yield we considered good back there. I told him the most farmers counted on 25 to 30 bushels / acre and for Barley they usually got 40 to 45 bushels / acre. They were amazed, and I thought they might want to call me a liar but Terry and Bob both joined in and talked about good crops and bad crops and about a danger that I did not think they encountered here. The straw on their wheat was no more that 12 inch tall. We told them that sometimes we would have very heavy rainstorms when the grain was ready to harvest, and the high winds and rain could beat the crop down to the ground and the loss of crop would be significant. I said that the short straw on their crops probably saved them from that sort of dilemma. They then asked me how high did the wheat grow on our Eastern farms?

When I told the 24 to 34 inches, they were
again clearly doubting my words. I told them the
straw was baled up after combining and was very
valuable for animal bedding. They told us to
adjust the cutter head to a height of 4 inches. This
only left 6 or 7 inches of straw on the head of the
grain. Cliff said this was enough for the grain to
feed properly in the thrashing section of the
machine, so we did not worry about it. We
started combining the next day and finished this
farmers crop in 2 days. We broke down the rigs
and loaded up for moving to the next job. The
farm we were headed to was located northwest of
where we were. Cliff said he was going to
combine up to Kansas and then start west to
Liberal Kansas. Cliff said he owned a small
house in Liberal. He said he had some work up
there, then he might go north to Nebraska if his
contacts there still needed grain harvested. Cliff
said his home was in Eads, Colorado and that was
where he intended to spend the winter. Cliff also
gave us some important personal information
about himself. Cliff said that he was a devoted
7th Day Adventist. He said he honored the
Sabbath, which for him was Saturdays. He told
us that from sundown on Friday until sundown of
Saturday he would be unreachable unless there
was a life and death emergency. He said that he

would pay us before sundown on Friday because they did not conduct any business on the Sabbath. The amount we had agreed on was 50 cents an hour. This was a standard farm wage in 1954. Payment was cash. We would finish up late afternoon on Friday. We could sleep under the combines, in the big truck or whatever worked for us. Work would commence on Monday morning. We cut wheat on several large farms, they called them Ranch's sometimes, after a couple weeks we ended up in Liberal, Kansas. This was very interesting. When we got to his house in Liberal, we parked the car and trucks and approached the front door of the house. Cliff said, I have not been here in close to a year. He then unlocked the door which opened in, as most front doors did in days gone by. He started to push the door open, and it took 2 of us to open it. There was at least 3 inches of very fine dirt/dust on the floor. The dirt was not wet or packed like it had been wet, it had been blown under the thin crack between the bottom of the door and the floor. The dirt was everywhere. On windowsills on furniture just everywhere! Cliff said this is plains dust storms for you. It took us hours and hours to put the fields back outside so they could go back to raising crops.

Welcome To Liberal!

Well, we had a good night sleeping in the house. But the next day got off to a bad start. The 3 of us drove into Liberal and drove down the very wide, and only, business street looking for a restaurant. I saw a restaurant on the opposite side of the street from the side I was driving on. The cars and pickups were all parked facing into the curb at a 45-degree angle. Well, that's O K I can park like that. There was a empty parking spot in front of the restaurant, so I went a little pass the parking spot then since there was no traffic on the street I turned left. And pulled into the parking space. We got out of the car and went inside. The waitress was friendly and showed us to a table close to the window. She took our order. A few moments later a Policeman pulled up in a squad car and walked around my car, looking at the back and I guess the Maryland license plate. He then entered the restaurant and although we were the only patrons in the place he asked in a loud voice, who's convertible is that parked at the curb? I stood up and said that is my car sir. He came over and said, "You know you parked illegally before you came in here" I must have looked at him like he had 2 heads and said "I 'm afraid I don't unterstand Sir". He looked at me and said, "You cannot pull across the street to park on the other side of the street." I thought about that for a couple minutes trying to figure out how people got from one side of the street to the other in Busy Liberal Kansas, but I did not dare question his clearly superior knowledge on this subject. I said that I was not aware of a more reasonable way to use that parking spot. He made a face that I knew was going to cost me money and said, "ignorance of the law is no excuse" and he started writing a ticket. I asked if I could get my registration from the car, and he said yes. He wrote the ticket then asked how long we would be in town. I knew the right answer was, "Not long sir" he said Well, the Magistrate hears traffic tickets on Saturday mornings. So, I said "that would be fine, and I would be there". He gave me the ticket and left. The waitress came to our table and said you are eating at the wrong restaurant. I laughed and asked, what do you mean? She said the Sheriff's brother owns the restaurant crossed the street. We looked over and saw the deputy parking his cruiser and walking into the Sheriff's brother's place. The thought then crossed my mind and I asked her "how do you park like I did today" she said most people would have parked the way you did. They call it "Jay Parking". I looked at my ticket and that was what I was charged with. I said I guess what it really means is get out of town before you get into real trouble. She laughed and said welcome to Liberal, Kansas. We told Cliff that we would not be going north with him to Nebraska. We said we were committed to continuing toward California. We did not tell him about the ticket and our concerns about the fine. Since it was Thursday, we said we would help him service the equipment or anything else he wanted us to do but we would like to be paid up to date so we could leave early Friday morning. Cliff was O K with this, he was obviously used to dealing with drifters and knew we would leave sometime soon. We were paid, put our gear in the car and quietly departed lovely Liberal Kansas early on that Friday.

We headed for the Colorado boarder which was only 50 miles west. I never heard from the Sheriff of Liberal again.

When we got to Colorado we drove to Denver. We had promised Tommy May's family that we would stop and see him if possible. Tommy had graduated from Sykesville High School a couple years before Bob, and I graduated. He was then in the U S Air Force and stationed at Lowery Airfield in Denver.

I think that Lowery later morphed into the present Denver Airport.

When we got to the gate at Lowery, they directed us to the Provost Marshall's office. He was able to locate Tommy and had him brought to the office to meet us and spend a little time with us. I thought this was very nice of everyone involved. We got a picture of him and Bob and I to show his family when we returned to Sykesville.

Forest Service Work

During discussions with different people in Denver someone suggested that we would be able to find work with the U S Forest Service up near Nucala on the western slope of the Rockies. This would be almost into Utah. Some research led us to our work destination, The Uncompahgre National Forest with a ranger contact in Montrose. The U S highway between Denver and Colorado Springs was route 85. We drove down to Colorado Springs on US 85, and took a detour up Pikes Peak, then U S 50 over the Rockies to Montrose. We found the Forest Service people that were fighting the Engelmann Spruce beetle infestation. They were looking for strong backed, weak minded young men to carry a 5 gallon spray pack on their back, (45 lb.) and carry another 5 gallon can (45 lb) of spray to refill the back pack from. This was to be done at an altitude of 7000 to 9000 feet. Now if you were a young fellow from Denver (5000 ft. elevation) you grew up with a little larger set of lungs than your neighbor from sea level Maryland. The Service had camps that were as high as 10,000 feet for the crews to live in. The camp we stayed at was nice. There were bunks on wooden floors in large tents. There were around 10 men in a tent. The latrines were out of doors but clean, there was a cafeteria tent for breakfast and dinner. Lunch was a nice package containing a sandwich, some cookies and maybe a candy bar. Everyone had a canteen and if you needed to refill it during the day you were provided with a community refill station set up. The camp setting was beautiful. We were just above a small lake that had Beavers in it. The one problem other that the very thin air was that it gets cold at night in the high Rockies! When we got up in the morning you would sometimes see a thin sheet of ice near the edge of the lake. We did not have heavy clothes. We had summer clothes from the East Coast. The food and bunk were part of the compensation package. The salary was what was probably the national average at that time. Fifty cents an hour! We rolled out at sunup, had breakfast and headed for the trees. The trees that were infested and given high priority were ones with holes in the bark where the beetles had bored into the tree. You sprayed the tree all the way around and up as high as 5 to 7 feet then went to the next tree. The spray left a reddish cast on the tree so you could tell which trees were already sprayed. We did this work for 2 weeks and it was killing us! Someone told us we could probably get a job over at Nucala. They said the Vanadium Corporation was hiring miners to mine Uranium. Well, we were not sure that we wanted to work with something that might have you Glowing at night, but we thought we would quit this job and go see what was up in Nucala. We drew our pay, said goodbye to our new friends and headed down off the mountain. We drove to Nucala to see some guys we had met with the Forest Service.

Water!

One of the strange things we encountered on the road to Nucala had to do with water. Where we came from in Maryland there were hundreds of small streams that fed into rivers which drained into the Chesapeake Bay. If there was a stream on your property you used the water to water your crops, water your animals, wash your car or whatever. Not so, on the Western Slope of the Rockies! We saw water flowing in streams alongside of the road and across fields, but this water was orderly and controlled. The streams were man made. There were gates on the edges to allow water to flow over into smaller streams at a controlled rate. Our newfound friends who had lived here all their lives told us that water was more valuable than gold. They said, People get killed over water! They said "water rights" had been allocated since the first settlers came to farm here. They said land was nearly worthless without water rights connected to it. Without water you could not farm or raise animals! When we arrived in the village of Nucala the big talk was about a Dance that was happening in Telluride on Saturday night. I asked about the distance to Telluride and was advised that it was around 65 miles. They said that was not 65 miles that you drove in 2 hours, but 65 miles of mountainous roads that required nearly 5 hours to traverse. But there would be girls to dance with, beer to drink.

Pool Shark

So, we planned the trip for Saturday. 4 of us drove up there. We stopped on the way at a hole in the wall bar for something to eat and drink. When we went in, we noticed a game of pool going on in the back. After our light lunch, Terry walked over to the pool table and was invited to shoot a round. There were 2 guys at the table and Terry said why don't you play with us Ralph? I agreed and selected a cue from the wall and put a dollar on the ledge with 3 other dollars. I was selected to break. Not only did I break, but I ran the table! When I finished everyone looked at me like I was Mr. Pool Shark! I placed the cue in the rack and picked up the 4 dollars. As I started for the door one of the losers said, art'n you going to let us try to win our money back? I said No, we got a long way to go, and we need to get moving. The 4 of us walked out while I'm sure that the losers were trying to decide if they wanted to test their skills at fisticuffs with us. Terry said, I did not know you were that good at pool. I said, That was the first time I shot a game of pool. I was lucky. I figured that it was a good time to stop. Remember in 1954 you could fill the gas tank for 3 dollars.

Wild West

Telluride was a string of buildings on a dirt street. There were hitching posts in front of most of the stores. I'v never been back to Telluride, but as I watch TV shows of the Rich and Famous Glad Flying around Telluride today, I'm sorry I lacked money and knowledge to invest at 1954 prices in this rundown town! The Dance was as advertised. But we were like the "Dog chasing the hubcap on a car, when the car stops, he don't know what to do with the cap."

Some of the girls might have been 'Willing 'but what are you going to do? Our answer was dance some more, drink some more beer and drive back to Nucala. A couple of days later Bob and I decided that the possibility of finding enough work crossing the desserts of Utah and Nevada to earn money to get to California looked bleak. So we packed up for the trip back to Maryland. This turned out to be a life changing decision for me as I will explain later. Terry decided he would give mining a shot and he would stay in Colorado. Bob and I had about 100 dollars between us. We decided that the best course of action was to plan on driving straight thru to Maryland. We had noticed that the Plymouth

lacked the power that it had when we started the
trip. We were talking to the mountaineers about
this and they asked if we had changed the Jets in
the carburetor when we got to Colorado. We said
of course not, why would we have done that.
They explained to us that at the higher altitudes
the air was much thinner and had less oxygen, so
you needed to reduce the amount of gas that was
dumped into the manifold because it was not
getting enough oxygen to burn completely. Well,
weather that was true or not did not matter at this
time because we were dropping down out of
these mountains to the plains and the car should
run better then. We left the next day at daybreak
and made our way back to Colorado Springs, then
north to Denver and then east on US 40. When
we got out of the mountains, we were still at an
altitude of 5000 feet. We had made a trip to the
Capital building to stand on the step that was said
to be 1 mile high or 5280 feet above sea level
when we first arrived in Denver. The high plains
gradually lost altitude on the way to the
Mississippi River. After we got to Colorado
Springs, I leaned the carburetor out by backing
the idle adjustment screw well out. Later in the
trip I removed the screw completely. To do this
Bob held the throttle at a very high idle. The
engine was rough but ran until the car got up to

50 MPH or so. This allowed a lot of extra air to mix with the fuel/air mixture. This is not good for the health of the engine, particularly older engines burning the quality of gas that was available in 1954. The engine designers counted on a certain amount of lead to be fed to the engine to assist in upper cylinder lubrication. The lead came from the gas sold in 1954. When lead free gas was forced on the market, engines were redesigned with hardened valve seats, valves were made of tougher metals and engine design in general improved to deal with lead free gasoline. My 1949 Chrysler engine was in self-destruct mode, but I did not realize it. But we were getting excellent fuel mileage. 22 or 23 MPG.

When I was down to my last 10 dollars Bob said not to worry, he had a 100-dollar bill that he had stashed for a rainy day. He said I think I feel some rain. We had to cash his 100 for enough gas to get to Sykesville. Driving through the night and then all day was tiring. The roads in 1954 were mostly 2 lane and they all went straight thru every town. No towns had bypasses until the Interstate System was built. That was not started until the late 1950's and not completed until the 1970's. Cars like my Plymouth did not have any features to make driving easier. Only expensive cars had automatic transmissions, power steering and air conditioning. We drove until we felt sleepy them, we would stop and trade off driving. When we got back it was not such a big deal. We had been gone about 5 weeks. The time seemed much longer when you were living it every day. Everyone wanted to hear about our trip, but no one was critical about us turning back without going all the way to California.

Life After High School

Bob and I moved into my bedroom with my younger brother. I went back to the hospital and asked for a job. They rehired me but I could tell that there was a cool atmosphere around rehiring me. I was offered a job at the Epileptic Colony.

The shift was nights, 11 to 7 am. I took the job but knew that it would have to be temporary. Bob got a job at the hospital, but I told him not to tell them that he knew me because it might cloud their thinking about hiring him. I think that some of the bosses thought that I had let them down by leaving when I did, after they had provided a job for me through high school. Maybe so, but life moves on. My car needed serious work. I took it to Billy Feezer for evaluation. Billy kept the car for a day then told me the bad news. The engine needed a major overhaul. He said it would cost $250. I had no choice. I told him to start on it. I bummed rides to work. The overhaul took a full week. Bob bought a 40-ford coupe for less than the overhaul on my car. When my car was completed, I borrowed some money from my mom, I had not collected my first paycheck, but I promised Billy the rest of the money in 2 weeks. I was back on the road. The damage on the engine was the worst I have ever seen on an engine that still ran! The lower section of 3 of the pistons had broken completely off. There was no skirt below the wrist pin boss on those 3 pistons. Billy and I could not figure out how the top part of those pistons kept from rotating in the cylinders and destroying the engine. The engine ran great after the overhaul.

Arlene and I picked up our relationship where we had left off. I was so glad to see her again!

Where Is OSHA?

The job at the hospital was not going well. I
did not like the work. I wanted to be working
outside. I wanted to make more money. And I
did not enjoy pulling peoples tongues out of their
throats to keep them from choking to death as
they were having a seizure. I was talking to my
uncle Arse about my problem, and he said why
don't you come down to the Soapstone quarry
where I work. I think they need a guy in the
stone mill. To put this situation in perspective
you need to know that after the Korean War
ended in 1953 there were a lot of military guys
returning to civilian life and looking for jobs. By
1954 the country was entering a recession. Jobs
were not plentiful. I knew the quarry and mill
processed a stone locals called "Soapstone" I
have also heard it called Feldspar. The stone had
a slippery feel. Some quarries cut this stone in
slabs 2 or 3 inches thick, and they made sanitary
tubs for basement or industrial use. I see Soap
Stone now showing up in designers' kitchens! I
went to the quarry before I quit my job at
Springfield and talked to the Superintendent
about work. He said the only job he had open
was in the Grinding Mill. He said all his quarry

jobs were filled. I asked him to describe the job in the mill. He said 2 people ran the mill at night. There was no day shift in the mill. During the day maintenance was done on the equipment and the grinding cylinders were refilled to run all night. The night shift started at 6 PM and ran until 6AM. 6 days a week!

72 hours. The hourly rate was 75 cents an hour. Time and 1/2 for over 40 hours a week equaled 32 more hours. Some quick mental math told me that I would be paid for 104 hours a week. That grossed out to $ 78 a week. That was more than the hospital, but a lot more hours. But it was a job. I said I was interested, so he walked me up the road 200 feet to the main mill building. There was dust everywhere. Dust was on the trees. The roadside rocks and brush on the buildings. The front of the building was open to the road, with enough setback space to allow a Tractor Trailer to back up to a loading ramp on the front of the building. If the tractor was disconnected and pulled away the trailer could be left, there without blocking the road. There was enough length to the loading ramp that 3 or 4 trailers could be parked their side by side at the same time. I never saw more than one there at any time though. Behind the long loading ramp, the building continued for a depth of 40 or 50 feet.

The roof of the building was maybe 25 foot high. The building was about half full of bags of Soap Stone Dust.

The bags weighted 90 pounds each according to the writing on the heavy-duty paper bags. We walked to the far end of the ramp and there was a pipe about 10 inches in diameter hanging down with a bag pulled over the end and a cut off lever in closed position. The Super pointed to the bag and said this station fills bags with #28 grade of stone. He said that means a screen having 28 holes per square inch in it would allow this size of stone to pass thru. I asked him what this #28 grade was used for and he said The stones you see on roofing shingles are #28 grade Soap Stone. The Shingle manufactures paint the stones and then sprinkle an even layer of then on the hot shingles. The stone embeds in the soft surface and stays there for years. He said we get around 150 bags of this stone each shift. You will either load an amount listed on the loading sheet for a trailer or move the remaining bags of stone from the nights run to the warehouse. A little farther along in the building was another bag filling station. The Super said the dust comes out of the mill and is bagged here. The dust is screened to 270 fine dust. That again is the number of holes in a 1-inch square of screen. The Super said that this dust had a lot of industrial uses. He said one use I might be familiar with is as a none stick barrier on rolled roofing paper.

I immediately thought of the powdery dust on roofing paper. The Guy you will be working with has worked at the mill for a number of years. He fills a bag then closes it with a 'Stitcher', then places the bag on a hand truck like this one here. And he points to a 2-wheel hand truck standing beside the bagger. The truck had 4 bags neatly stacked on it. He said this hand truck will hold 10 bags. It balances well, he said, when you tilt it back, stop as soon as the handle weight feels balanced, then you can push the truck to the ramp of the trailer or back into the warehouse. By the time you load the bags into the truck or carry them up into the warehouse and return to the bagger the other hand truck should be loaded. He then asked, Are you O K with all of this? I said "Sure"! The Super led me back to the office and we filled out some paperwork and he got me on the payroll. A few people drifted in and out of the office while I was there. I knew some of them, he introduced me to the others. Everyone welcomed me to the job. I knew a lot about the Quarry operation from visiting my uncle when he was working. The Quarry was just up the road from the mill by a couple hundred yards. The quarry had been worked for a number of years. The floor of the quarry extended about 200 feet away from the road.

The mouth of the quarry in the high hill side was maybe 150 yards across the back wall of the quarry had to be 200 feet high. During the week 1 or 2 men would be drilling on the face of the quarry from the foot up to the ridge with the surrounding woods. The woods had to be cut back 20 or 30 feet from the face to keep trees from falling into the quarry. The drillers used pneumatic air hoses to operate the drills. They would start with a 2-foot drill bit, then move to a 4-foot bit, until the hole was 20 to 22 foot deep. They started drilling 8 feet back from the edge at a slight angle back. The face of the quarry sloped back at about 75 degrees. When they reached the finished depth, they would put a plug in the hole to keep it from getting any dirt or stone in it. They would mark it with a small flag to find the hole later. A series of holes in a line across the face were drilled, then they moved down the face 15 feet and drilled another string of holes. The drillers worked from Monday to Thursday. On Friday they loaded the holes with Dynamite. An electric detonation cap was placed in the bottom of a stick of dynamite. The wires were taped to the side of the stick of dynamite and brought up to the other end of the stick. This way the cap could not pull out of the stick.

They would then lower the dynamite down into the hole by the electric wire pair connected to the cap.

They would carefully extend the wire until the dynamite was at the bottom of the hole. They would sometimes have to gently push the dynamite to get it down. The wire ends were taped so as not to touch during handling. More sticks of dynamite were placed in the hole until the required amount was in place. Then several hands full of wet mud were shoved into the hole. This forced the explosion to go down and out. All the holes were loaded and on Friday the wires from all of the holes were lead together outside of the quarry entrance. In early afternoon traffic was stopped on the road and the wires were connected to the Detonation Plunger, this was an electric current generator, the blaster pushed the Plunger handle down rapidly and a charge of electricity was sent thru the wires and the face of the quarry was shot out into the floor of the quarry. The full face for about 8 feet back moved out and fell to the floor of the quarry. There was usually a lot of dirt, dust and some small stones that showered onto the road. Several guys would clean up the road if necessary. This would provide stone for a week or more depending on mill operation. Every morning one of the crew experienced in handling dynamite would have to breakup some large boulders into a size that would fit into the mouth of the stone crusher at the mill. To do this, a couple guys would pick a boulder closest to the road and examine it for the best place to set a small charge to shatter the boulder. They had been doing this for years and could quickly select a place and determine if they needed a quarter stick or half stick of dynamite. When they had the location for the charge they would place the piece of a stick, it seldom required more than that, on the boulder with an electric cap in the dynamite. They would then place a large handful of mud from the quarry floor or a close mud puddle or a bucket of water from the Piney Falls that flowed by the mill. This handful of mud, to my amazement made all of the force go down into the boulder and split it to pieces. They would "Cap" 5 to 10 boulders and then clear the quarry, stop traffic, and with all the detonation wires brought back to the Ignition Plunger up the road in the clear, they would shoot the boulders and when the dust cleared there would be a nice bunch of smaller size rocks. Then everyone could get to work. One of the first jobs that the shot crew did was to follow all of the wires back into the jumble of broken rock and see if they could trace the wires to the remains of the end that was connected to the blasting caps.

This was not always possible but occasionally, they would find a stick that did not detonate. They would carefully remove the cap from the stick of dynamite and safely dispose of the cap. What they did not want to happen was to have the shovel bang against the unexploded dynamite and injure or kill someone. My uncle Arse operated the Diesel-powered shovel. We always called it "The Steam Shovel". I could never get over that name. He would load dump trucks and they would make the short trip, 200, 300 feet to the rock crusher. The trucks would dump their loads then return for another load of stone. The crusher pulverized the stone and fed the small pieces of stone and dust into a giant hopper which fed the rotating mill. As the mill rotated and tumbled the stone it was ground to the sizes that were screened out for bagging.

When I arrived for work at 6 PM my new boss, instructor and companion for 12 hours a night, 6 days a week, Jim, took me under his wise guidance. He said, think about everything you do, before you do it. There are a lot of ways to get hurt here. If you get hurt, about the most you can expect around here is some Iodine and a band aid. So don't get hurt.

Jim was a large man, but not fat. He was as strong as an Ox. I never asked his age, but he had to be 60 or so. He told me to complete the loading of the truck. He said it's all #270. No #28 on this truck load. The bags of #28 accumulated much slower. He placed them on a different hand cart and when it was full, I would wheel it to the section of the warehouse reserved for #28. When he placed the 10th bag of #270 on the cart I wheeled it to the trailer truck, wheeled it to the front of the trailer and set the cart up straight and slide the load of bags off the cart and up against the forward wall of the trailer. It looked like the pile of bags would have to be about 20 high to fill the trailer to a load line someone had drawn on the side of the trailer marked "270 dust." When I went back to the bagging station the next cart only had 5 bags on it. Jim said over the noise of the mill, go rest on those bags of dust, I'll holler at you when it's full". This started a drill for me that lasted as long as I worked there. I would move the cart of bags, return the empty cart then lay down on the last warm bags of dust from the mill. The stone got fairly hot as it was tumbled. I could go to sleep almost immediately and would sleep until Jim gently kicked me on the foot to wake me.

The Dust was as thick as fog. We had simple paper masks that we wore. The masks had an elastic band that held them on your face. The hanky that I had tied at the back of my head to cover my face did not prevent much dust from being inhaled either. I would spit the dust out, I would blow it out of both sides of my nose and when we took a break at the office I would use the air hose on my head and face and blow out more dust. Then blow dust off my clothes. Then use the water hose to clean my face and nose. The dust was never ending. There was no OSHA in 1954. Had there been, this place would have been long ago out of business, at least the way they were operating. But in defense of the Owners and Operators they would say, "You don't have to work here". "There are plenty of men looking for work who would do the job and not complain" When 6 AM came we shut the mill down, walked down to the office for the last time on that shift and cleaned up again. After a few days my car looked like everyone else's car there. Almost white, the inside was dusty, everything was dusty! I was still living with my parents and my mother commented on the dust, she had lived near the mill for years and did not think any more about long term health concerns than a 18 year old boy did.

"LSMFT" - 'Lucky Strikes Means Fine Tobacco '

This was the advertisement slogan used by Lucky Strike cigarettes. All the cigarette manufacturers had catchy advertising phrases. Nearly every man smoked. At least one member of every family filled the house with smoke. I had never started the habit of smoking for 2 reasons. First, I was a non-conformist. All the kids I went to school with smoked. It was the "Cool" thing to do. So, I didn't smoke! You could buy cigarettes 1 or 2 at time from most stores or Filling stations. They charged 2 cents apiece for them and doubled their money on a pack of cigarettes. I thought it was a dirty habit plus, I didn't want to spend what little money I had on smokes. My father smoked, both my brothers smoked, but I did not, nor did my mother. So, the dust at the mill job was not enough to make me look for other work. Arlene and I went out every Saturday night. This was the only night I had off. We would go to a dance if one was happening close. We might go to movies. But what we both wanted to do was find a secluded place to park and talk and kiss and plan a little on our futures.

My father would ask me every once in a while, if I would like for him to try and get me job with The C & P Telephone Company where he was a Line Foreman. I, being the non-Conformist, didn't want to just follow my father into a job. We did not talk about 'Careers 'in those days. You got a Job, and you went to work.

People were not afraid of work; they did not think that the world owed them a living because they had decided to grace the world with their presence. Bob Bruce was living with my family at that time. Bob had his nice 40 Ford Coupe, and he also bought a 1949 Harley-Davidson motorcycle. I would ride the 'bike 'from time to time. Arlene liked to ride with me, but her father was very upset about it. Carl thought I was farm trash, and he would rather see the 'Apple of His Eye 'do a little better. He told Arlene once, "If you think anything about your life you will stay off that Motorcycle" I never thought that 20 years later I would be saying the same thing to a dinner table full of our kids! As luck would have it the worst that happened to us on Bob's bike was dropping it over off the kick stand. The long nights went on until late October. I had been in the mill since Mid-August. When the Superintendent asked me if I would like to go on day work. I jumped at that. He said he needed a driller in the quarry! This was 5 nine-hour days and 4 hours on Saturday. 49 hours was less money than 72 but I was being dragged down by the long weeks in the mill. I figured that I was moving a cart of dust every 25 to 30 minuets. That was 10 times 90 pounds or 900 pounds. I was working 12 hours a night so that added up to around 11 tons of dust with a break thrown in that I was moving each night. Did I want to go on days, you bet your butt I did. Drilling was easy work compared to the mill. I enjoyed the outdoor work. The guys in the quarry were fun to work with. The work lasted thru November then the mill was notified that they were cutting back on production because of a slowdown in the economy. They were going to let several people go. Since I was the last one hired, I was the first to go.

Merry Christmas

Well, where do you look for work three weeks before Christmas? How about a big company that does a lot of business around Christmas? Hello, Montgomery Wards. Monkey Wards as we kidded about it was one of the largest mail order/catalog companies in the world. As luck would have it, one of their largest stores was in Baltimore. I drove down to Wards as it was called for short and applied for a job. They asked if I could start that day! Well, yes since you mention it, I' m not doing anything today except looking for work. The job was hectic. I was led to a workplace where boxes were setting around opened, partially filled with toys, clothes everything that's in the Wards Catalog There were shipping bags torn open merchandise spilling out of them.

What is going on here? There were conveyer belts moving all this disorganized stuff along. There were a lot of message tubes that people launch canisters full of papers in. A young man maybe a year or two older than me came up and said, "Boy can I use your help". I said what is this all about.? He said, when shipments to customers are damaged in shipping, whether at

the post office or by anyone else handling our
merchandise It is returned to this department.
Our job is to try to find a shipping order or
anything that will let us reassemble their order
and resend it to them. He said we start by placing
stuff that comes in and looks like it was in the
same shipment in a box to start reassembly. If we
have the shipping papers, we are in good shape.
We look thru all the stuff we have and put the
items that seem to be part of the order in the box.
When we find that something was lost and not
returned to us, we contact that department and
reorder the item to include it in the order. He
said when all we have is the mailing label, we
contact Mail Order sales, and they provide us
with the shipping list for that order. We can build
the order from that. The priority is to get these
orders to the customers in time for Christmas.
Now you must know something about the size of
this Montgomery Ward facility. The building
was a Humongous white building trimmed in
black that was located on the end of Monroe
Street in West Baltimore. The footprint of the
building must have been 2 acres. The building
must have been set on a 4- or 5-acre plot. The
building was 5 or 6 stories high. The building
housed a large retail area as well as the giant mail
order operation. I had shopped there with my

parents on several occasions. 30 years later I saw the twin to this building in Oakland, California. Mail Order was big business back then. Many people were too far from large cities to have the selection of goods available to them that were at their fingertips in the Wards catalog. The job paid 65 cents an hour and I had to drive 25 miles to Baltimore, but it was a job. The work was interesting and challenging. We were working 10-hour days so there was some extra income to offset the lower wage. This job lasted until the first week in January of 1955. They then said the job is over and our regular staff can take over from here. Well, it got me through the Holiday season. I was beginning to formulate a feeling about life that reflected on my personal self-confidence, when someone might comment on the conditions or quality of a job, or more important, whether the management approved of my performance, my dress or demeanor my answer was always the same!

" I was looking for a job when I came here and I will be looking for a job when I leave". Unlike so many people I meet today, particularly those who are out of work, I never considered a job as under my 'Station in Life'. I was willing to work at jobs some considered 'Menial 'or 'Beneath my Social level'.

To point out what I mean, I remember a situation thai happened when I was a Second Level Manager at an At&T office in Maryland. We let the one 'Apparatus Cleaner' we had on the payroll 'Go' for sleeping on the job. Later in the day I noticed that the Test room area and the area around my desk needed sweeping. I asked the 1st line supervisor who was responsible for this function to see if he could get the place cleaned up a bit. He looked around and saw a Test Board man that was idle, and he asked the young man to please get a broom and sweep the area. The young man was not sure what to do, He had never been asked to sweep the floor before. He told the supervisor that he did not think that Sweeping Floors was on his job description. I overheard the comment and thought I would use this as a teaching 'Moment'. I said to the Supervisor, "that's OK Woody, I'll take care of this," I walked to the cabinet where brooms were stored, opened the door, and selected a nice 3-foot push broom. I then commenced sweeping the floor. There were 5 or 6 vocational employees, a couple of Supervisors, and 2 clerks in the immediate area. They were all rather Dumb Founded to see the "Central Office Chief "performing menial work. One of the Supervisors approached me and asked me to let him sweep. I quietly said to him, let this progress. I said in a conversational tone, "please get a dustpan to pick up the sweepings". While I was sweeping, the 'Shop Stewart 'that is, the Union Stewart showed up and asked me what I was doing. I said I was performing some much-needed work. He said that is not what you are paid to do Mr. Baker. I said I agree with you, but it is work that needs to be done and I make the same money for doing this that I make for Managing this office with 75 employees working here. I said if I was asked by my boss to perform work that was in the class of a higher pay scale then I would probably object. But to be asked to do something that was well within my skill level and below my pay grade I would not think twice about doing it. If that was the way the Company wanted to spend their money it was OK with me. I continued, "If it was my Company, I would hire someone in the lower pay grade, like an 'Apparatus Cleaner 'to get the work performed in a more cost-effective manner. I then pointed out that we would be looking to hire a replacement Apparatus Cleaner in the next several days, but in the meantime, someone had to sweep the floors. The Shop Stewart was sharp for a young man. He said. "I think anyone here would be glad to let you get back to more important work, can I have the broom to finish what you started? What I tried to imprint was the value of work. All work is good. A man should be compensated for the work he performs. He should not be cheated. But if the only work available required lower skills than you possessed and you were eminently qualified to perform the work that was available, and you were willing to work for your going hourly rate at the lower skilled level work then you should take the work until a better job came along. There was a saying that we used in the Cable Department when I worked there that stuck with me until this day, when describing a work operation, we would laugh and say "It's all in 8" meaning you pay me for 8 hours of work in a day and I will give you 8 hours of work. Who cares if the work is at the top of my pay skill or sweeping floors?

Are there any of these people left today?

Social Security Administration

I do not remember how I found the job at Social Security Administration. It could have been a tip from someone or an ad in the newspaper. It certainly did not come from the Internet or TV. Very few people had Tv's, and TV was not stooping so low as to peddling jobs. Computers numbered about 3 in the whole world. Those 3 required the space of a complete building each. I remember driving to downtown Baltimore. Social Security (SS) was in a number of buildings in Baltimore. The main building was The Chandler Building on Pratt Street. They had been in the Chandler building since the 1930's when the Social Security act created them. Across the street from the Chandler Building was the Harbor. There was a pier for car parking opposite the Chandler building that had to be 300 feet long. West of the parking pier was the Power Plant pier. To the East was another pier or 2 then the right turn into Little Italy. The Chandler Building was nearly a block square and 12 stories high. SS occupied many of the floors in 1955. I enter the building and was interviewed, then given a test and told that I would have to pass a physical. You could not be employed at any company or government agency unless you were in perfect health at that time. I don't know why they cared so much. No one had Health Care as part of their employment package except maybe the Military. After I was hired, I reported for work at 4 PM to start working on the 4 to 12 PM tour. I worked the evening tour for the full time I worked at Social Security. I was led to the 3rd or 4th floor of the building. The floor was full of IBM machines. All the machines were dealing with little cards about 3 1/4 inches wide and 7 3/8 inches long. The cards were thicker than writing paper but not as thick as cereal box cardboard. I found out later that the cards had 80 columns of rectangular holes, arranged in 12 rows. These cars stored the earning records of all the U S citizens who were covered by the SS program. My first job was operating a Collator. I loaded cards removed from card trays which were about 2 feet long and loaded them into a feed hopper on one end of the machine and continued to refill the hopper as the cards were fed along a tract on the top of the machine. Small metal brushes positioned above the cards made contact with receptors thru the rectangular holes in the cards. The machine gated the cards into vertical collection bins based on the information derived from the cards. The machines were electromechanical in their method of operation. There were boards larger than a book plugged into the end of the machine that had a large number of Jumper Wires connecting a matrix of holes together. This wiring "Instructed" the sorting operation. An early form of "Programing". The system was designed around the collection of individual earning data for employees on a quarterly basis from their employers. The data was reported under the heading of the employee Social Security number. This numbering scheme, of 3 digits followed by 2 digits, followed by 4 digits has weathered the test of time. The first 3 digits originally could narrow down the geographical area in the country where the card holder applied for their card. The second 2 digits created a group number which included 10,000 employees, 0001-9999. I think that most of this was still true in 1955 when I worked for the SS Administration. I believe that over time numbers retired by deaths have been recycled and reissued. One segment of the numbers has been reserved for Railroad employees since when the laws were passed in the 1930's that made SSA responsible for administrating the Railroad Employees Pension Plan. Numbers in the 7XX series were reserved for this purpose. When employers reported quarterly earnings data to

SSA, clerks would create IBM cards representing the data for a single employee for 1 quarter. If the employee worked for 2 or more employers in a quarter, then there would be multiple cards generated under that single SS number for that quarter. The job that I and a number of other collator machine operators had was to arrange the quarterly cards for 1 SS number in order for them to be processed by a IBM Tabulating machine which would create a summery card that was then carried forward with the quarterly cards until the end of the year. As each quarters earning were reported, new quarterly cards were created and after being joined with the year-to-date summery card via the collating process, a new summary card was produced. After the last quarters data was received and the processes were completed for that quarter a printout was printed and available for the personal that provided management of the payout process. This was generally how the records were handled in the 1955-time frame. The work was interesting as I learned more about the overall system and how we fit into the big picture. I think that a career at SSA would have been a good choice If I had stayed there. The recent recession of the 1930's affected my parents severely and their attitude was passed down to me. A young man should get a job with a company that would weather a depression, either a good job with a utility like the power company or the telephone company or the State or the Federal government. Jobs with manufacturing companies like, General Motors, Fisher Body, American Can and other big employers in Baltimore paid a good deal higher hourly rate, but they laid off for months at a time to retool for next year cars or because of a decline in the economy They didn't have solid retirement plans like the utilities had. I hired on with SSA for 60 dollars a week.

We were paid twice a month. I was required to contribute to the Federal Employees retirement plan. We had sick time and vacation time accumulate the same way that the state of Maryland's plan worked. I liked the work and drove my old 49 Plymouth to work every day. I soon realized that these cars days were numbered. When I received my first paycheck, I asked my mother to sign for me at a car dealer to get a new car. I was still 18 years old in January of 1955. You were not considered human back then until you were 21 years old. We went to a Plymouth dealer located on Edmondson Avenue in Baltimore to look for a car. The Salesman showed me a new Plymouth Savoy 2 door sedan. It was sharp, it had a two tone green paint job, a

V-8 engine and a stick shift. An AM radio and heater rounded out the options. They quickly removed my old car and I never saw it again. I'm sure they were ashamed to have it on the premise. With a new job that looked promising and a new car I was Styling! I liked the people I worked with at SSA and made good friends with several of them. I was still living at home waiting for Arlene to graduate from school and I now worked 5 days (evenings) a week, so I had both days of the week ends off. We took long drives on the weekends and had an enjoyable summer that year. My health seemed to be great. I never worried about it.

My Father's Line of Work

As the summer was slipping away my dad asked me again if I would like to get a job at Chesapeake and Potomac Telephone Company. He was a supervisor there and he said he thought he could arrange to get me hired if I wanted the job. The thought of working out of doors was appealing and I made a life changing decision and told him I was interested. But I would have to give SSA 2 week notice that I was leaving. I said I would not give notice until I had a start date from C&P. He set me up with an interview, and I took a physical at 320 Saint Paul Street, C&P's main building in downtown Baltimore. When all of this was completed, they said to report on September 5, 1955. For work. I told Social Security that I was resigning to take a job with C&P. Everyone I knew at SSA wished me good luck in my new endeavor. I started with The Chesapeake and Potomac Telephone Company at their plant garage in Catonsville, Md. There were 2 Line crews assigned there. These were 7-man crews. The number 1 crew worked for Bob Holman. The number 2 crew worked for my father H Otis Baker. They did not want to put me in my father's crew and that was fine with me. I knew that if I worked for my father, I would draw the worst assignments automatically. If there was a rock hole to dig, it would be mine, if there was a pull of open wire through a bunch of blackberry thorns it would be mine. So, I started my career in Telephony in Bob Holman's Line Crew. Bob was A good man. I knew him and several of the other linemen from hunting small game with my father or through visits to the garage with my father. Bob and the linemen in his crew were top of the line. I knew I would learn a lot from them. The 7-man crew trucks had a regular cab that the driver and the Foreman rode in. Behind that cab was a larger cab with a door on the right side of the cab and a full width bench seat that 5 men could spread out on. There was no glass in the window openings between the 2 cabs. This allowed all 7 of us to hear the driver and the Foreman discuss the job as we drove to the work location. C&P did not have lineman helpers, or grunts as they were called. All six of us were linemen. But our pay was quite a bit different. Top Lineman pay in 1955 when I went to work for C&P was $90 a week. I started at $37.50 a week. That was $24 a week less than my salary at SSA. I thought this was worth it because of some offsets and because I felt that I would get overtime pay and their

retirement plan was the best in the country. I
knew that I would see pay raises on a regular
basis at C&P so I was satisfied with my decision.
I also was glad to get outside to work. There was
a lot of home building going on in the suburbs. A
lot of our jobs were to install the utility poles and
attach the telephone equipment, such as strand to
support phone cables, the cables and also the
distribution terminals that were later connected
into the cables by a splicing crew. Splicing crews
were in the same garage we were in but in a
different department. The engineers who wrote
the job orders we worked from would sometime
indicate that a pole should be 'Stepped'. This
meant that we would have to drill holes in the
pole at certain heights and distances apart so and
install pole steps so that an Installer Repairman
could easily climb up the pole to the height of the
cable to work on telephone lines accessed in the
terminal.

All these poles were usually what were called
'Joint Use' This meant that the Electric company
would have their wires and transformers on the
top of the pole. To accommodate this
arrangement poles 35 foot high would be on the
order. We knew that 35-foot poles had to be set
in a five-foot hole. We were to install our cables
20 foot up the pole. The top 10 foot of the pole

was for the electric wires and transformers that the power company would install after we were finished with our work. We also placed anchors and guy cables on corners of the route where the pole line made a turn. This was to keep the load on lines from pulling the corner or end pole and causing it bend or break toward the strain. These equipment units were all shown on the job order we worked from. Before we left the yard in the morning, we loaded a 2-wheel trailer with the correct number and size of poles for the job. We also drew from the supply room, anchor rods, anchor plates and other necessary hardware for the job. When we got to the job, The Forman and one of the top linemen would walk over the job and mark where poles were to be set and anchors placed if this had not been done by the engineers. A couple of the lineman and the driver would start setting up the derrick on the back of the truck. The lowest man on the totem pole, me, would get a digging set off the truck and proceed to the first pole hole to be dug. The digging set consisted of a 5-foot shovel, a 9-foot digging bar, this bar had a point on one end a spade about 2 inches wide on the other end. The bar weighted 40 pounds by itself, before you picked up the other 3 tools. There was a 8 foot straight spade and an 8 foot spoon shovel to scope dirt from the bottom of the hole.

Some pole holes needed to be 6 foot 6 inches deep. The depth varied with the length of the pole. Equipped with this digging set which weighed more than I did, at my fighting weight of 125 pounds I would start digging. I really did not mind digging holes. It was just a small part of an interesting job. The derrick was mounted to the back of the truck by 2 of the linemen. It had 2 cables led to it. One was the derrick cable that was used to lift the derrick off the ground and to position the height of the derrick and pole that was being set. The other cable was the winch cable that was used to pull things and to lift poles and lower the pole into the hole. When setting poles, they would be left in the hole as the setting operation went from one hole to the next with the poles. After the poles were in the holes a couple or 3 men would come along and tamp the pole in. To do this, 2 men would get a couple of Pike Poles off the truck. These poles were 2 1/2 inches in diameter and 10 or 12 foot long and had a 2-inch pointed spike on one end. The 2 men would get on the 2 sides in which the pole was leaning and using the pike poles would push the pole to a near vertical position. The third man would sight the pole from first one side then 90 degrees around to that side and instruct the pole holders until he was satisfied that the pole was vertical. While this man observed that the pole remained vertical one additional lineman would be needed to start shoveling dirt in around the pole. He would have to stop after a half dozen shovels full and use the tamping bar to pack the dirt around the pole. After the hole was filled and tamped up 2 or 3 feet from the bottom the pike pole men could lay the poles on the ground and assist the man who was hole filling.

By then the man sighting vertical could return to the pole and help finish filling and tamping the hole. This may sound complicated but for a trained crew poles went up quickly. The only thing that could ruin your day was a rock hole. If you ran into a pole location that was so rocky with boulders or a slab of rock, you might have to have a qualified demolition person come to the job site and use a little dynamite to 'adjust 'the hole or contact the engineers and ask then to reroute the poles somewhat. This did not happen often in our area of operation.

C & P sent me to 1 school in September of 1955. The school was a 4-day school for New Linemen. In all the time I worked for C & P it was the only formal training they ever offered to me other than driver training. All other training was 'On the Job Training'. I will say this for C&P, they had some of the best instruction 'Manuals 'for any company in the USA. These manuals were The Bell System Practices or BSP's. The problem was that even though there was a set of them that involved most work we would be involved with kept in the office in the garage, the most that was available in the field on the truck was a partial set. You might be able to read them on a rainy day, but not when you had work to be done. OJT from coworkers was the answer. I was learning to work 'Aloft 'on climbing 'Hook's. Hooks were strapped to your legs, and you were careful not to bring a leg down carelessly and stab yourself in the leg. You would slap your leg against the pole and put you weight on the foot. You could feel the hook dig into the pole. You then straighten that leg but did not let your knee go up against the pole. If you did let the leg, go against the pole the hook would most likely Cut Out. This would drop you down the face of the pole rapidly. This could never end well. You next lifted the other leg up like you were climbing a set of stairs. You would bring that leg against the pole and place weight on it. As you lifted yourself to that new height you paid attention not to let the leg move in against the pole and when you were doing this properly you would be standing up straight holding on to the sides of the pole not to keep from falling backwards, but to steady yourself to pull the other foot up as you progressed up the pole. When you reached the working height you would bring the lower foot to the height of the upper foot, set the hook then disconnect one end of your safety belt and reach it part of the way around the pole and steady yourself with the hand holding the belt while you reached with the other hand an took hold of the end of the belt and brought it back and snapped it into the 'D 'ring on your work belt. You then looked to see that both ends were properly engaged in the belt 'D 'rings, and you could lean back. If you had just climbed a 50-foot pole, the sight from the top should be very good. Also, safety was not just taught it was preached. You never got into a motor vehicle with climbers on. You might end up stabbing yourself or someone else.

Driving was a big deal with C&P as it was with all the Bell Companies. I found out in later years that these companies were 'Self-Insured'. This was one of the big reasons that they wanted excellent drivers. They actually issued their own driver's license. You had to have a clean State of Maryland license as well as C&P license to drive one of their vehicles. Backing always required that you have someone watch behind your vehicle as you backed if there were 2 or more people in the vehicle. When driving alone they required that you walk around to the back of your vehicle and check for children or obstructions before backing. We held safety meetings in the garage monthly and tailgate meetings a couple times a week. Attendance was only next to safety. When I worked for the State and for the Federal governments, I found that most people treated sick time just like vacation time. The only difference was you did not want to talk about the nice day you had at the beach on your sick day! With Bell System companies like C&P, they expected you to be at work every day. They expected you to be on the job 10 or 15 minuets early. You did not come to work and then go immediately to the Crapper for 15 minuets. You better get up early enough to Crap on your own time before you come to work. If you needed to go after you were on the job for a few hours that was to be expected. They did not allocate a certain number of days per month to sick or vacation time. You received 1 week of vacation time after 1 year of service. After 2 years you got 2 weeks. Paid Sick time was at the discretion of management. If you had a couple years of service and were a good employee, you could receive up to 1 year of Sick Leave before you were put on Disability. They treated good employees well. They gave marginal employees an opportunity to find employment elsewhere. The people that I worked with were all at least High School graduates, some had a year or 2 of collage. Most of the linemen in my crew had attended Loyola High School in Baltimore or City High School. Graduates from those schools in 1955 received a far better education than the average high school attendee in today's schools. They were on my butt continually about my grammar. They would correct me until I started to sound like I understood Proper English. These guys also dressed nice for the type of work that they performed. One day in the first week I was in the crew I came in with a hole in the leg of my pants. Before noon someone had grabbed at the hole and tore it much larger. I was flabbergasted! I screamed what are you doing? The guy answered as some of the other guys looked on, 'We don't come to work looking like bums' 'I thought that you might get a 'hole free' pair of pants if you could not ware that pair anymore' Someone else pointed out that a tear could snag on a pole step or other protrusion on a pole and cause me to get hurt. I improved the type and condition of my clothes as I improved my

English. Open Wire was still used to provide phone service in the rural parts of our work area. Open Wire was just that. A pair of bare .109 diameter wires connected to a pair of glass insulators. They might run for a half mile or more to a farmhouse on 3 or 4 poles that the property owner had to pay to have installed to get phone and probably electricity to their house. That pair might connect to an open wire run that went some distance towards the central telephone office before it was connected into a cable to complete the trip to the central office. If there were a number of open wire circuits on a pole, they would be carried on Ten Pin Arms. A ten-pin arm was about 10 foot long and had 10 wooden pins inserted in holes on the top of the arm. The pins had a crude thread cut into them. Glass insulators were hand screwed onto the pins, the wires were held against a grove in the glass insulator with 12-inch lengths of soft wire that were wrapped around the open wire on one side of the insulator and drawn tightly across the face of the insulator opposite the side that the open wire passed the insulator on. The other end of this 'Wire Tie 'was wrapped tightly around the open wire on the opposite side of the insulator. 10 wires or 5 pairs, a Pair being required for communication, were attached to each 10-pin arm. The arms were bolted to the pole in the middle of the arm. 2 metal straps, each about 3 feet long were bolted to the arm at one end and to the center of the pole at the other end. This supported the arm and kept the arm stable. Our crew was called out on a weekend to repair storm wind damage. We had some work to do on an Open Wire to cable termination pole. The open wires were terminated on the cross arm and jumper wires went to a cable terminal. The cable terminal was spliced into a cable that went down the pole and went underground. There was a 'U' shaped metal guard over the underground cable run. There was a second underground cable that came up the pole and went in the opposite direction from the pole. This second cable also had a cable guard on it. I was going to climb the pole on 'hooks' to examine the terminal for lightning damage. As I started up the pole, I saw that there was plenty of space between the 2 cable guards for me to place one of my feet in as I climbed the pole. It was warm out and I was only wearing a 'T 'shirt on my upper body, with dungarees covering my legs. When I nearly reached the height where I would stop climbing and hook my belt and examine the terminal. I attempted to set my foot on the side between the cable guards and there was no pole there! The guards had been slowly becoming closer together as I climbed, and I never looked down to check on this situation. Everything that happened in the next several seconds went to slow motion, but there was nothing I could do to prevent what was happening except reach out with both hands and try to grab the pole and stop my decent to the ground 15 feet below me. I only fell about 2 feet when my 'T 'shirt caught on the top edge of one of the cable guards. The shirt stretched, then tore and I continued down. My head was enough to one side that my chin missed the edge of the guard. Had I caught my chin on the guard I could have broken my neck or caused other significant injury. In a second, I was on the ground, still standing. My feet had dropped about 7 feet after the shirt tore, enough to cause injury, but I must have landed well and was just shaken. One of the older linemen was near the pole waiting for me to tell him what I had found. He looked at me and not knowing if I was injured or not was not sure what to say. Before he could say something smart to reflect on my stupidity, I blurted out. 'It looked OK so I took the fast way down' I think that incident and my response made me an authentic member of the crew. I was asked to describe my 'decent 'at the next tailgate safety meeting, but no more was said about the incident.

A Ghost From The Past

I was enjoying the line crew and telephone work. Thanksgiving passed and near the end of November I decided to perform a tune up on my car. I bought ignition points and parts for the distributor. I planned on working on the car in my father's driveway. After dinner on a Friday evening with the hood open, I covered one of the front fenders with a work blanket and leaned into the engine compartment and removed the distributer cap, points and rotor and was just straightening up when I felt a strong urge to cough. When I coughed, I felt warm fluid rush out of my mouth. I knew right away by the silvery taste that it was blood! But this could not be right because this was a lot of blood. I put my hand to my face and when I looked at my hand it was covered with blood. I went into the house and my father was sitting at the kitchen table watching a small TV that was on top of the refrigerator. He looked around to where I had just entered the kitchen from the other side and saw the blood. He said what has happened to you. I said 'I coughed and started spitting up blood. My mother was working at her evening job at the State Hospital. My brother Donald came into the kitchen, and we went through the same questions. I said would one of you please call Dr Gau and ask him what we should do. Dr Gau was the primary Doctor for Sykesville. His son Claude was in my high school class, his daughter, Daniele, was in Arlene's class at school. My older brother Guy was married to Jo who was Dr Gau's nurse. Donald called the Dr's office and Jo answered. Don explained the situation to Jo, and she went to talk to the Dr who had patient visiting in progress at that time. Dr Gau said to remain quiet, sit down and he would come to see me in 30 minutes or so. In our community there was no Emergency Squad, there was no hospital or medical facility in the county. The closest hospital was in Baltimore, 30 miles away. In 1955 Drs still made house calls so we were not surprised when Dr Gau said he would come to the house. Someone put a blanket on a stuffed chair in the Living room for me to set in. I set and mopped up blood until the Dr arrived. He could not determine what was causing the bleeding, but he said I don't believe you are losing enough blood to have you rushed to Baltimore tonight. He said to lie quietly, and he gave me a shot of Penicillin. He said he would return in the morning to see how I was doing. They made a temporary bed out of the sofa in the living room for me to spend the night on. The next day Dr Gau returned and said that the blood color indicated that the blood was coming from my lungs. He thought that the flow might have diminished somewhat, and he wanted me to remain quiet until Monday. Just eat soups and juices. On Monday my father went to work, and he reported what had happened to me. This was a report to the District Office. They told my father not to worry about my job but keep them advised of my condition. They said I would continue to be paid while the Doctors were determining my situation. That took a big load off my mind. When Dr Gau visited me on Monday, he said that he had spoken to a specialist in Baltimore before he came to our house. The specialist was a Doctor of Internal Medicine. That Dr asked Dr Gau to have me come to his office on Charles Street in Baltimore that afternoon. My mother worked evenings so she was home at that time, and she said she would drive me to the Internist as soon as we could get ready. When we arrived at the Internist office, he examined me as well as he could with the tools he had in his office. He said that I would have to go to University of Maryland Hospital right away so they could do X-rays and other tests to determine the reason for the continuing flow of blood. My mother packed me back into her car and drove the couple of miles to University Hospital. When we went in and they saw the blood the recent activity had restarted, they took me straight to the Emergency Room. The staff did some X-rays and blood tests and then decided to put me in a bed until they could sort out the test results. Meanwhile my mother filled out paperwork for admission. I had no Health Insurance because I was removed from my parents Blue Shield, Blue Cross plan when I reached age 18. I had not been at C&P long enough to start coverage. Either later that day or the next day I met Dr R. A. Cowley for the first time. Dr Cowley was Head of Cardiac, Pulmonary Surgery for the hospital. He asked me some questions, checked me over and then said they would perform a test the following morning where they could look inside of my lungs. They did not offer me anything to eat the next morning and around 8:00 am they wheeled me to an operating room. Dr Cowley had several other Dr's around him. I guessed that one was an Anesthesiologist. He advised me that he would be controlling oxygen that I was receiving during the procedure. I only understood why he told me this when they got started with the procedure. I was strapped to the table and they had me swallow a solution that numbed my throat. Then they inserted a Stainless-Steel tube that was about 3 foot long and 3/4 inch in diameter down my throat and into my left lung. They told me later what they had done during the procedure. They could look down the tube with a light, snip samples of tissue and inspect the far reaches of my lung with this tube. The downside of this procedure was I could barely get any air around the tube to breath. I was strangling, being asphyxiated, and suffering serious pain all at the same time. They returned me to my room when they were done and gave me some Percocet, a substitute for Morphine. It still hurt like hell. The next day they operated on me. After the operation I was in terrible pain even with the drugs. The results of the operation were described when my head was clearer a couple days later. What they found was a significant quantity of Soapstone dust in the small bronchi in the bottom of the left lung. The dust had caused the bronchi to deteriorate and bleed. They were not going to heal. They removed the lower lobe of the left lung. The left lung has 2 lobes. The right lung has 3 lobes. I guess the space that would have been used for a 3rd lobe if there was one on the left lung, was used by the heart. All in all, the loss of the lobe only reduced my lung capacity by 20 %. Before the operation they had me perform some lung capacity tests by breathing into a balloon type device. The 5-lobe capacity was judged to be nearly 5 liters. Weeks later after I could breathe without too much pain, they determined my lung capacity to be nearly 3. 5 liters. I never smoked so my "new" lung capacity was enough to let me live a normal life afterward. I SCUBA dived and free dived to fish and work underwater on boats without ever thinking that I had diminished lung capacity. Healing after the operation was more complicated back then than it is today. In 1955 the standard procedure for entering the chest cavity was to make an incision from the sternum/ breastplate in the front to the backbone in the back of a person. They would then cut a wedge of bone from the upper rib of the cut front and back, leaving a small portion of cartilage on each end of the rib. Then they would use mechanical opening tools to force that broken rib away from the remaining lower ribs until an opening large enough to work thru was created. The surgeons could then get a good look at what was right and what was not right. Dr Cowley said that one of the first things they discovered was that I had a large Aneurism on my Aorta. They repaired/reinforced it with a section of plastic tube. Dr Cowley told me a couple weeks after the operation that he doubted that I would have lived more than a couple of years before the Aneurism would have ruptured. He said that if that had happened, the only chance I would have had to survive would have been for it to rupture while a Surgeon was looking at it with me being opened at the time! So, this leads back to my decision to return from Colorado and to get a job in a dust laden stone mill. Had I continued in a job like Social Security, no dust, no reason to look inside my chest cavity, well you get the idea. The pain was severe. I had tubes draining fluids from my chest, I was cut halfway in too and all that trauma was trying to heal. 2 days after the operation Dr Cowley was on rounds with a group of residents and he stopped to explain to them why a 3-hour operation took 6- hours. I was lying on my back, and he was standing at the foot of my bed. He reached over the foot of the bed and motioned for me to take his hands. I did not know what he was thinking or planning to do and of course I trusted him, he had saved my life. Dr Cowley was a large man, I took his hands, and with one quick motion he pulled me up straight in the bed. I thought he had pulled me in two! I know I must have screamed, he said you cannot just lay there, you have got to get up and move around. You are going to be fine.

A few words about Dr R A Cowley. He went on to be the Father of Emergency Medicine. He was the person that 'Coined 'the term 'The Golden Hour' he said that your chance of surviving a traumatic accident was greatly enhanced if you could be given emergency treatment in the first hour after the injury. He had been a medical doctor in the US Army during WW2. In 1955 he was head of the Cardiac/Pulmonary department at University Hospital in Baltimore. He went on to convince Governor Mandel of Maryland to joint/use Maryland State Police Helicopters to bring trauma victims to the new center he was establishing called 'The Shock Trauma Center' at University Hospital in order to get them there within 'The Golden Hour' He saved my life and thousands of other lives. Maryland has State Police Helicopters located all over the state that they label Trauma Hawks, the crews of those helicopters are all pilots and EMS trained State Police Officers. The call signs for the choppers are 'Trooper 1,' 'Trooper 2,' 'Trooper 5 'etc. These helicopters serve the dual use of Medevac and Police duty. Maryland was the first state in the U S to put the State Police into this business. I was released from the hospital after 2 weeks. I was sore but could get around. I stayed with my older brother and sister-in-law for a couple weeks and by that time I was getting around very well. The young heal rapidly! C&P held my job for me, for which I was eternally grateful. With only a couple months of service they could have easily let me go. Back then if a 19-year-old applied for a job and had told the Dr. at his physical he had a lung removed, it would have been the door! If you had any type of medical anomaly, you were toast. I went back to work in the District Office on Edmondson Avenue in West Baltimore. I filed BSP (Bell System Practices) pages. The BSP booklets were 3 inches X 6 inches and were loose leaf. You could remove outdated pages and insert updated pages. Very boring, but it was work. I was waiting for my next Medical to get a release to go back to line work! I was also seeing Arlene a lot. Donald had put my car back together while I was incapacitated. When the Company Dr cleared me for work it was supposed to be 'Light 'outdoor work. Within 2 weeks I was climbing poles and throwing the 40 pound 'D 'spinner across the face of the pole. The young are not too smart . I guess that's why they do better as soldiers. The Big Crew I had been working in had replaced me while I was recovering

On Our Own Again

Since management wanted to do something different to deal with the Electric Company transfers and other jobs too small to send a 7-man crew on they decided to create a 2-man crew. They had an old 7-man crew truck they used for backup when either of the 2 full time trucks were down. They decided to give that truck to my Cousin Oatie and I. We were to use this truck to clean up the backlog of transfers and any other small jobs that came up. This was one of the best work assignments I had as a young man. Oatie and I had worked together on many different jobs as we grew up and we got along very well. There was never a question of who the boss was. We were always equals. Sometimes I drove the truck, sometimes Oatie drove. We loaded the truck with miscellaneous pole line hardware, like 2 and 3 bolt clamps, pole steps, drop wire strain relief devices and other small parts that would be required to finish a transfer to Bell System Specifications. We picked up a stack of transfer orders from Bob Holman the first day and went to work. What we typically found when we got to the job identified by a order was a new pole with electric wires and equipment on the top.

Strapped to the side of the new pole would be a cut off old pole with telephone cables and maybe steps to the cable height if there was a terminal on the pole. There might be drop wires connected to the terminal and tied with wire to the pole. We would transfer the old equipment to the new pole then remove the supporting straps that the Electric company linemen had left to hold the old pole up. When the old pole piece, which was usually no longer than 20 feet was bare of equipment we would shove it into the back of our truck, put a red flag on the 4 or 5 foot that was hanging out and go on our way. When we returned to the garage at days end, we unloaded the junk material and old poles, cleaned up the truck and turned in the finished work reports. The first few days Bob Holman, the Line Forman we reported too, said we were doing a good job. He said he had checked a couple of our jobs out after we had completed them, and they were good. We worked transfers for several more days. One day we saw a Baltimore Gas and Electric crew replacing a joint use pole that was quite old and had been chosen for replacement due to deterioration. We stopped to talk with them. They were quite friendly and when they found out what our job assignment was, they had some suggestions for us. They told us that they

were very knowledgeable of Bell System
standards, and if they had the materials such as 2
and 3 bolt clams, pole steps, drop wire strain
relief devices and other miscellaneous materials
they would be glad to complete simple Telephone
Company transfers and remove the old pole when
they left the job. The BG&E supervisor said that
in most cases it required more of their time to
leave a partial completed job safe for C&P to
finish than it would require to do the Tel Co work
and finish the job before they left. We came to
an agreement with them that we would make a
delivery to them of a quantity of materials that
they would need to complete the transfers before
they left the job. Another bit of information they
passed on to us was that they usually cleaned up
the work area and tossed scrap copper wire ends,
soda bottles and trash in the top of the pole hole
before they put the last few shovels full of dirt
around the pole. They mentioned this because
they saw that we had a collection of scrap copper
and soda bottles in the 5-man crew section of our
truck. Neither company tolerated employees that
were dishonest and certainly not employees that
stole Company property. There was a saying
back then at the Telephone Company that the
fastest way to get fired was to Mess with Ma
Bells Cash, Copper or Ladies. Before widespread

Direct Distance Dialing or DDD by the customers themselves, all long-distance calls were placed by operators. This required a large number of women, (No men in this job) to set these calls up for customers. Management frowned on male employees spending time with female employee, particularly on the job. My how times have changed. C&P had very little copper wire on the job so if Oatie and I collected scrap copper left by the BG&E Co. that was fine. We were not collecting and selling C&P wire. The deposit on Coke and Pepsi and other soda bottles was a couple cents each. We would have 30 or more bottles in the back cab every week. Our scrap copper would amount to 25 to 50 pounds a month. Copper was worth $.50 /lb. We gathered several boxes of clamps, bolts, drop ties and any other material that would be used in transfers from the supply room, and we drove them over to BG&E's garage. We did this early enough to catch the crews before they went out on their jobs. They were happy and we waited to see the results of this newfound cooperation between companies. A couple of weeks later Bob gave us a sheaf of transfer orders from BG&E and we drove off to complete them. As we had hoped we started to find jobs that were completed to Bell System Specs. The first day we turned in 10 or

12 completed orders, Bob took a look at them and then in front of the other linemen and my father who shared the office with Bob, he asked us if this was a joke, he said if so, I'm not amused. We said No Joke. The work was performed by BG&E. He looked at Oatie and I and waited for a better explanation. We told him about the deal we had made with the BG&E Foreman, and we reiterated that they suggested that it would make their work go faster. The other linemen looked at Oatie and I with a completely different look than we had seen before. A couple said that was a really good idea. We said we didn't do it to get out of work, we were talking to one of the crews and they suggested the arrangement. Bob said it was O K with him and he thought we would let it continue but would not involve higher management because that might cause more problems than we needed.

A Gift or Punishment?

A new Line Truck was delivered to the Catonsville Garage during the summer of 1956. Normally a new concept vehicle like this would be assigned to a senior employee. But why was it assigned to Oatie and I? The reason became clear to us quickly. This turned out to be a lot more work than a 7-man crew. The truck was built on a Ford 1.5-ton bed. It had a standard cab with a bench seat. Basically a 2-man cab. The Line Utility bed was standard with cabinets accessible by doors on the sides of the bed and 2 cable winches inside the bed up against the back of the cab. What made this truck unique was the folding derrick mounted on the back of the truck. And the Power Take Off (PTO) drive on the back of the truck. The derrick had 2 legs mounted on fore and aft pivots in the back of the bed. One of the winch cables led thru one of the sheaves on the top of the winch was attached to a pad eye on the truck back. This cable was used to lift poles and tools like the hole digger that was stored in the truck bed. The other winch cable controlled the height of the derrick. The hole digger was crude by today's standards, but it worked well. The digger was built around a truck differential that might have been designed for a light truck. The power input shaft of the differential was connected to a telescoping driveshaft that connected to the back PTO (power take off) of the truck. There was a lifting ring welded to what would have been one axel shaft output side and the other equivalent of a axel shaft had a fitting connected to it that rotated when power was applied to the driveshaft. The fitting was designed to accept a shaft on the end of a digging auger. There were 3 or 4 different diameter augers provided with the hole digger. Attached to each side of the differential were points of attachment for steel support rods of 3 inches or so in diameter that would reach to the back of the truck and could be connected to a pair of pivot points with pins. These rods kept the assembly from rotating while the digger was drilling a hole in the ground. To dig a hole, the digger was suspended from the winch cable over the location where a hole was to be dug. A proper size auger/bit was inserted into the fitting on the digger and a safety drive pin was inserted in a hole that went from one side of the drive coupling, thru the auger shaft and out the other side of the drive coupling. A safety pin was inserted in a hole in the drive pin to keep the pin from coming out of the assembly. This pin would shear off if the auger encountered a rock or other obstruction that stopped the auger from rotating. A new pin would have to be inserted after the remains of the broken pin were removed. The P T O could be reversed if necessary to help free up the auger if it jammed. The System worked well when you could position the truck over the pole or anchor hole location. Many times, we were sent to a job where 2 or 3 of the holes were in suitable locations and the rest of the holes had to be dug by hand. So much for automation! We were doing a lot of small jobs in support of the big line crews. A job might have 3 to 5 poles and associated anchors with cable strand, cable and other equipment included. Bob would ask Oatie and I to set the poles and anchors because the TeleLcct truck with it's folding Derick and Power Take Off driven hole digger should be able to make short work of the pole and anchor setting. It was interesting work, and it was mixed in with transfers and other small jobs.

Wedded Bliss

Spring and early Summer of 1956 was an exciting time for Arlene and I. She would be graduating from high school in June and there was a lot happening. Prom dance, a group of Arlene and some of her friends went to Ocean City, Maryland for a long weekend and I went with them. We had a great time, maybe too great! Arlene told me in early July that she thought we ought to get married. I thought it was a great idea, but her parents still thought she could do better in life than a Farm boy who did not have a family farm coming to him. We talked to my parents and one of my aunts who lived in Virginia about the pressing need to get married. My aunt and a couple of cousins who also lived in Northern Virginia said that we should come to Virginia and get married. Arlene was 17 and I was 19 years old. In Virginia that was old enough to get a marriage license without a parent's permission.

My relatives in Virginia put the whole wedding together! We invited Arlene's parents, but they were to upset with the pair of us to participate in the wedding. I took several days of vacation time, and we packed up the '55 Plymouth and headed to Occoquan, Va. My parents and other family members from Maryland drove down in their cars. My aunt Mickey was living on base at Quantico Marine Base. My uncle was a 'Lifer 'in the Corps. Mickey's daughter, Kay was living with her mother. My cousin Sylvia and her husband John Sugars were living nearby. They arranged a church wedding for Arlene and I and I was forever thankful that they loved Arlene and I enough to do this for us. I felt bad that Arlene's parents did not chose to attend the wedding, but I realized many years later why it hurt them so for Arlene and I to get married under the circumstances that we did. It seems that Arlene was, as they used to call them a short-term baby. In today's culture of people living together and raising families out of wedlock, having babies at 15, or 16 and continuing to attend high school, it probably is difficult to imagine the 1950's stigma associated with being pregnant when a couple got married. There was a saying when I was a young man that the first child was susceptible to being born at 7, or 8 months. Girls that became pregnant while still in school were asked to drop out of school. I think that in today's promiscuous world they provide childcare for the children of schoolgirls. I guess this is better than throwing them out into the world without the diploma

needed for most jobs. After we returned to
Maryland from our short 'Honeymoon 'we leased
an apartment in Catonsville for $75 a month.
Arlene's parents gave her the bedroom set from
her room at home and other people gave us a
chair here and a small table there and before long
we had enough furniture to allow living in our
new apartment. Arlene had a job in the C&P
business office near where we lived. We did not
use any family influence to procure the job. She
just applied and was hired.

Cable Department

The line work was slowing down in late summer of 1956, and they had to cut back on the number of linemen in the Catonsville Garage. Since I was the junior man, they offered me a job as a Cable Splicers Helper. I said sure that would be a good job. Cable Splicers top salary was $10 a week higher than Lineman pay. The problem that I was not aware of was that in the lineman job pay raises continued with good job performance to top pay. The Splicers Helper job went to a level $25 less than top pay. To get the top Splicers pay you had to be promoted to Splicer. This would not present itself as a problem for a couple of years. When I reached top Helpers pay the company was in a recession and I remained at top Helpers pay for almost a year. But that did not stop me from taking the helper's job. I really liked splicing. The Splicing foreman in the Catonsville garage was Mr. Buresy. He assigned me to a splicer that worked from a Tool Cart. Tool Carts were used for splicers throughout the city. The cart contained all the tools needed to perform the cable splicing job. The cart also had some supplies like lead for wiping joints between the cable sheath and the cable sleeve. The sleeve was a larger diameter lead tube that was used to cover the splice where 2 or more cables were joined.

There was a heavy cast iron pot that contained 25 pounds of lead that was stored on the cart. When a splice was to be 'closed 'with a sleeve in a Manhole no flame could be used because of the danger of explosive gases from the underground conduit system. Splices had to be 'Wiped 'close with molten lead.

We carried a pressurized kerosene single burner stove on the front of the cart that we set up on the sidewalk and heated the lead pot on. It could take an hour or more to melt the lead and bring it to a temperature that could be used to wipe lead sleeve joints. Later on they changed to Propane stoves. The carts were left on the job site when we went home. Crime was not a major problem in Baltimore in 1956. There were some sections of the city where you would have a tool cart broken into and the lead pot stolen. We would report this to the Police, and they would go to the local scrap metal shop and would often find the pot shaped chunk of lead that the thief had knocked out of our pot. The Junk dealer would know the crooks name and give it to the police. The junk dealer would usually offer the lead back to us, but what we wanted was the cast iron pot. I think that if the Telephone Company tried to operate out of Tool Carts today, the complete cart would be liberated the first night it was left unattended. When working from a Cart you would drive to the job site in your own car and meet the splicer who had driven his car to the site, and you would go to work. The Cable department was divided into 2 sections under 2 different Forman. One section was called Construction. They spliced large cables and worked from carts. The other section was called Cable maintenance and they had trucks. Buresy's crew was a Construction crew. We did some small aerial jobs, 1 to 3 days on a location for a while then we went on a job that was to splice a new 900 pair trunk (main connector) cable between the Longwood office in west Baltimore to the main telephone building located at 320 St Paul Street in downtown Baltimore.

One of the first small jobs I was assigned to was with a splicer whose name I'm not sure of. I think his last name was Ruck. We met on a job he was finishing up by himself late in the day. It was too late to call the move truck to take our cart to the new location so the splicer said that we should go look at the new location and call the lady in the district office that scheduled the move truck from a pay station on our way. He would ask that the move truck move our cart first thing in the morning. We said we would meet the truck at the new location at 8:00 am. There was no cell phone service in 1956 so most of our communication was from pay phones. Pay phones were found everywhere. They required 10 cents, 1 dime when I first started to use them. Later they jumped to 25 cents, or a quarter. The good thing about most of the calls we made, like to the district office for a move or to a Central office to talk to the Test Desk, was that they were recognized by the telephone equipment as Official Business Calls and they returned our coins to the coin slot. This meant you needed to carry a coin for phone use all the time, but you usually got it back after the call was placed. There were other odd stories about the pay phones. One tricky way to get dial tone on the pay phones in the mid 50's was to go to the back of the phone booth if you had access to the 'Drop" cable that fed the booth. If you could stick a straight pin into the side of the neoprene covered wire and touch the "Tip" conductor in the cable and then ground the pin against the metal frame of the phone booth that would do the same thing that the coin did when dropped into the slot. You would then get dial tone. Another situation we encountered in some of the more

'Seedy 'areas we worked in was the Coin Return Collection Route. Older Pay Phones didn't have a 'Flip Down 'coin return box on them. They just had a small hole in the bottom of the equipment face those coins returned to due to the call not being completed or for a number of other reasons. The coins would fall into a small holding area in the bottom of the phone and the noise would get the customers attention. The customer would stick a finger into the hole and retrieve their coins. Enterprising people would shove a wad of paper up in the coin return hole far enough that you could not see it. Then when coins were returned, they would hang up on top of the paper and the customer would not have his money returned and most often he would cuss the phone company and walk away. Periodically our entrepreneur would patrol his collection route and remove the wad of paper, pocket the change and reinsert the wad. He would continue to the next payphone on his collection route and repeat the process. There were fights over what phones belonged to what 'Businessmen'. Bell Labs designed a flip box for the bottom of the coin return slot that fixed the problem. The coins dropped into the collection box and you had to flip it down to get the returned coins out, but you could not reach up into the slot to jam it with the box open. We still checked the coin return every time we used a pay phone and quite often found coins that had been returned after the customer left the phone. Ah! The joys of Pay Phones. Another form of communication was to use the 'Butt-in-ski 'set. This was a hard rubber covered one piece phone set designated as the 1011B Test Set. This handset had a pair of wires about 6 foot long connected to it.

The end of the wires had spring clips attached to them. You could connect the set to any phone line that you had access to and place a call. We would often climb a pole that had steps on it and a distribution terminal on it and listen to each of the telephone lines to see if anyone was talking on them. When we found a line that had Dial Tone, we would place our call. If the customer attempted to use their phone, we would advise them that we were telephone company employees and were testing their line for reported service problems. If they said that they did not report a problem, we would say that our automatic test equipment reported a condition, and we were investigating. This was usually good enough for them and we would get off their line as quickly as possible. We did have equipment in our Central Offices that periodically ran tests on cables checking for faults such as 'Shorts', 'Crosses ' and 'Grounds ' on conductors in the cable. These would be caused by damage to the cable sheave that allowed water to soak the conductors. Lead cable sheaves were regularly damaged by squirrels in areas where trees were near the cables and by rats in the city areas where cables were run down the side of a pole and into the underground. In both cases the rodents were hungry for salt. The lead sheave of the cable contained lead acetate, a salty tasting chemical that the rodents hungered for because they thought it was salt. We often found the lead damaged to the extent that the conductors were exposed. This allowed water to enter the cable and short the conductors together and fail the phone service. We got to the new job site and since the pole was stepped it was easy to reach the cable terminal, so the splicer took his 1011B and climbed to the terminal height and called in for the move. We were scheduled for first thing in the morning. The next morning, we met the move truck got our tools out and went to work. I worked with this splicer for a week or so. During this time, I found out that he was having a lot of problems with a business he was involved with. He told me he had brought a Bar on York Road in North Baltimore. He said he had a partner in the deal who was supposed to open the place, 'keep bar', and close the place. He said he would run the place on weekends. He said that the partner was stealing from him big time and he was going to have to do something about it. He never told me what his plan was. I came to the job one morning and Bill was not there. I waited for a couple hours for him to show up, but he did not make an appearance. Around 10 am the Splicing Forman stopped by and asked me what was going on. I told him that Bill had not come to work, and I did not want to leave the job site to find a phone to call the Forman because I thought Bill would show up. We did not have Cell phones or other forms of communication at the cart. I could not get to the Buttinsky because I did not have keys to the cart. The Forman was not upset with me but was quite upset with Bill. The Forman sent me to another job to help a different splicer. Bill never returned to work. He had 10- or 12-years' service with the company and we all thought he was being foolish jeopardizing his job. But later I heard bits and pieces of what was transpiring, and it was interesting. Bill thought that C&P would fire him for not coming to work. He thought that He would receive a Severance Payment for the years he had worked there. C&P took the position that he had 'Abandoned hie Job 'and they did not owe him anything. I don't know for sure how this situation worked out but, I was paired with another splicer and life went on. We would get jobs on hilltops in Brooklyn, (a suburb of Baltimore) in November when the wind was blowing 40 miles per hour and the temperature was 15 degrees and we were freezing our butts off. The splicer said the Engineers laid out the job's 6 months before we were sent to do the work. So, the Engineers were on this hill site on a pleasant breezy day in June and here we were in November. Later when I was working in steam tunnels under Union Memorial Hospital in June we decided that this job was engineered in December.

New Digs

Arlene and I found out that the apartment we had rented in Catonsville was too expensive for us to keep. She was sick most of the time with her pregnancy and could not work. I was making $45 a week before taxes, medical insurance and Social Security. That left me with 30 couple dollars a week. $130 a month. $75 for an apartment killed us. We had to eat, and I needed gas and car expense money. I was not upset with her about not being able to work, that was just something that had to be dealt with. I never have been one to place blame for situations, I have always been a problem solver. So, the solution I proposed to Arlene and my parents who loved Arlene and I unequivocally was that we find a small house trailer. We would place the trailer on my parents' property and live in it. I felt that we could find a 30-foot trailer at a reasonable price. Everyone agreed and I started a search. I found a nice 30-foot house trailer that had a double bed in the bedroom. One of the 2 doors opened into the area where the bed was located but that was fine. There was a small bathroom forward of the bedroom, then the kitchen then the back 3/8's of the trailer was occupied with a small table and chairs and a sofa across the front of the trailer. There was a second door that opened into the living room area. The owners wanted $1800 for the trailer. My parents paid for it and I agreed to pay them back at $40 a month. The trailer owner had a truck that could move the trailer and he moved it to our lot for a few dollars. There was no zoning in Carroll County against trailers at that time, so we set it 75 feet behind their house and off to the side, for sewage disposal I dug a hole behind the trailer about 8 foot deep and around 6 feet in diameter. I used my father's pick-up truck to get a load of #2 stone and I put 2 foot of stone in the bottom of the hole. We then set a 55-gal steel drum in the center of the hole. We used an axe to knock 5 or 6 holes in the bottom of the drum before it went into the hole, and we knocked several holes in the sides of the drum. We then filled the hole up over the top of the drum with stone. Before we covered the top with stone, I cut 3 holes in the top. 1 hole was for a pipe that stuck up above the ground level for sewerage input. The next hole was for a 1-inch pipe to be connected to a vent pipe that was led up above the top of the trailer and bent into a 90-degree loop and cut off with 4 inches hanging down. This was the vent pipe. This let air out of the tank when sewage went in. Due to its height, you seldom smelt any aroma from the pipe. The third hole had a cap on it but was there so we could "dip stick" the tank to see if it was filling up. We figured that, if necessary, we could have a 'Honey Dipper 'come in and pump the tank through this hole. After the stone covered the tank, we leveled it up with dirt and I threw some grass seed on top. A short length of pipe from the trailer toilet discharge to our Septic tank completed this part of our hook up. Next was water, electricity, and phone. We dug a ditch from the back of the house that gave us access to the crawl space under the back porch. Under the porch we had access to a water hook up and Phone extension, we ran a 3 wire # 8 gauge buriable cable for electricity. When these were connected, we were good to go. We moved into the trailer near the beginning of September 1956.

We moved our few pieces of furniture from the apartment and stored some and gave some away. I felt a load off my back. I knew that if we were caught short for the trailer payment my parents would let me catch up the next month.

New Hot Wheels

I was still driving my 1955 Plymouth. It was nearly 2 years old and I was starting to have to spend money on repairs. Cars were not as well built in the 50's as they are today. You would be lucky to get 80 thousand miles from one before you needed major work on it. I stopped into Wilcox Chrysler, Plymouth on US route 40 on my way home from work one day in December to get a part. A salesman handed me a mimeographed sheet of paper that announced the availability of Plymouth's new V800 performance package in any model of their 1957 cars. This would be the same as the special equipment installed in the new 57 'Fury car. The engine was a special 318 cubic inch displacement block, a high lift cam, high compression heads, 2, 4-barrel carburetors, dual exhausts, 290 horsepower. More than the 265 HP ford, more than the 283 HP Chevy. It also had wider wheels, heavy duty torsion bars on the front suspension and asymmetrically positioned heavy duty Leaf springs on the rear. There were many more tidbits, but I had seen enough. I ordered an all-white Savoy 2 door hardtop with the V800 package. Solid white, nothing more. This was the lightest body in their lineup. They said it would take 4 to 6 weeks before delivery. Arlene was 6 months along with Jeff, although we did not know the baby was a boy. The only hint was the 'Old Wives 'tale about how much a boy was kicking! My time as owner of the 57 'Plymouth was relativity short. I wanted to race the car. The closest Drag Strip was just being built at Aquasco, Md. This was down in Calvert County Md. 90 miles away. Most of the local racing was conducted on the roads around Baltimore. Of course, this was illegal, but everyone was doing it. The local 'Hang Out 'was the 'Pig and Whistle 'drive-in on US route 40 near Ellicott City. Guys with 'hot 'cars would drive thru the parking lot, maybe stop then spin their wheels, and go on. When you parked, if your car was new to the scene, some guys would drift over and want to know what it 'had in it'. You could open the hood or tell them the cost of looking was to race you and beat you for say '$10.' We had some regular sections of road that we raced on. The offer might be 'I'll run you from the poles to the bridge. ' This meant we would go south on route 29, which was a 2-lane road to a pair of poles on opposite sides of the road marking an under-road pipeline, and a bridge over a small river 3/4's of a mile farther south. There was very little traffic on this road at that time. We would wait until the road was clear in both directions and then take off! I only had the car for a week before I found out that I had missed a very necessary option. The rear axle ratio was too high. That would improve gas mileage but not performance. Who bought a car with 2, 4 barrel carburetors expecting good gas mileage. The worst problem with the 3.31 rear in the car was that the clutch and transmission could not take the strain. With a lower ratio axel the rear wheels would spin or the car would move out faster with less strain on the driveline. After I had returned the car to Wilcox motors twice for repairs to the clutch, they told me that they knew I was racing the car and Chrysler would not repair the driveline under warranty any longer. As luck would have it, I was working part time at the Amoco gas station, and I could use the lift there to work on my car.

I opened an account at Parts Wholesale, the Chrysler parts outlet in Baltimore. I was not sure what axel ratio would be optimum, so I started with a 4.81 ratio. What a mistake! That rear got you off the line fast but then you ran out of engine. By the time you were in 3 rd. gear at 40 MPH the engine was redlined. This Plymouth only came with a 3-speed volume shift. No 4 on the floor for Plymouth until early 60's. 2 days later I was back at Parts Wholesale picking up another rear ring and pinion gear, this time 3. 91 ratios. This was the ratio for V 8's with overdrive. This ratio was just right. It let the engine reach maximum RPM of 6000 but got you there quickly. We raced every make of performance car in 1957. We raced 270 hp Chevys, 265 Fords, Studebaker Golden Hawks, Pontiac's with 3, 2 barrels. We beat them on the road, and we beat them on the track. We had a few tricks we used on the road, but on the track, you were inspected so no Hanky Panky could be used. The closest race we had was on the track at Aquasco. When we went to the track, we drove the car on its own wheels. This was what almost everyone did. We would take another car to carry parts and tools. The pits were dirt, it was a dirty place. We would have a spare pair of 16-inch wheels with tires that had very little tread left on them and were inflated to 70 pounds of air pressure. We mounted them on the front wheels, using the bumper jack. These tires would have less friction and drag because of less surface area on the ground. The rear tires were mounted on the original 14-inch diameter, wide rim wheels that came with the car. We lowered the air pressure in the rear tires to 18 lbs. We wanted maximum surface area on the rear wheels but did not want the wheels to turn inside of the tubeless tires. We removed the air filter cartridges from the dual air cleaner covers, and we loosened the tension on the fan belt so that the pulley on the crankshaft would slip inside of the loop of belt when the engine RPM was advanced rapidly. This removed the drag of the water pump and alternator during the rapid acceleration phase at the start of the race. This could provide you with up to 8 horsepower more for acceleration. The hazard of this operation was that if you loosened the belt too much it could possibly jump off the engine pulley and wreck the radiator or cause serious damage. We also jacked up the front of the car and loosened the spindle nuts a fraction to let the wheel turn more freely. While we had the car up we would back the brake shoes off the drum to stop them from dragging. The closest race I remember happened at Aquasco. We had run a 265 Ford powered Mainliner, their lightest body and whipped him, we raced a 270 Chevy in a Belair Hardtop and beat him by a full car length. We then were matched up with the only other V-800 Plymouth we ever came across. It was a black 2 door sedan, Plaza. This was not a "Hard Top'. The owner told us later that it was the first time he had been beaten. We only beat him by half a car length. He wondered if we had modified the engine or anything. He said he was running the same 3.91 rear that we were. I told him a few things we were doing to get an edge because he was a fellow Plymouth owner, but we did not give the store away. We ran a Studebaker Hawk that day and dusted him soundly. I still have that little Super Stock trophy for winning the fastest SS car trophy. We continued to race on the roads. We had accumulated 3 different intake manifolds for the engine. We had the 2, 4-barrel manifold, we had a single 4-barrel manifold, and we had a 2-barrel manifold. They were all good for different types of racing. The 2 barrels would get you off the line like a rocket ship. One of the advantages of the suspension on the V-800 package was the rear spring geometry. The axel was placed forward of center of the spring's length. The right spring had 6 leaves while the left only had 5. The geometry allowed less 'spring wrap 'and better traction on launching. We used this to our advantage on several occasions. One night we were at the 'Whistle" looking for 'action'. I had the 2-barrel carb on the engine that night. Some guys from East Baltimore were nosing around and they had heard about a fast white Plymouth that hung out here. We told them that this was not the car, we just had dad's car. They wanted to see the engine, so I told my friends that I had an idea to take $20 from them. We showed them the 2-barrel carb and said that we would race them but only on a short track, say 1/5 mile. They had a 245 hp Ford Fairlane. I knew that the Fords had a problem with traction and would probably spin their wheels at start. I knew the perfect place to race them. There was a half mile of straight road on route 99. And on the end that I wanted to start there was a wide piece of roadway that was covered with road Tar. The tar strip was at least 10 foot wide. I told the guy who was going to start us to position us on that tar patch. The guys from East Baltimore did not know the territory so we told them to follow me. About 10 cars and the 2 race cars drove up to the race location. A guy we knew was holding the money. I pulled up and got my rear tires just on to the tar patch. I don't think the other driver noticed the difference in the road surface. When the Starter who was standing in between us raised his arms, I floored the 2 barrel and popped the clutch. I knew the Plymouth would not spin. It shot forward and I immediately was 2 car lengths ahead and leaving the wheel spinning Ford. I was approaching halfway to the finish, and I saw the Ford coming on like a freight train. I kept my foot in it and beat him to the finish flagman by 2 or 3 feet. I knew the roads in the area well, so I took a turn off Rt 99 and circled thru some back roads. When I got back to the start line there was a State Trooper outside of his car talking to the Ford driver and some of the spectators. I drove by at normal speed, and no-one pointed me out to the police as a race participant. We drove back to the Drive In and waited to see what had happened. It turned out that some of the people that lived along that stretch of 99 were upset with the drag racing in front of their houses. I think that was inconsiderate of them, but they had the Maryland Troopers Barracks phone number ready to launch when we set up to race. I got my race money and the guys from East Baltimore got a ticket and I cheated death that time.

The Long Arm Of The Law

My Road Racing career did not last long. I was racing on the night that my first child, Jeff was born. It seemed like the natural thing to be doing to me. But some people have criticized me for that over the years. The way it happened was that Arlene told me she thought her water had broken and that I should call Dr Gau. When I called him, he told me to take Arlene to Sandy Springs Hospital in Olney, Maryland. This was about 25 miles from our home. I drove her there and when Dr Gau arrived, he spent some time with Arlene then came out to talk to me. In 1957 men did not hold their wife's hand while they delivered children. The husband sat in a little waiting room for hours and waited to be advised that he was now a father. Dr Gau said that since this was Arlene's first child the delivery would probably take some time. He said I could go home and then give the hospital a call in the morning to see how everyone was doing. I left the hospital and drove to the Pig & Whistle to see if anything was happening. The next day I called early in the morning, and they said that all was well, and we had a Boy. I continued racing, working for C&P and part time at the Amoco station. I had some other good races but one night I made a major mistake. Maybe it was a blessing. But it cut my road racing off forever and that turned out to be good in the long run. There were more important things to concentrate on like being a good father and husband and earning a satisfactory living. The life changing event started out innocently, I stopped at the Pig & Whistle coming home from the filling station job. There was a guy there that I had always wanted to race, Roger. Roger had a 270 Chevy that was fast. I thought I was faster. We decided to drive out US 40, to the west for 10 miles or so and have a go at it. We were not betting on the race we both thought that we had the fastest car and we wanted to settle the question. Roger had someone riding in his car with him. He wanted me to get a rider to make the load seem the same. A young man said he would like to ride with me. I said hop in. We took off and drove west on US 40. We drove beyond Marriottsville Road and there was a long stretch up to Maryland route 32. US 40 was a divided highway with turn around cuts in the divider every 3 or 4 miles that would let you change from the west bound lane to the east bound lane or to let you exit on a side road. In the middle of this stretch a road came into US 40 from the right. The road was a back road that led over to route 99. We lined up side by side on the 2 west bound lanes and hit it. As we sped past the side road on the right, I glanced up the road, I was in the right lane, and I saw a State Trooper setting off the highway by a hundred feet. He had his head lights on, and they swept along my car. We were doing about a 100 mph or faster and I was leading by a half a car length. The cop pulled out and started after us. I kept it floored and was really leaving the cop. Roger grabbed the first turn to the left and started back east. The cop never hesitated, he kept on after me. With route 32 coming up fast I thought that I had opened enough distance between me and the cop that I could take the cloverleaf off the dual hi way and speed away on route 32. What I didn't think about was the amount of time I would be circling on the cloverleaf with the patrol cars lights on my side. I also knew that although Roger's 57 Black Chevy was one of maybe, 20 in the area, my White hardtop Plymouth was the only one in central Maryland. After I got on to 32. I hotfooted it away and the cop did not try to keep up with me. I thought, well I will drive home, get my father or mothers car and take this kid with me back to the Pig and call it a night. After taking a roundabout route home I turned onto the road in front of my house and there was a Maryland State Police Cruiser parked across the driveway. Well, so much for being a smart ass. I told the guy riding with me that I would talk to the cop and then take him back to the Pig. If I had been by myself, I might have denied everything, but I could not trust this kid to back me up so that did not seem like a good idea. I figured it was better to take the medicine. The cop was friendly, he relayed what we both knew, but I would not tell him who I was racing. He was not to upset with that because he said he would get him another time if he kept racing on public highways. He wrote me a ticket for speeding to elude the police, racing on public highways and exceeding 100 mph. I said, is that all you can think of? He said give me a few minutes. I said no that's good enough. The fine was $300. That was $300 in 1957 dollars. More like $3000 today. I signed for the ticket and left to take the kid back to the Pig. I knew that I was going to lose my driver's license as a result of this escapade. That meant that I had to determine how I was going to get to work, where would I get the money for the ticket, and what was Arlene going to say.

Life Goes On

I continued to work with different splicers thru the fall of 1956 and early 1957. Some were working out of cable trucks. These were Pickup trucks with a utility body on them designed to store supplies and materials. They also had a ladder rack on the side that we carried a 28-foot wooden extension ladder on. The ladder was heavy when compared to today's aluminum ladders. The nice thing about the weight of the ladder was that when you placed it against the cable strand or a building side it tended to stay where you placed it. I fine today's lightweight aluminum ladders tend to 'drift 'when I set them up. Back in the 1930.s and 1940.s Bell System ladders were painted dark green. After the telephone companies had a few broken ladder incidents they decided that a ladders condition could be monitored more closely if it was bare wood. So, by the early 50's most of our ladders were bare wood. We were taught to carry a ladder in a way that I find makes the job easier. When one end of the ladder was dropped down off the truck you would walk up to the underside of the ladder and place your shoulder against the lower side and walk forward holding the lowest side of the ladder against your shoulder. When you positioned yourself properly your shoulder would be at the center of gravity of the ladder. You could then reach down with one hand and lift the full weight of the ladder and balance the ladder on your shoulder and walk wherever you needed to go with the ladder in a nearly vertical position. Of course, you had to be careful of overhead obstructions.

I have carried those damm 28-foot ladders for hundreds of yards down right-a-ways behind houses where there was no road access. When earning 'Blood Money 'locating cable troubles and repairing them in the middle of stormy nights. Today when I pick up a 24- or 28-foot ladder some people will question the way I handle the ladder, but it is still the easiest and safest carrying method.

12 Hour Nights

In early 1957 I was assigned to a splicer who was working on a Trunk cable being placed and spliced between the Longwood office in West Baltimore and 320 St Paul Street, the headquarters building for C&P in downtown. This was a 900 pair 19-gauge pulp insulated lead covered cable. The manholes were in the roadway of Mulberry Street. This was the East bound side of U S 40 thru Baltimore. The manholes could not be opened during the day because it would have closed 1 of the 3 lanes on this critical route thru Baltimore. We were allowed to open the holes at 6pm after the heavy traffic of the day had lightened up. We set up our cones and placed the manhole guards around the hole and started our generators to give us light and went to work. I had not worked on any job for C&P that had planned overtime built into the schedule. We would occasionally pick up an hour here or there of overtime but to be told we were going to be working 6, 12-hour days a week was unheard of. This was an important job to C&P. Overtime paid time and one half. So with 20 hours OT for Monday / Friday and 12 hours for Saturday that was 48 paid hours plus the 40

hours regular time I was paid for 88 hours a
week. At $1.20/hour my gross was $105.60.
This was and incredible amount of money. I was
beginning to feel that I had made the right
decision to leave Social Security for C&P.
There were 3 or 4 splicing crews on the job. The
manholes were about 2 blocks apart. Each hole
was a mystery waiting to be explored. When you
opened a hole, you did not know what you would
find. Even if the splicer thought he had been in
this hole a few years ago things could have
changed. The first thing we looked for when we
drug the cover off was 'Is there water 'in the
hole. Most holes in Baltimore were relatively
dry, but there were gushers. A gusher would
require 1 or 2 pumps. Even a hole with a foot or
two of water required us to call the move truck to
bring us a pump. We always asked them to bring
2 pumps because many of the pumps were
unreliable. Most were powered by Briggs &
Stratton 4 cycle engines, but the Homelite pumps
were 2 cycle, which required mixing oil with the
gas and they never ran good if they ran at all. We
always got out our 'Bliffy Sniffer 'the flammable
gas detector and checked the hole and the cable
ducts leading into the hole for gas. Everyone
smoked back then, except me! You were not
allowed to smoke in manholes even if they tested

gas free. But most of the old-time splicers smoked in the holes. One of the helper's jobs was to stand at the top of the hole, ready to get whatever the splicer needed to perform his work. Also included in that job was to keep a sharp lookout for the foreman. The foreman visited each splicer at least once a tour. The foreman liked some of the crews more than others and they might stop by a couple times a shift to 'Shoot the Sh-T 'with the splicer and or helper. Whether the splicer smoked in the hole or not they did not want the Forman sneaking up on them. Some of these older splicers were from a different Era. I knew one splicer who was a perfectly dressed gentleman. He rode the streetcar to work. The helper would be at the cart and usually had the hole open for him when he stepped off the Streetcar. He wore a suit and tie to work.

When he got to the cart, he would remove his suit coat and overcoat if it was cold, and he would fold them neatly then place them in a compartment he reserved for his clothes in the front of the cart. He would remove a set of white coveralls from the cart and pull them on and he would ware his tie with the coveralls. I had a splicer that I worked for who was hard on helpers. When you first started helping him, he treated you like you were another tool in the cart. If you looked down into the manhole while he was working on the splice, he would stop what he was doing and reach across the hole to some supplies that were stacked there and he would pick up a 'rubber blanket', this was a cloth fabric blanket about 30 inches long and 18 inches wide that was coated with a rubbery material. The blanket had brass grommets in the edges to tie it in place with. Our cord of choice, provided in wound balls was a oil'y cord called marlin. We used it to tie blankets over splices, to hang blankets in front of cable ducts to deflect water draining from the duct or for any other job that required a line for tying. He would lay the blanket over the splice in front of him and look up and ask you if there was something you wanted. If you said 'No I'm just watching 'or something like that he would tell you to clean up the cart. He would say 'I will call you if I need you'. This was a form of job security that went back to the days of Guilds. After you worked for him for several months, he might start to explain work functions and procedures to you. The work at hand on this job was there in front of you when the hole was opened. There were 2 cable ends coming out of cable ducts on opposite sides of the hole. The first thing to do was secure the interior of the hole.

Place rubber blankets on the walls behind where the cables would be when you worked on them. Next was to route the cable ends neatly from their duct to the point on the wall where they would lay on supports attached to the wall. There were usually cable racks in the holes, and you could pick the best rack for your cable. You did not want to hog the available space, because there would be more cables coming thru these holes and you might be the guy who was cussing some Jackass that used more space for a splice than was required and was now making your job difficult. Splicing a new cable like this was straight forward. A 900 pair cable had 9 separate groups of 100 pairs of wires. Each group of 100 pairs had different colored silk like ribbons and you could pull the groups out of the bundle and start splicing the ends of a group that matched the color in the other cable end coming into the hole from the opposite side. You had to leave enough slack in the first layer of groups in the back of the splice so that the next groups would fill in the area in front of them and make a nice even splice. To splice a pair of wires you brought the 2 ends together leaving the proper amount of slack, then did a half twist of the pairs around each other.

You then used your splicing shears to cut off both pairs 4 inches from the twist. You then slide a wax saturated cloth sleeve over both conductors of one pair. You then pulled the one side of the pair over the side of the splicing shears and with your thumb pressing down on the wire pair you cut the insulating paper away from the pair of wires. You did the same with the other pair, then pulled a single conductor from each pair and quickly spun the 2 ends 8 times. You did this in a manner that resulted in the outer 5 spins being tight together and the remaining 3 being looser. Single conductors were marked so you could identify the two wires from each other and connect them so that the 2 conductors were not transposed in any of the splices. You flipped the shears in your hand and cut the end of the wires off so that the twisted splice was no longer than 1.5 inches. You bent it down flat against the now joined wires and slid the waxed sleeve over the bare splice. You did the same thing to the other conductor. You now had a spliced pair. When you became productive you could effortlessly splice 100 pair of conductors in an hour. We would tie the bunch of 100 sleeved pairs together with string we called 12 cord. It was waxed cord that was incredibly strong and provided to us in rolls that were 6 inches long and 2 inches in diameter. A square knot in the center of the sleeve bunch secured the group. To make the work go faster we usually would take the hundred pair group on one side of the splice and slide selves on all the conductors. When doing this you had to be careful not to separate conductor pairs. Splitting pairs would cause much gnashing of teeth and wailing when the cable was 'Buzzed "for continuity at the end of splicing.

Community Affairs

12-hour nights are long. The splicer is busy in the manhole, and I would just stand around the manhole guards. Sometimes I would be leaning on the guard and in the early evening some black kids might walk up and watch what we were doing. This was the "colored" section of Baltimore. When the splicer was closing a splice, he would dump a quart of powdered Desiccant from a Blue can over the splice before he carefully wrapped the splice with 2-inch-wide Muslin. Muslin was a light loosely woven material available in sheets or in rolls. It was provided in a plastic wrapper meant to keep it dry. The insulation on the cables at that time was paper or pulp. You did not want to leave any moisture in the splice because it would negatively affect the quality of transmission of the telephone signals. When the kids saw the splicer dumping the Desiccant on the wires, they were curious and might ask why he was doing that. The standard answer was that he was putting Sugar on the wire so that you could 'Sweet Talk 'your girlfriend. That always got a laugh out of the kids, and we would talk about their schoolwork or what sports they were involved with. I never encountered any animosity toward us or our work in those days. We were living in these people's front yard, and we got glimpses of their day-to-day life. Some of it was entertaining and understandable. One hot night when everyone had their windows open to try to catch some breeze, I overheard a funny discussion. It was around 4 AM and I heard a gruff manly voice stage whisper, "What time it be" this was followed shortly by a female voice, "The little hand it be on the four and the big hand be on the 12, it be time to get up". One evening the Patrol Officer who walked the beat we were on stopped to talk. He said he just had an interesting discussion with a fellow down the block. I asked what it was about, and he said the guy was upset and came out of his house as the Officer was walking past his steps. He told the Officer that he needed some help in getting his wife to return home. The Officer asked why she had left, and the fellow told him I think she is seeing another guy. The Cop told him that this was not something that the Police would normally be involved with, but the Officer said he asked the fellow how long they had been married and the grieving man said, 'Well I don't have no papers on her, but we been living together fo '4 years"

The Cop said I felt bad for the guy but I could not do anything about that.

Trap Line

We worked our way east on Mulberry Street and as we got close to Fremont Avenue, we were in what was considered the poorest section of town and most libel to be a problem area. There was a Public School on the North side of Mulberry St., and we were working on the South side of the street. We had been in this hole for one night and I noticed rats crossing the street on a regular basis. I saw that the school yard was 4 or 5 feet higher than the sidewalk. There was a chain wire fence on the edge of the schoolyard for the full length of this wall. The wall had pipes about 4 inches in diameter protruding 1 inch beyond the face of the wall. They were about 3 foot up off the sidewalk. They were clearly drainpipes for yard runoff. The Rats were using these pipes to get from the school yard down to the sidewalk and were then crossing the street. My trapping experiences came back to me, and I thought it would be fun to trap some of these loathsome creatures and dispatch them at night with a manhole hook. When I was at home that day after work, I gathered up 4 or 5 #1 steel traps and put them in the trunk of my car. After the splicer was settled down to splicing that night, I cut some Marlin into 6-foot lengths and tied a

piece to the ring on the end of each trap's chain.
I waited until midnight and the traffic was down
to a few cars every couple minuets and no-one
was on the street. I then set a trap in each of 4 of
the pipes. And tied the end of the Marlin to the
chain link fence. I had no more than returned to
the cart when the first trap went off. I saw a rat
caught by a leg dragging the trap on the sidewalk.

I grabbed the Manhole hook, put on my gloves,
and ran to the trap. One good whack on the head
killed the rat. I released the dead rat from the
trap and picked it up by the tail and tossed it out
into the street. I continued to catch rats every
couple minutes and before long I had 15 or 20
rats spread across the street. I then realized that
this was not such a good idea and I better gather
my traps and put them in the trunk of the car.
Luckily, I got the traps put away and was leaning
on the manhole guard when the Beat cop stopped
by. He looked out at the dead rats just as a car
ran over one and swerved. He asked me, what
did I think was going on. I told him I had no
idea. The rats just started running from the
school yard and into the street. I said maybe they
were poisoned. He said he hoped they did not
cause an accident. I agreed with him an he
walked off. When Banbury came out of the hole
he said, "what the hell have you been up to

Baker?" I said What Me? Ban said, "don't do that again". I said I was just trying to clean up the city a little. It did get a little dicey about 5 am when traffic picked up and every other car was squashing a rat. I was glad to close the hole and go to the White Coffee Pot where we met all the other crews at 5:45 after the holes were all closed. We got some laughs from my escapade, but we all realized that I would probably get fired if the 'Big Wigs' found out.

Marine Architect, Not!

If we were closing a splice on a temporary basis with the intention of going back into it to do more work in a few days we would put a waterproof cover on the splice made from CR Tape, a flexible rubber with a very sticky side that was covered with sheet plastic that was removed when you wanted to cover the splice. The sticky side would stick to the cable sheath and the edges would stick to each other. It would remain watertight for a long time. This rubber covering was available in rolls of 20 feet and was 3 foot wide. I took 2 rolls of it home with me once and tried to make an inflatable rubber boat with it. What a mess! I thought that I could carefully remove the backing material on the areas that I wanted to mate together and leave the backing on the rest of the rubber to keep it from adhering to sections of the interior that were to be expanded to create the flotation. As the tube sections expanded the rubber still attached to the plastic pulled loose inside of the tubes and stuck to parts of the tube that I wanted to remain free to expand. It turned into a uncontrolled glob. There was much more to inflatable boat manufacturing than I knew. I decided to stick to wood and plastic.

My splicer, Banbury and I moved to a hole on the corner of Mulberry and Paca. This was a unique hole; The hole was well out under the street and there was a manhole in the sidewalk as well as one in the street to enter the hole from. You could open the hole in the sidewalk and go down a ladder to a tunnel that led out to the main cable run under the street. There were cables coming into the hole from several directions and C&P must have felt that they would need better access to this hole, so they spent the money to provide the sidewalk access to the hole. This made working in the hole more of a concern because of ventilation and gas possibility. We had a gasoline blower forcing air into the hole when someone was working in the hole and the helper was more vigilant than in a regular hole. There was an Amoco service station on the south /east corner of the intersection. I went to talk to the operator of the station the day we moved the cart on the job and asked him if I could park my car in one of the stations parking spaces. During our discussion I told him I was looking for a part time job that would fit around my C&P hours. Because of my experience with cars, he said he would give me a try. Since we could open this hole from the sidewalk, we were working there during daylight hours. I started working at the

Amoco station from 5:30 PM right after I got off from C&P, till we closed the station at 11 PM. The rest of the holes on this job, until we finished at 320 St Paul St were in alleys or side streets, so we stayed on days until the cable was completely spliced. I pumped gas, serviced cars and light trucks and enjoyed the work. After we went to days a lot of the overtime stopped so this 2nd job money was very helpful.

The ExTerminator

We had one last situation that happened on that cable job that I remember as if it happened yesterday. We finished in a hole not to far from the main C&P building on St Paul St. The move truck hauled the cart to the next hole in an alley west of Charles Street, there was room to park the cart without blocking the alley. The move was just before quitting time at 6 am, so we were still on nights at that time. After the move truck left, Ban said let's take a look in the hole before we leave. I set the hole guards up around the hole with a couple safety cones guarding the perimeter. I pulled the cover and the inside of the hole looked like it was alive. There must have been a thousand roaches surfing around in the hole. We found roaches in manholes all the time, but I had never seen this many before. Ban stepped back and said get me a roach bomb from the cart. We carried roach bombs that contained DDT which was still commonly used at that time. We reached in the hole and sprayed around where we could reach then I gave Ban a second bomb and he taped the trigger open and threw the bomb into the hole. We slid the cover back in place and stored the cones and guards and left the job site at

5: 50 or so to go to the coffee shop. When we arrived at 6:00 PM that evening we opened the hole and the first thing I noticed was that there were no more than a few dead roaches in the hole. I went down first and picked up the empty spray can and the dead roaches and brought them out with me and placed them in a canvas trash bag we kept in the back of the cart. We continued setting up the hole and preparing the cable ends for splicing. After we had been there for 30 minuets or a little more, a door on the building beside where we were set up opened an a well-dressed man stepped out. He looked at our operation and then said, were you fellows here last night? I said, 'We left the tool cart here then went home. I asked him what the problem was, and he said Oh, nothing I was just wondering. He then went back into the building. About an hour later a guy who was a worker by his dress came out the door with a trash can and set it where the trash must have been picked up from. He then walked over and said, are you sure you guys didn't do something here last night and I said no, nothing at all why? He said when we came in this morning the kitchen was overrun with roaches. We have no idea where they came from. We were both looking down in the hole where Ban was working and I said Hey, Ban have you seen any roaches in this hole, he looked up and saw the guy and me and he said in a nonchalant manner, naw, not in this hole. The guy left and went back into the restaurant, and we did not even talk about Roaches within earshot of that place. But we got a lot of laughs about it at the coffee shop. I felt a little bad about this misfortunate situation, but we did not feed the roaches. The restaurant must have provided access to enough food to keep them alive, so it was not our problem.

Life On 'Shank's Mare'

My Grandfather, Westley Baker never drove a motor vehicle in his 91 years. He walked, rode a horse or rode with someone who was driving. Sometimes when he was asked how he was going to get from one place to another, he would respond "I guess I'll be riding Shanks Mare" It took me a while to figure out what he meant, but my mother explained the term for me. People referred to the lower part of their leg as they did to a horse's lower leg, the Shank. Of course, a mare is a female horse, usually the best sex to use for a riding horse. He meant he would be walking. That's what I would be doing for nearly a year.

When this job was finished, we were moved to Brooklyn, a southern section of Baltimore on the South side of the Patapsco River. I knew that I would lose my license as soon as I appeared in court a couple weeks after I received the ticket for racing. I started making plans. My uncle Putts worked in the Brooklyn / Glen Burnie area. He was a Installer /Repairman. He drove from his house 2 lots up the road from my parents' house thru Brooklyn to Glen Burnie every day. I made arrangement to ride to and from work with him.

Since I could not drive, I wanted to get rid of the 57 Plymouth. I asked my brother Donald if he wanted it. I said all you must do is take over the payments. He reluctantly said yes and drove it for a couple of months. He then told me he did not want the car anymore. I said OK, if you follow me and our mother who would drive the car for me, down to Wilcox Chrysler / Plymouth I will turn it back in to them

When we got there and told them what we wanted to do, one of the mechanics came up from the back and told the salesman he wanted the car. The salesman said I will take care of this just sign these papers. I signed and we left. I never saw the car again. But I was car less.

Even though I didn't need a C&P license to work on a tool cart I knew I had to turn my License into my boss when I lost the Maryland license. I told My new boss, Mr. Moxley, who managed the crews in the Brooklyn area the story and he said he would keep me on a tool cart assignment until I got my License back. I thanked him and analyzed my situation. The job in Brooklyn would last for over a year. The job was to convert the phone service in Brooklyn from old technology central office equipment to modern # 5 Crossbar equipment that would allow the customers to make Direct Distance Dialing (DDD) calls to any place in the US. A new Central Office had been built on Hanover Street a couple blocks south of Patapsco Ave. 10 or so large cables came down Hanover Street from different parts of Baltimore and turned east on Patapsco and went east 10 blocks to the corner where the old Central Office was located.

We would be splicing a number of cables leading from the new central office to a manhole on the corner of Hanover and Patapsco. The number of cables was enough to carry all the traffic that was presently going to the old office and some new capacity leading back to Baltimore. The first couple months were spent in the first manhole on Hanover after cables left the New Central Office. We half tapped new CO cables to existing cables passing thru the hole on their way to the old CO (Central Office). Half tap means, we identified individual pairs in the thru cable then slid the sleeves back and then spun a pair going to the new office onto this thru pair. Now that pair appeared temporarily to the Cable Head at both the new and the old CO. In the new office the ends of the pairs were insulated so they would not affect service still being provided by the old CO. At the time of Cut

Over of service from the old CO to the new CO the old CO would rapidly disconnect all of the cable pairs coming into the old CO and the new CO would rapidly remove the insulators and put those cable pairs in service. This process was repeated many times throughout the country as new COs were placed in service and old COs were removed from service. The big work was in the manhole on the corner of Hanover and Patapsco. We were in that hole for about 9 months. All the cables that came down Hanover from Baltimore and turned east on Patapsco continuing to the old CO had to be half tapped to the new cables pulled into the hole from the New CO. This was at least 10 cables of sizes up to 2100 pairs. After the half tapping was complete on a cable the splice that now had 3 cables going into it was wrapped in muslin and given a temporary cover of CR tape to waterproof the conductors. We would cover the splice with a rubber blanket and go to the next splice.

The arrangement of riding with Putts was working O K but I felt Arlene and I had to make a better living arrangement. She had never applied for a driver's license. Young girls were not like they are today. If you lived on a farm, you probably got a license because you would be more useful on the farm if you could drive a truck

to Southern States to pick up feed or run other
errands for farm business. But Arlene could walk
to school, her parents shopped and took care of
household business, and she did not need a
license. We got her license for her in 1959. But
in the meantime, I had to ask my father or mother
or someone to take us places like food shopping,
Dr's visits, and such. So, I suggested to Arlene
in early 1958 that we get an apartment in
Brooklyn, move there and sell the Trailer. I
could walk to work or use public transportation.
We could do the same with Shopping and Dr's
visits. I had found a Loan Company, (Shark)
across the street from the manhole on Hanover
and Patapsco that would lend me $300 dollars to
pay the traffic fine. I would have to pay them
back in 12 months at $35 a month. Yes, I know
that is $400 pay back. A usury rate, but I was not
going to ask my parents or Arlene's for the
money. We found a very nice apartment 10
blocks from the manhole I would be working in
for the next 5 - 7 months. We rented the
apartment; it was one bedroom on the second
floor. I told the manager of the apartment's that I
would paint all the rooms and sand and refinish
the floors if he provided the paint. He jumped on
that offer like a Robin on a June bug. I got a
couple friends to help me sand the floors and then

I varnished them. We did them on a weekend.
The next weekend we painted all the rooms and
the stairway down to the front door. The next
weekend we moved in and put the trailer up for
sale. The apartment was nice. The neighbors
were nice, and the job was going well. We were
not making any overtime and I could not work at
any part time jobs because of no transportation.
This made money short, but we were hanging on.
The manhole in Brooklyn was across the street
from a White Coffee Pot. We had Electricity in
this hole. This was unheard of. This was like
working in your living room! What happened
was that when we went into the CO manhole just
down the block from the new Central Office, they
pulled in an electric cable to give us lights. It was
great. When we opened the hole at Hanover and
Patapsco, we saw that the line crew who had
pulled in all the cables from the central office had
also pulled in an Electric cable to this hole.
Having a Christmas Tree in a manhole for the
holidays was going to be unbelievable. The
foreman told us, do not leave anything connected
to that electricity when you are not in the hole.
But to be able to run a blower to clear the air in
the hole without listening to a noisy generator
was beautiful.   Arlene and I moved into the
apartment around January of 1958. Jeff was 10

months old. I missed riding with Putts. He was a character. He had been a cook on Submarines in the first world war and lived thru the war. That was an achievement. He could crack 4 eggs, 2 in each hand, simultaneously, and drop the egg yolks and whites in the skillet without breaking the yolks. I had trouble doing that with one egg. He told me many stories about the telephone company and its employees over the years. He said he knew an Installer who did some work for a group of Bookies in south Baltimore. The bookies had rented a small house very close to the main track of the railroad running between Baltimore and Washington. There was a Telegraph open wire pole line beside the track. There were several 10 pin arms on the poles and the bookies had identified the pair that carried the horse race results from the racetracks at Bowie and Upper Marlboro Maryland to the News Papers in Baltimore. They had paid an employee of Western Union for this information. The Bookies then engaged a coworker of Putts to climb the pole closest to their house and tap the pair, run the tap wire down the pole and bury the wire as it was led to the Bookies house. The Bookies got hold of a surplus 28 RO teletype. They had the guy from C&P connect the wiretap to the teletype and they had all the race results at the same time they were being received by the newspapers. There seemed to be enough time between the receipt of the results and the dissemination of race results via radio and newspapers for an unscrupulous Bookie to lay a few discreet bets before the race results were publicly known. Putts said his coworker almost got his butt in serious trouble one night when the Bookies called at 2 am and said that he must get to the pole where the wire was tapped and remove the illicit connection before it was discovered. They said Western Union linemen were working their way down the line from Washington, looking for a wiretap! The telephone worker raced to the pole and removed the tap and the wire on the pole and in the ground and cleaned the site up and got the heck out of Dodge before WU got to that pole.

He said another side job he knew a guy had done was to rearrange some phone service at a Beauty Shop location. He said the Beauty Shop had 2 phone lines for business use. They also had 2 lines for personal use in the house. The Beauty Shop was a legitimate operation but there was no need for 2 lines to handle their customer calls. There was a large 2 car garage behind the house that had been converted into a Bookie operation. Phones were the life blood of this type of operation. C&P would not install 3 phones in a garage. When the Vice squad was looking for Bookie operations, they looked for multiple phone lines going into a house or garage. The 4 lines going into the Beauty shop did not raise suspicion. What the C&P guy did on his own time was to dig a shallow ditch from the house to the garage and he ran taps off 3 of the house phones to the garage. They hooked up the phones in the garage, disconnected the ringers on those 3 phones in the house and the Bookies were in business. Putts could entertain me all the way to work and back home with his stories. Sometimes I wondered where he got the detail on these little deals he seemed to know about.

When we were moved in and living in reasonable comfort, I would walk the 10 -12 blocks to work rain or shine. C&P issued good rain gear to outside employee's whose job required them to be in the weather. I would carry my rain gear home if there was any threat of rain. Sometimes I rode the Baltimore Transit Bus that drove up and down Patapsco Ave. This kept me out of the rain for 9 blocks of the distance. Shopping was a little more trouble. There were not many Super Markets in 1958. There were food stores that had grown beyond the type of store I had grown up with. When I was growing up you entered a store and went to the counter and told the storekeeper what you wanted. They would walk to the rows of shelves behind them and select your product and return to the counter and ask you what else did you want. When you were thru, you paid and left with the purchases in a paper bag. The store we bought food from in Brooklyn was large enough to have 3 or 4 cashier lines. You served yourself as you do today in many stores and then paid at the check-out cashier. Then you hoped that you had not bought more than you could carry. That was usually controlled by lack of money to make too large a purchase. One incident I remember vividly was the week that we were flat broke. Friday was payday. The Foreman had to visit each crew on Friday, and we hoped he was early, to give us our paycheck. So this week on Wednesday, Arlene told me we were down to a jar of Peanut Butter with a few table spoons left in it. 4 or 5 potatoes, a few slices of baloney and a half a loaf of bread. There was a half a quart of milk. Jeff was O K because he was still eating some canned baby food as well as a few bites from the table. We had Baby food. When you were out of money and 40 miles from anyone we knew. You had to persevere to survive. What made things difficult was without any savings and no such things as

Credit Cards, they didn't exist in 1957, you were on your own. When we moved back to Sykesville, we found that we could run a tab for food at the local store if you paid the full amount each week. When credit started to become available in the form of Credit Cards my older brother warned me 'do not charge for food' He said If you charge for a car or furniture, you get to use the product while you are paying for it. But if you charge for food, you will have long ago flushed it down the toilet while you are still paying for it! My brother is very wise! We did not have a bank account at that time in our lives. When I was paid, I would take the check to the Bank on the corner and by then we were recognized by everyone in the neighborhood as 'The guys in the manhole 'and they would cash the check for me. I think they charged 10 cents to cash the check. Sometime that fall Arlene announced that we were going to have another child. This was not a surprise, since we now knew what was causing this situation among men and women and we had not stopped doing it!! There was no reliable prevention for pregnancy except abstinence. And that was not on the list of acceptable solutions for a young couple. We knew this would cause a problem that we would have to deal with in 6 or 8 months. The apartment was limited to 1 child. They could not ask us to leave until the baby was on the scene. But we would have to think about our next move. Meanwhile we located a nice Dr. with an office on Patapsco Ave. within walking distance. The splicing was on schedule we were going to have the cables Half Tapped and tested in good time for the Cut. As spring started to blossom, I often thought that a set of wheels would make life easier. I walked down Patapsco Ave. toward Baltimore at lunch time one day and a block from the manhole there was a used car lot. They had about 15 cars on the lot and on the front row was a 1948 Studebaker Starlight Coupe. This was the car that when it was introduced it 1947 had everyone talking about the car that looked the same from the front or the back. Well, that was an exaggeration but they were different. I asked the salesman the price and he said $100. I thanked him and decided that I should check with Department of Motor Vehicles and see if I could get my license back. When I called the DMV and asked about reinstating my license, they said not a problem. I had been without my license for almost a year, and they said that was good, just re-apply and they would give it to me. I had to go to the DMV in Glen Burnie, so it took some help from my mother to come to Brooklyn and

take me to DMV. When we left, I had a valid
Maryland Driver's License. My next stop was at
the used car lot, and I bought the Black 2 door
Studebaker coupe. This turned out to be one of
the most economical cars I ever owned. When I
drove home and asked Arlene if she wanted to go
for a ride she was delighted. There was a lot of
interesting things and places to see in the area
where we lived. We would put Jeff in a blanket
lined container on the back seat. Cars did not
have seat belts in them until the 1960s. There
were none of the safety features of today's cars
other than safety glass in the windows. This was
basic transportation. The longest afternoon drive
would be out to Fort Smallwood at the entrance
to the Patapsco River from the Chesapeake Bay.
This was one of 4 or 5 forts built to protect
Baltimore Harbor. The most famous of these
Fort's was Fort McHenry where the 'Star
Spangled Banner 'hung during the War of 1812.
We would sometimes drive down to the
waterfront and find a quiet place where we could
drop a couple crab lines in the water and try to
lure some Atlantic Blue Crabs to the surface so
we could net them. We could now drive to
Carroll County to visit our parents and friends on
weekends. I was only working 5 days a week
now, no overtime. Arlene and I were now

welcome at her parents' home. The hard feelings over the circumstances of our marriage were forgotten amidst the joy of a grandchild. Jeff was a joy to everyone. Summer was in full blossom, and we would set on the steps of our apartment and talk with our neighbors while the children played in the large grass area in front of the houses. We had one troubling incident that occurred that spring. My cousin Carl from Sykesville was visiting us for a few hours on a weekend and he had his younger sister Debbie with him. Debbie was around 5 years old. Jeff was just over 1 year old. A neighbor from across the Cull-de-Sac had a daughter about 8 or 9 years old and she was a bully. Arlene and I, Carl, and 4 of our close neighbors, were setting on our front steps. Jeff and Debbie were playing around our steps when the girl from across the way joined them. Before long, pushing and shoving started, and Debbie was knocked to the ground by the Bully. Debbie got up crying and I grabbed the culprit and smacked her ass. She ran home and before long her parents and her came down the sidewalk screaming at all of us. They wanted to know who had struck their child. I spoke up first and told them she had tripped and fell. Of course, she denied that she had fallen, but all my neighbors spoke up and supported my claim. The couple collected their Brat and went home. I felt that we would hear more from them, and we did. That night about 2 am the phone rang and when I answered it there was no one on the line. I immediately knew that this was a call from my upset neighbors. I knew that the fellow worked at night, and it was no problem for him to call us in the middle of the night. I tried to get his phone number from information, but it was an unlisted number. On Monday I walked around behind the row of houses where the troublesome couple lived, and I climbed the stepped pole behind their house. It was easy to follow the drop line from their house to the pole and trace it into the cable terminal. I identified the pair number the drop was connected to, and I had all the information I needed to get their phone number. Later in the day I went to the Trouble Desk for the Brooklyn area and while I was talking to the guys on the trouble desk, I glanced at the cable books. The cable books listed the cable pairs and the phone number serviced. It was easy to associate the pair in the terminal with a phone number. As luck would have it, we were working on some live circuits that week and were on nights for 4 nights. We had a phone in our manhole because of the length of time we were to be in the hole. That night around 2 am Arlene called to say that she had a call with no-one on the line. I immediately called the number I had pulled from the cable book and a sleepy voiced woman answered. I provided some heavy breathing then hung up. A few minutes later Arlene called again and said she had just received a call with no-one on the line. I said go back to sleep. I then called the number again. I figured that like Pavo's dogs it would take a couple repeats of this charade for them to catch on. We did not receive any more phone calls of that nature. I figured that his wife must have told him she needed to get some sleep so cut the crap.

Two For the Price of One

There was a Bull Roast planned for June 7th a Saturday. Outside Plant Bull Roasts were not to be missed. They would have sliced roast beef sandwiches, Steamed hard crabs, beer, soda. There would be card playing, and most important an opportunity to say hello and maybe speak to the Second level managers and The Big Kahuna, The District Manager. We were all sure that He reported to God. The festivity would start at 10 AM at a Hall in Glen Burnie. We knew the baby would be coming soon so we had asked Arlene's mother to watch Jeff for a few days as the delivery date approached. On Friday evening, the 6th of June, I took Arlene to a regular scheduled visit with her doctor. We thought that the baby was very active in the last couple of weeks, and I was really concerned by the amount of weight that Arlene had gained with this pregnancy. She was as big as a house. Arlene's normal weight was 110 to 115 pounds. She weighted 165 at the Doctors that evening. She said she felt fine but wanted to have the baby. When the Doctor was finished with his examination, he told us that the baby was close to birth, and he would not be too surprised if it was Twins! Well with that on our mind we went to bed. Early next morning Arlene said she thought she needed to go to the hospital. The Hospital that the Doctor had scheduled us for was University of Maryland hospital in Baltimore. The same Hospital where I had cheated death 3 years before. Around 6 AM Arlene said her water had broken and we got up and got dressed. We piled into the car and drove to University Hospital. I parked the little Studebaker and helped her to the admittance desk. They took her away after giving me a phone number to call later. I went home and wondered what was happening until around 9 AM. I called and they informed me that Arlene and the Twins were doing fine. The first had been born at 8 am and the second twin had arrived 20 minutes later. They weighed 12 pounds. One weighed 6 pounds 1 ounce; we named her Vivian Yvonne. The second weighed 5 pounds 15 ounces. We named her Cheryl Lynn. They told me I could probably take all 3 of them home on Monday. They said visiting hours today would be at 2.pm. I called my mother and Arlene's mother and filled them in on everything. I told them I would see them at the hospital. I then went to the Bull Roast. This was directly associated with earning a living. That was only second to family, and I could not see family until 2 PM. We did not have the twins home more than a couple days before the Apartment Management gave us official notice that we had to vacate the apartment. We had 30 days, so we were not put out on the street. The timing of our need for a place to live aliened perfectly with a situation that my parents were facing. They had decided that they wanted to live closer to my father's work location.

He was working out of the Pikesville, Maryland service center. They were looking to buy a house in Sudbrook Park near Pikesville. They did not want to sell their home on Brangle Road in Marriottsville because they planned on retiring into that house in a few years. I told them we would love to rent the house and property from them and would be responsible for all maintenance on the place. The rent we agreed on was reasonable and within our budget. We had a plan. They proceeded with their house purchase, and we waited to hear the date we could move. Well, the Bull roast went fine I took a box of Cigars that had pink bands on them that said TWINS. I found the cigars in a drug store on my way to the Bull Roast. I opened the box and removed about half the cigars and left them in the car. I knew that once I opened that box of cigars, they would all be gone in 5 minuets! I wanted some for family and friends that were not telephone people. I had a good time at the Roast, I did not drink much in those days, just soda. So, I met everyone I thought I should shake hands with, and of course I had the joy of making the birth Announcement and this led to the Second level manager and the District manager congratulating me and asking about the mother's condition. I felt this was more contact than I would have ever had without the Birth Announcement.

End Of Brooklyn Cutover

We were wrapping up the cutover of the Brooklyn exchange. After the cut over, the splicers had to go back into the half-tapped splices and cut out the unused cables, then place permanent covers or sleeves as they were called on the splices. In the manhole closest to the new CO, we had cables that were half tapped to the South bound cables that passed the entrance to the new CO and continued down to Patapsco Ave. and then east to the old CO. Now that service was provided by the new CO, we disconnected those cables running to the old CO. The line crews would come in after we were finished with our disconnects and they would remove all those old cables from the ducts. The hole with the major work was the one at Patapsco and Hanover. When we were finished disconnecting the old cable that ran to the old CO, we would fit a lead sleeve to the remaining cables left from that 'bridging 'of cables from the city that were connected to the cables from the New CO and have them ready to be 'Wiped". That meant pouring molten lead on the joint between the cable and the sleeve and 'wiping 'it with a heavy piece of material while you were wearing very thick gloves. The molten lead bonded to the sleeve and the cable to make a strong waterproof joint. The sequence that the splicer used was to push all the lead wiping out to the end of the job. He did the disconnect, then closed the remaining 2 cable ends together, fitted the led sleeve over the splice then covered the sleeve with waterproof CR tape and then placed a rubber blanket over the splice and moved on to the next splice.

After all the old cables were cut out of the 'bridges 'and laid back ready for the line crews to remove the old cables we would wipe all the joints. This was a tedious job, and we would have to heat lead for 3 or 4 days continuously to 'wipe 'all of the splices. Actually, the splicer wiped all the splices in 2 days. He then put rubber blankets on all the finished work and uncovered the work 2 or 3 splices a day. I kept the lead pot hot for the total time. All the tools and material were there and if the foreman looked in the hole on his daily visit, he would see the splice being 'wiped'. Each day more splices were uncovered and after 5 days all the work was exposed and done. Now you ask why? Well, this was part of a game that I saw throughout C & P. Don't do more than the job required to meet a satisfactory productivity result. If you worked too fast, then a new level of expectation was created, and you would now have to meet that performance level. A year or so later I was working in a splicing trouble crew, and we would have small jobs assigned to us that we could wrap up and leave quickly if we had to go on a trouble call. When we would leave the office in the morning almost all the splicers, I worked with would do the same thing. They would examine the work order then hold it up to a strong light and see if they could read what was under the 'White out' covering a block of data at the bottom of the order. The block was filled in by the engineer who wrote the order, and it gave the number of man-hours that was allocated to do the job. A lot of small jobs would have 16-man hours in the block. The Spicer would look at the order and say, 16 hours. This job will not take more than 4 hours for the two of us to do. We'll knock it out and then Goof off for the rest of the day. This was before GPS tracking of vehicles or tracking of the route and miles covered in a day by the truck. To understand this attitude, you need to understand the method for measuring productivity that was used and accepted thru out the Bell System. The C&P Company was a wholly Owned Subsidiary of the AT&T Company. AT&T and its Subsidiaries were the

Bell System. Labor in the Bell System was measured on Work Units Per Hour. Through exhaustive studies the length of time necessary to perform all of the individual work functions required to operate the Bell System telephone Plant was gathered and then broken down into arbitrary units named 'Work Units'. Productivity was then measured by how many Work Units you could complete in an hour. I do not remember the exact figures but if the satisfactory target was 8 Work Units (WU) per hour. Then at the end of a month all the WU's on completed work orders for a foreman could be added up and then the total number of productive man-hours, of his work force could be divided into those total WU's and that Foreman's productivity performance for the month was established. Productive hours discounted time spent in meetings, work on trouble locating and clearing, and time required to meet the demands of unanticipated delays unrelated to the tasks that were measured. This was a learning lesson for me that helped me solve nationwide service degradation problems in future positions of responsibility that I held in the AT&T company. The reason that the 'grunts', the guys on the ground, played this game of limiting productivity as they explained it to me, 'The Newbie 'was if

we bust our ass today, we will drive the WU
performance up from 8 to 10 then next month
they will expect everyone to deliver at that new
higher rate. Maybe next month the cards will not
fall in the same sequence and there would be no
way we could do a better job. But we would all
be punished because we did a good job last
month. I thought this was an oversimplification
of the situation, but I saw where they were
coming from. I was allowed to be a sort of non-
voting observer of the process at this time since I
was just a Helper. I did not make decisions in
any of these actions.

Back To The Homestead

In early August Arlene, Jeff, the Twins and I moved from the apartment in Brooklyn to my parents' house on Brangle Road in Marriottsville. As soon as the twins arrived, we were under pressure to vacate the apartment. We knew the rule, Only One Child. The house on Brangle Road was the home I had lived in from 1947 until Arlene and I were married in 1956. The house had been expanded with a small, 15 feet by 8-foot enclosed back porch. It was more like an Arctic Entrance than a porch. There were windows on all three walls. The side connected to the house, contained the back door of the house and a window that opened into the kitchen. This window sash was left in the raised position all the time, except the dead of winter. There was a hanging locker in the corner of the porch to hang winter coats and rain gear in. The other main occupants of the porch were a washing machine and a gas clothes dryer. After Arlene and I moved in we made room for a 15 Cubic foot chest freezer on the very crowded porch. There was a small hand sink in one corner which was good to wash your hands when you came in from working. The house had one bathroom with a tub but no shower. I added a shower head to the tub after we moved in. I don't think my parents ever used a shower. When we were through adding our touches to the house the porch was little more than a covered walkway to a very small kitchen. But it was as close to ours as any living quarters would be until we bought our first house. My parents had added a powder room in a corner of the larger of the two upstairs bedrooms.

There was a toilet and wash sink. This was great, since it meant, you didn't have to run down the steps in the middle of the night to tinkle. The bedroom at the top of the stairs was open to all traffic using the steps. This had been the bedroom that my brother Donald and I shared. Before we moved into the house Donald had graduated from High School and had joined the Air Force. The twins would grow into this bedroom as they grew out of basinets. There was a small room on the first floor in the back corner of the house that was 10 foot long and 6 foot wide that we used as a bedroom for Jeff. We were set! I drove the little Studebaker to the Brooklyn area and also to the new work location at Barkley St. One thing I did to improve the reliably of my transportation was to buy a second 1948 Starlight coupe. This Studebaker was Green and in rougher condition. I bought it because the owner said the engine was in very good condition. I got it for $ 75. The engine in the black Studebaker was burning oil and getting noisy. One of the nice things about the homestead was it allowed me to work on my cars. My father had built a chicken house a hundred feet behind the house. He was no longer raising chickens when they moved, and the chicken house was very clean inside. I decided to make a workshop in it. The building was built off the ground on 8 telephone poles buried in the ground 3 feet deep and sticking up 3 feet. There was a pole at each corner of the building. The building was 20 foot long and 8 foot wide. The other 4 poles were placed evenly 2 on each side of the front and back between the corners. There was a set of steps at one end to a small landing then thru a door into a 4-foot-wide room that had been used to store feed, then a second door into the main area of the building. I built a work bench across the distant end of the building. There were 2 windows in the side of the building facing the main house and 2 windows in the opposite, or back side of the building. In the middle of the back side was a door. The door had been used to let chickens walk down a ramp into a small yard when Dad had chickens there. The ramp and yard were gone. Electricity was extended from the house via a pair of wires leaving the house at a height of 10 feet off the ground and attaching to the side of the building. The 110 VAC was good enough for lights and small power tools. Before winter came, I purchased a 1 kw gasoline generator and set it inside of the building. I wired an arrangement to connect the generator output to the wires going to the house. We often lost electricity during snowstorms. When this happened, the oil-fired furnace would not run. Also, the refrigeration was lost. I knew that if the electricity failed, I could throw the main feed breaker to the open position and disconnect the house power from the Baltimore Gas and Electric lines. I could remove the screw in fuses for all the circuits except the refrigerator and the furnace and a couple light circuits and start the generator up and we were back in business. The total load of all those appliances was less than 1000 watts. So, we were good. Cooking was with bottled propane gas, and we had 2 100-pound bottles connected to the house. One of the first changes I made with the Shop building was to sink 4 poles into the ground outside of the side door on the shop. 2 were close to the side of the building and were 2 feet on either side of the center door. This placed them about 8 feet apart considering the width of the door. Since the distance between the front wheels of an American car are approximately 5 feet, I set the other 2 poles 5 feet farther out from the first 2 poles directly in line with them. We then placed a plank of oak 3 inches thick and 9 feet long by 12 inches wide from one of these poles to the other parallel with the length of the building. We ran 2 more oak planks of the same dimensions from the top of the poles on the end closest to the shop end where the work bench was. What we had created was a drive-up ramp that would position the front of a car beside the shop door when the car was driven up on the ramps. We then dug a hole opposite of the door aligned with the center of the door and set a telephone pole that went 4 feet into the ground and stood 10 foot above ground. We bolted a 4 X 6-inch beam to the pole at the same height as 2 inches above the door into the shop. We cut a 4" W X 6 "high hole in the wall of the shop above the door and set the beam from there to the pole. The end of the beam inside of the shop was placed on a reinforced support in the shop. We were now ready to pull car motors and reinstall motors. The motor from the Green Studebaker was the first motor we removed. We removed the hood from the car before we pushed it up onto the ramp. This took a little help by having the Black Studebaker on the other end of the ramp with a rope connected between the cars. With one person driving the black car and one person steering the green car and me standing beside the pole supervising as the car came to rest directly under where we intended to hang the chain/falls for lifting the engine. We pulled the motor and drifted the car down off the ramp. We then swung the motor into the shop. This was the first of many engines to enter the shop that way. After going over the engine, changing plugs, points, ignition parts we pulled the black Studey up and reversed the process. I now had a Black Studey with a better motor. Another change we made in the Studebaker was to cut a piece of 1/4" plywood to fit on the back seat of the car and extend up to the back of the front seats. I screwed a pair of hinges to the front corners of the piece of wood and screwed a leg of 1" X 2" wood just long enough to reach the floor on each front corner. This supported the front of the plywood that overhung the seat edge. I also screwed a pair of folding lock springs between the sheet of wood and the legs. When the legs were pulled down the spring locked open and kept the leg from collapsing. Arlene took over and made a couple inch thick pad to cover the complete plywood sheet. She would also put blankets on the bed for more comfort and warmth if needed. We could then throw all 3 kids on the back pad, and we were off. When we first moved to Brangel road Jeff was 18 months old and the twins were 3 months old. Of course, there were no seat belts or child seats back then. You could carry a kid on the roof if you wished too.

Things were much handier for Arlene. There was milk and bread delivered by Koontz Dairy several times a week. I had not taught her to drive but it was on the schedule. We could see her parents much more frequently. My Aunt Elaine lived next door and she was a great help for Arlene. My parents were doing well in their new house in Pikesville.

When the Brooklyn cutover was finished My splicer and I moved to one of the worst work situations I had faced up until then. A cable was being spliced across Hammond's Ferry Road along the southern suburbs of Baltimore. The road was bordering wetlands and the line crew was just ahead of us placing the conduit run and then pulling in the new cable for us to splice. If I remember correctly, it may have been one of the first cables, we placed Splice Cases on. The splice case was a 2-part Aluminum casting. The 2 halves were interchangeable on each end of the case which was about 30 inches long for full size cases there were 2 half round cutouts in the casting. Try to picture a 3-inch round cable laying in the cutout and the other half of the case pressed against the first half and then bolt the 2 halves to gather. The end of the cable would be in the case, and with some waterproof material wrapped around the cable before we bolted the 2 halve's together we would have a watertight seal around that cable. Now let's take it apart because some work must be done inside of the case before, we close it up. The 2 ends of cable to be joined in the manhole were cut to the correct length that would fit in the new splice case after the splice was complete. If there was only 2 cable ends to be spliced, then a single cable case was used. If there was a need for a 'Bridging 'cable to be connected to the main cable, then a case with 2 holes on each end was used and the 4 th entrance hole to the case was filed with a watertight plug. The new technology was interesting but the real problem with this cable run was the water. When we open the hole water was nearly up to the top of the hole. The cable ends were almost touching the manhole covers under side. We opened the hole while the move truck was still there. When we saw the water the move truck driver unloaded a pump and some hose sections.

We told him to stick around while we started pumping the hole. When the pump was started the water level receded much slower than we liked. The typical duct arrangement was 6 ducts in a stack of 3 pairs of ducts. When the run required more ducts for more cables the run was built out in increments of 6 ducts. This was a 6 duct run. When the top pair of ducts was exposed water continued to flow from them as the hole was drained. After the hole was drained to the point that only 1 foot of water remained in the hole the water flowing into the hole from the lowest ducts looked like it was going to hold the water level at 6 inches or a foot. We talked about working in the hole and decided that we could place our 3-way box/stool in the bottom of the hole and place the splice high in the hole and if the pump did not fail, we could do the splice in one day. But we needed a second pump that we knew worked! Hooked to hoses tested and ready to start. We called the dispatcher and asked her to have the foreman come by to look at our situation. We called this procedure of involving management in the decision-making process, 'Holding hands and all jumping off the cliff together.' The thought being that if things went 'Bad', management could not bail on the situation and say" Gee I would not have done it that way" or some other 'Let me escape from the responsibility for this course of action". We got the second pump and all the necessary closing materials for the new splice cases and pumped the hole, we kept both pumps running and we knocked out the splice in the 600 pair cable by end of the day. The cases were interesting to work with. One thing that I hung onto for 50 years was a ratcheting 7/16" wrench made by Snap On for this particular use. The wrench could be flipped over and used to loosen a bolt as well as for tightening the bolts. The wrench was only about 3 inches long, no doubt to keep the craft from over-tightening the bolts. We still had problems with over tightening and wringing the bolts off. You then had to get the broken piece of bolt out to place a new bolt in the hole. The case would leak if a bolt was omitted. The Cases really sped up cable work in the underground. No wiping of joints! All the holes along that run had water in them. We were glad to finish the job.

A New World!

When we were complete with that job. Moxley said there was a request for a splicer's helper from the Barkley Street Garage in north Baltimore. He said his workload was falling off and he thought that I might want to volunteer to go up there before things got so tight in the Glen Burnie Garage that I was forced to take something less desirable. I know he liked me and was being sincere. I asked him if he would get my C&P driver's license back for me before I left. He said he would, and he did. Fall of 1958 I reported to Barkley Street. It was just around the block from the Stadium where the Colts played. There were 2 cable foremen there. Bob Seigler had the Construction splicers with their tool carts and Ralph Warehime who supervised the Cable Trouble crews. They covered all of north Baltimore. From Pimlico to east of York Road. When I got there, I was introduced to the splicers and the Helpers. They seemed to be an easy-going group. I was assigned to Bob Seigler's crew. He asked me if I had ever driven the Move Truck. I said no, but I would be glad to do that job if he wanted me to. He said the man who was presently driving the truck wanted to get some more splicing experience. I told him that I had been in a splicing crew for a couple years and I liked splicing, but The Move Truck seemed interesting, so I was looking forward to it. There was some amount of competition in the realm of the Helpers because no new splicers had been made in a few years and you had helpers who were at top helpers pay and could not get a raise unless they were promoted to Splicer. I was not quite at top helpers pay yet so I was not a threat to any of the helper's senior to me. When Bob Seigler, my new Forman was finished with paperwork associated with my move to Barkley Street and I had met nearly everyone Bob led me to the back of the garage. There was a screened area maybe 20 feet by 20 feet with a screen door that could be locked. Inside of the screened area were pumps, blowers, generators, manhole guards, safety cones and other assorted gear. It was just piled up in a ugly mess. Beside the storage area was a couple year old GMC 1-ton pick-up truck. Bob gave me a clerical loose-leaf notebook. The first few pages had phone numbers for the offices in the garage, the main numbers I needed, that of the District Office secretary who recorded all the move requests and passed them on to me. And notes that the last move truck driver had made on the condition of the truck, and the condition of the equipment under his care. From what I could observe the equipment was in poor shape. Bob said give the District Office a call and she will get you going. Bob showed me where the gas pump was for filling the truck with gas and for filling the gas cans that I would deliver to the splicers with the equipment. I called the district office and introduced myself to the secretary. I told her I was the new Move Truck driver. She said that was nice, if I got by the District Office please stop by and meet everyone face to face. I said I would. I then asked her to tell me how we were going to operate. She said to call in first thing every morning so she could give me orders that she might have for moves that day. She said to check with Bob Seigler at start of business for anything he might want me to do. There were no cell phones at that time so everything was done thru relayed message

I knew a little bit about North Baltimore, but my best assistant was a good, detailed map of Baltimore that was in the glove compartment of the truck. I found a couple chest like boxes in the bed of the truck. They had some material that splicers might need on the job. I thought it would be helpful if I had a good selection of materials to give the splicers when I moved them. There was a supply room in the garage, as there was in each garage, I picked out several small items that would be helpful when I made a move and stored them in the boxes in the truck bed. The next thing I did was wash the truck with a hose and soap and water in the garage. I cleaned the interior and the work bed. When I got my first move from the clerk, I was off to the races. I had to look up the locations on the map for where the Tool Cart was located and where it was to go. I met the splicer and his helper, we hooked up the Tool Cart to the truck and I followed them to their new location. After we were disconnected, I asked them if they needed anything. They said no-one had ever made an offer like that to them with a move. I said I was on a Tool Cart for 2 years and I thought it would be a good idea. They stocked up a few items and sent me on my way. If I was across town from the garage, I often would hang out in that area for an hour or two waiting to see if any work would turn up near me. If things were quite for a couple calls to the office I would drive back to the garage and get to work on my clean up and equipment service work.

One morning I came in a little early and went to the Move Truck before going to the boss's office for daily orders. When I was in the back of the garage, I saw a face that I knew from Marriottsville. I walked over to the night mechanic who had not left to go home yet. I said, "Hello George, I did not know you worked here". George Albert Shipley was 15 years older than me, but I knew him and all his family. George said, "I have worked for C&P for years. "He told me he serviced all the motor vehicles in the garage." Of course, the work had to be done at night because the vehicles were in use during the daytime. I asked him who services the pumps, blowers, and generators in the storage room. He grinned and said, "I am supposed too, but I really don't have time to service them properly, so I work on them when they report that one is not working." Today we refer to that as "Corrective Maintenance". The best way to minimize corrective maintenance is to conduct "Preventive Maintenance". I asked George about parts like spark plugs, oil, filters for the equipment. He said I have some parts and the maintenance manuals on my work bench. I told him that I would service the equipment if I had access to parts. I said it would be better for me to take equipment to the Splicers that worked and would continue to work, rather than chase my tail making multiple trips to the same Splicer because the equipment stopped working. So, we struck a deal that I would exercise the equipment on a regular schedule, perform routine maintenance using the parts and materials on his work bench and leave him a record of work done. I would leave any piece of equipment that required more extensive maintenance than I had time to do beside his work bench with a request for service. After I was Move Truck Guy for 3- or 4-months comments about the improved performance of pumps and generators and blowers filtered back to Bob Seigler, my boss.

He walked out to the equipment crib one day and asked if I was keeping up with the moves. I said I called in at least once an hour to the District Office and if someone needed to contact me direct, they could call on any of 3 different phones in the garage. I said If I heard a phone ring for more than a couple time I usually went and answered it. I then asked him if he or Ralph Warehime's phone rang would they call for me on the garage Intercom. He said certainly. Bob asked if I wanted to work on construction rather than drive the Move Truck. I was beginning to get the feeling that Move Truck duty was not a job that most of the Helpers wanted anything to do with. When I was talking to Bob Seigler as he looked in on my corner of the garage, he said I wish that every new employee I got came off a farm. I asked him why? He said they know how to work, and they like to work. That was one of the nicest compliments I think I ever received. Bob told me and the crew one day in the morning meeting that he was getting a "Newbe" helper, and he was going on the move truck. He said Ralph is going to help Carl Hokemeyer. He will spend a couple days with the new Move Truck driver before he moves to help Hokemeyer. So, I provided more of an introduction to the Move Truck world than I was offered but that was fine. Then I went back to a Tool Cart. Most of the work in this area of the city was aerial. The cables were small, around 100 to 200 pair and a lot of the work was cutting in terminals. We did an underground cable occasionally. I moved from this splicer to another splicer, Al Fiedler.

Al was a good splicer and a gas pressure expert. C&P had been involved in a service protection plan for several years that revolved around using Dry Nitrogen gas to pressurize the old lead cables. The amount of pressure applied was around 5 pounds/ sq. Inch. The concept was good and simple. If you soldered a threaded boss on a cable sleeve and screwed in a nipple that contained a Schrader valve you could inject low pressure Nitrogen into the cable. To do this injection we carried a large Nitrogen bottle to a pole and locked it to the pole with a chain. We had a regulator on the nitrogen and a cover locked over the regulator. This kept an honest person from changing the pressure or stealing the setup. We then ran a hose up the pole to the fitting on the cable. Some cables were pressurized right where they left the Central Office. These were pulp insulated cables. When water penetrated the lead sheath and soaked the pulp insulation, the conductors became 'shorted ' together and were no longer capable of carrying telephone conversations.

The gas keeps a positive pressure inside the cable and if a small fault developed in the cable sheath the gas would leak out and keep moisture or water from entering the cable. Our normal method of locating faults in a cable was to fine the 'wet section of cable 'and open the cable, dry out the wet area with desiccant then close the damaged area up with a temporary CR tape cover or close it with a lead sleeve or a splice case. The choice of closure was determined by the cable type and its age. Sometimes the trouble report was not very definitive. The central office test man might tell us that he had at least one hundred phones out of service in a certain area of the city. He would usually suggest that it looked like it was a certain cable. We would then ask him to

have the 'Coils 'pulled from a specific cable pair.
The coils provided isolation of the central office
equipment from the cable pairs but allowed talk
to go thru them. When we placed a high voltage
charge on the faulty pair, we did not want the
charge to enter the central office. We would have
the 'Frame Men 'place a warning sign near the
cable pair termination on the frame warning
people that we were about to apply high voltage
in this cable, so stay clear. We would usually go
to a pole where the cable pair was connected to a
subscriber's phone wire and lift the subscriber's
line off the cable pair. We then went to the
Central Office to do the Break Down. This test
set was The KS 141003 L5 Break Down Test Set.
(630VDC) 2-foot-long X 1 foot wide and 6
inches deep. The set had 14, 45-volt batteries in
it. The best place to do the break down was from
the Central Office because you could leave the
set there having it send test tone out on the cable,
and you did not have to worry about someone
stealing the set. After you hit the pair with 630
volts you would usually weld the two wires in the
pair together at the point where the cable was
wet. You would then use the ohm meter on the
set to get the round-trip resistance to the shorted
fault. We knew the distance in feet per Ohm for
each gauge of cable by heart. The resistance in

Ohms could be multiplied by the number of feet/ohms to get an estimated distance to the fault. If the cable was a 24-gauge cable and the resistance read 215 ohm's the distance to the fault was 5380 feet or 1 mile. Now you would look at the cable record books as see where 1 mile took you. You would turn the tone transmitter of the test set on then you would drive to a location closest to a mile away and get your head set and coil on a pole and start walking the cable holding the long pole up in the air and moving the coil along the cable listening to the tone in the head set you were wearing. When you had the coil over the fault in the cable it would be loudest. Just beyond the fault the tone would be very low or gone. You now knew where to open the cable.

If the cable went underground finding the location was more difficult. You would open a manhole on the cable run and identify the cable and then listen for the tone. If the tone came into the hole and left the hole you moved on to the next hole. If the tone did not come into the hole, you went back to the last hole and listened there. If the tone left one hole and did not sound in the next hole the fault was probably in the section between the holes. The best thing to do then was to see if there was any obvious damage source in the section between the holes, like construction or digging. The next procedure would be to open the cable in that manhole and locate the pair with the tone emanating from it to the test set. You would cut the pair and measure forward away from the tone source and toward the short you had caused with the 'Breakdown set' That resistance should give you the distance into the cable section to the fault.

That was where you would tell the construction crew to dig!

Trash By Nash

My adventures in transportation continued. I was not really looking for a newer car, but My brother Donald asked me if I wanted the 1952 Nash Statesman, he had owned for a couple months. The interior was like new. I took it for a drive. The car seemed to be OK, so I took ownership of it from Don. Nash automobiles were built by the Nash-Kelvanator Corporation. Kelvanator built and sold refrigerators and other household appliances. One of the unique features of the Nash cars was that the backs of the seats could be reclined to make beds in the car. Nash had advertisements showing the typical American family of four covered in blankets and sleeping in a camp site in their Nash. Of course, most parents of teenage girls did not want their daughters going on dates with a Rutting young boy in the family Nash! My Nash problems did not involve morals. They involved questionable engineering and poor design. The first problem I encountered involved the exhaust system. Car owners today never think about the exhaust system of their new car for the first 10 years of ownership. During the 1950's, 60's and 70's mufflers and tail pipes rusted out and needed to be replaced in as little as 6 months from new car purchase. There was no 'Aluminized 'coating to extend the life of the system. But design did play a part in durability. The exhaust system on cars and trucks was divided into 3 parts. Bolted to the engine against the exhaust ports of the cylinder heads or the side of the engine block depending on engine design was a rather rugged cast iron exhaust manifold. Bolted to the exhaust manifold was a heavy construction exhaust pipe. The other end of the exhaust pipe slid into a muffler and a clamp held the two items together. Leaving the muffler and continuing to the back bumper of the car was a lighter metal exhaust pipe. The farther away from the source of the hot exhaust gases that you got the lower the temperatures and the less stress on the system. A few days after I bought the Nash, I started the engine, and it made a sort of rumbling sound. I opened the hood and took my first GOOD look at a Nash exhaust system. The noise was emanating from the point where the exhaust made a gentle 90 degree bent down from the engine on its way to the muffler. There was an obvious crack in the pipe at that point. The startling revelation that dawned on me like a bolt of lightning WAS, there is no exhaust manifold on this engine, there is no exhaust pipe on this car. What Nash Engineers had done certainly in the interest of cheapening the car was to make a very long tail pipe, broken at the muffler. The pipe that ran from the engine was of the same gauge metal as the tail pipe. There was no exhaust manifold. The tail pipe made the bend where it now was cracked and ran straight along the side of the engine block. This was a 6-cylinder Flat head "L" design engine. The exhaust ports were Siamese, 2 ports sharing 1 opening. The side of the block was cast with a half-moon boss surrounding the port with the high point of the sides of the half-moon being at the top and bottom of the port. The exhaust pipe had 3 rectangular holes to match the 3 exhaust ports in the block. The pipe was laid against the Block with the 3 holes aligned with the 3 ports. There was a 5/16 stud above and below each port, a common exhaust pipe clamp bottom section was placed over the pipe and 2 nuts held the pipe against the block at each exhaust port. In credible! In-credibly cheap and in-credibly poor engineering. I could understand the tail pipe rusting out at 22,000 miles but not the exhaust manifold. Well to fix it I was going to have to take the whole exhaust system out to Arthur Ruck the local welder, machinist, and metal repair shop. He was located at Ruck's corner where Days Road dead ended into US Route 26, better

known as Liberty Road. I tied the exhaust system
on top of my black Studebaker, put a few dollars
in my pocket and drove out to Ruck's Corner.
When you arrived at the shop you had to look
around to find Arthur. He might be on a
Caterpillar tractor, a big truck or anywhere on the
place. The best way to find him was to look for
welding flashes. When I got Arthur's attention,
he looked at the exhaust system and said NASH.
I said yes. He said I can weld it but it won't last
long. I said I now understand, but it will not have
to last long because I don't think I will have the
car for long. Arthur laughed and said just take it
to the welding table. He made a sleeve to
encompass the bend for several inches on each
end of the crack and welded it together. I asked
him how much and he said $4. I paid him then
tied the pipe back on the top of my car and drove
home. After I had bolted the exhaust system
back onto the Nash and started it up it was quiet
and drivable. I drove the car to work for a few
weeks and it seemed to be a nice car. The next
anomaly I encountered with the 'Trash by Nash '
happened while Bob Bruce and I were on a short
trip to Sykesville. I went around a curve at a
reasonable rate of speed, and the car felt
squirrelly, and the engine sped up. I let up on the
gas, then stepped back down on the gas and the

engine sped up but the car did not. I checked that
the car, which was a 3-speed manual was in gear
and it was. I drifted to the side of the road and
got out. When I walked to the back of the car I
saw that the left rear wheel was up tight against
the side of the wheel well. I thought, how could
that happen? Bob came around and looked at the
wheel and we discussed the situation. I said the
wheel and axle must have drifted out together.
So, we got hold of the side of the car and started
rocking the car and trying to pull the back of the
car to the left. We got lucky the wheel and axel
didn't come out far enough for the wheel to slip
off the brake shoes. Had that happened when I
applied the brakes the shoes would have
expanded far enough to let the brake hydraulic
cylinder come apart and bleed out all the brake
fluid and have a total brake failure. It did come
out far enough for the splined end of the axle to
disengage from the rear end. That was why I had
no power. When we rocked it back the axle must
have aligned with the rear end and slipped back
into the drive section of the rear and the wheel
disappeared back under the car. We got back in
and I started the car and let the clutch out easy
and the car started to move! We drove home and
we found that if we turned to the right the axle
remained in place. When we turned to the left the

car slipped off the axle splines. A turn back to the right would reengage the axle. Well, we made it to my workshop where we jacked up the back of the Nash and determine the necessary repair. When we had the rear of the car up on stands, we removed the left rear wheel. Without the body limiting the wheel, the brake drum and axle could be easily pulled away from the rear end assembly. What stopped me from removing the complete assembly was the brake shoes remaining bearly in the brake drum, brake lines and emergency brake cable. Careful examination showed the problem to be that the axle seal plate which retained the axle bearing in the rear end housing had been wore thru by the bearing rotating in the housing. The inside of the bearing did not touch the seal plate, but when the Race, or outer shell of the bearing became partially seized to the inter bearing race because of scored bearings the total bearing began rotating. We replaced the bearing, and the axle housing was still good enough to hold the outer race without allowing it to rotate. We put it back together and were mobile again. I soon made the Nash someone else's problem

Vince Sabitino

At work I had been assigned to the splicer that I would spend nearly all the rest of my time in cable working for. I was moved from Bob Seigler's construction crew to Ralph Warehime's Trouble /Maintenance crew. The splicer who I was assigned to work with was Vince Sabitino. This worked out very well for both of us because Vince lived just 8 miles down the road toward Baltimore on the way to work.

We could carpool. I learned quite a bit about the telephone cable business from Vince. I also learned quite a bit more about the politics of the cable personal. What I mean, is, who is 'sponsored 'by who, what is the cost of having a sponsor and what is the advantage of having a sponsor. I had a little taste of sponsorship with Nepotism. My father got me my job at C&P. My father's relationships with various higher managers secured my employment when I was hospitalized 1 month after I was initially employed by C&P. I have always believed that an off the street employee in the same situation would have been let go at that time. But the relationships that Vince pointed out amazed me even when compared with what I knew of the power of nepotism. Vince would point out a splicer and say, 'He's one of Warehime's 'inside guys 'I said what do you mean' Vince said 'You know, he paints and does little things inside the house for Ralph.' I said 'You got to be S——-ing me '! Vice said 'No, that the story' He went on to point out 'Outside men 'They did yard work and other things like house painting. I said, 'Vince I 'v heard enough, I just want to be paid for what I know and what I do.' Unfortunately, I did not work in an environment that functioned that way until I transferred to the AT&T Long Lines Department in 1960. But until that time I continued to learn about telephone work, people, and parenting. Altogether it was Character Building.

The company was trying to minimize cable failures on the older cables. One of the things they were doing was removing rings that supported cables that may have been placed in service 15 or 20 year prior. These were lead sheath cables and over time the cables would ware away the lead where they laid in the ring. The rings were placed about a foot apart. The plan was to remove the rings and spin a wire around the cable and strand to support the cable. To do that a lineman would climb a pole and place a cable chair on the support strand.

The cable chair was a device that had a metal frame with 2 wheels on the front of the seat, a wooden seat and a line hanging in a loop below that the workman could support his feet on. The lineman would climb off the telephone pole at cable height onto the chair facing the cable and get comfortable! Someone would walk along the ground and pull the chair and lineman along the cable run. The lineman in the chair would reach behind the direction of chair travel and first place a hanging pulley on the strand, then remove several cables supports rings. The cable would sag down onto the hanging pulley. The lineman would continue this procedure until he reached the next pole. Now behind him the cable was supported by the hanging pulleys. The line crew might strip 2 or 3 sections of cable from the supporting rings then stop. They would then return to the beginning of their work and a lineman would climb the pole and they would hoist a 'D" Spinner up to him. This tool weighted 40 or 50 pounds. The bottom of the spinner was open, and the lineman would lift the Spinner over the top of the cable and set it down on the strand and loosely hung, supported cable. The spinner had a roll of fine wire loaded to it and the lineman would place a one bolt device on the strand near the pole and attach the end of the wire coming from the spinner. Now the ground hand would start pulling the spinner along the strand toward the next pole. The trailing section of the spinner rotated as the device was pulled along the strand. The wire would wrap around the cable and strand as the spinner moved forward. The cable was drawn up tightly against the strand and the hangers were pushed ahead of the spinner as it was pulled to the next pole. A lineman would be waiting on that pole to remove the collection of hangers as the spinner was drawn to the pole. When the spinner was within reach of the lineman he would reach out behind the spinner and use a hand clamp to temporarily secure the spinning wire so that it would not go slack and let the cable drop. He would then pull a couple feet of slack off the spinner and lift the spinner off the cable and swing it between his chest and the pole and set it on the opposite side of the pole over the strand and cable. After placing a permeant 'Bug" on the strand where the spinner wire was temporarily terminated, he would make a permeant termination on the 'Bug". He would then secure the cable with a cable strap and spacer where the cable approached the end 'Bug'. The cable would be allowed to sag a couple inches as it passed the face of the pole then after the spinner was pulled away from the pole heading for the next pole, the lineman would secure the wire on the terminating 'Bug 'for the next span, place a cable clamp and spacer and he would move on to the next pole to repeat the operation of 'Throwing the Spinner'. The famous American Artist Norman Rockwell captured the act of a Lineman Throwing the D Spinner in his painting "The Lineman". In that picture the lineman was terminating the spinning wire before he threw the spinner across the pole between his chest and the pole face to the next span. Replacing rings and spinning the cable cut down on holes in the cables caused by ring ware. We also inserted resin in old 'F 'type access terminals to allow us to pressurize the cables. These old terminals would leak the compressed nitrogen because the terminal faces were not pressure tight. 'Damming terminals was a messy stinky job. We could do a terminal in about 2 or 3 hours if the weather was good. You could not do it in very cold weather or rainy weather. But it was work we did while waiting for a trouble report. They were jobs you could close quickly to go on a trouble. Once we pressurized a cable the very next thing, we did was start looking for leaks in the cable. We would put pressure on the cable at the Central Office or out in the span, then watch to see if it held the pressure. Usually, it did not hold pressure. We would then take readings along the cable route and chart the drop. This would hopefully lead us to the general area of the leak. It was tedious work. But it was gratifying when you located a leak and were able to repair the cable before it got wet and failed.

We called everyone by their last name. I was Baker, Vince was Sabitino. When Sabitino got upset with a supervisor or someone he would remind me that he was Siciliano. He would say, that guy is on thin ice, I can have him 'Rubbed out" for 50 bucks. He really looked like he could. His wife was a sweetheart. We would get called out during a storm at 10 PM and I would drive to his house and either ride with him to the garage or we would drive in my car. But it was not unusual to work all night and come home at 9 or 10 the next morning. Connie would always invite me to breakfast. I watched her fry eggs in olive oil. I loved her cooking. I'm a pretty good cook today and I still fry under a low flame using olive oil.

Vince became my son Jeff's Godfather when we had Jeff Baptized in the Catholic Church. I was doing good by my standards at C&P but I could tell that even though my job was secure, I would probably wait a long time before I was

promoted to splicer. I really never thought
beyond a job as splicer. The economy was weak
in 1958, and '59 and C&P talked about laying
craft off. We heard rummers that you could get a
transfer to Southern Bell in Florida if you applied
for one. We did not know of anyone who had
done that, but Florida sounded good on cold
winter days. I mentioned the thought of
transferring to Florida too Arlene and we both
came to the same conclusion, how in the world
would you make that happen even if the transfer
was offered? We did't have the money to pack
up 3 kids and move to Florida. So, I kept on
doing what I had been doing. I was happy living
in the Brangle Roadhouse. I had nearly an acre
of land for my garden, a nice workshop and all
my high school friends close by. Arlene's
parents were only 5 miles away. And my brother
lived close. I was forever building contraptions
and working to improve the homestead.

The furnace in our house had been fired by coal
when my father installed it in 1948. Around
1954 he had the local fuel oil dealer install an oil
burner in the bottom of the furnace and they
installed thermostatic controls to make it
automatic. The setup was not very efficient like a
purpose designed oil furnace would have been.
The hot air was distributed by convection, you

know, hot air rises and draws cold air in from the basement floor. The upstairs where the bedrooms were was cold in the winter. I noticed in many of the buildings we were in and out of during work that the big ones were heated by large rectangular furnaces hanging high in the building. Most of these burned Natural Gas. When I had the chance to look at one closely, I saw that half of the box was a large drum type fan. I thought that if I had the fan end of one of those heaters I could cut a hole in the side of my old coal furnace and slide the fan section up against the furnace and I could control the fan with a thermostat and we would be much more efficient and hopefully warmer. It did not take me long to locate a company in Baltimore that had quite a few used oil and gas heaters that were in various states of repair that I could take a look at. When I told them what I wanted to do they found a unit that had no burner in it, but a good fan, The price was right. I think it was less than $100. I loaded it into my father's pickup and took it home. I cut the bottom housing in half, leaving only the fan section to be placed against the hole I had cut in the bottom apron of the furnace. There was a working thermostat in the unit I had just bought. I placed the temperature detector in the bonnet of the old furnace. When the air in the bonnet rose to a temperature of 130 degrees the blower turned on. When it fell below 110 degrees the fan shut off. The nice thing about this arrangement was that the original coal stove had furnace stones lining the fire box. The oil conversion did not remove or change them. So, the oil fire would heat the stones and the blower would continue to run from the heat drifting up from the stones for a while after the oil burner shut off. The oil burner was controlled by a thermostat in the living room of the house. The fan was sensing heat still in the furnace. This fan housing also had a place to put a large filter. This provided us with much cleaner air than we had been getting off the basement floor. I also installed a humidifier in the bonnet of the furnace that sensed the humidity on the first floor and controlled the water flow inserted into the hot air. There were times when we were short of money, and I could not call the oil delivery people and have them deliver fuel oil. I would watch the gauge on the oil tank which was in one corner of the basement and before we ran out of oil I would take 1 or 2 , 5 gallon cans and go to the local Gulf Oil filling station and buy 5 or 10 gallons of Kerosene for 18 cents/gallon and pour it into the fuel oil tank. Kerosene is # 1 fuel oil, the furnace used #2 fuel oil, but I don't think the furnace knew any difference.

We interchanged the 2 fuels in diesel engines all the time.

Talent Saves Money

Arlene's mother was one of the finest Seamstresses in the country. She made all of Arlene's clothes and gowns as Arlene was growing up. All of Arlene's friends envied the clothes she wore and knew that they were not something that their mothers could go to the store and buy. Arlene learned well from her mother. She made everything that the children wore. We got some of the cotton cloth she used to make clothes from friends who bought animal feed from Southern States Cooperative. They used to sell feed in sacks that were made of nicely decorated cotton material. She made Identical clothes for the twins, matching clothes for Renee when she came along. Arlene also got involved in curtain making. There was a woman who lived 15 miles down Liberty Road from us who had a large curtain making operation. Arlene started sewing for this woman. There was a lot of math involved in the pleating dimensions and amount of material required for different spans, I provided the math help. She sewed. I felt that we were perfectly matched to raise a family and provide a level of living far better than my salary would provide for. We did just about everything for ourselves. We seldom paid anyone to do things for us. The first summer in the Brangle Roadhouse was 1959. I wanted to raise a garden and we were going to freeze vegetables to last a year. We had bought a 15 sq. ft. chest type freezer and had shoehorned it onto the back porch. One of the first items we bought to stock the freezer was a large selection of beef. I think we bought a side of beef cut, frozen and labeled. This turned out to be a great bargain. We did learn some things from the exercise though. We found that we preferred beef of the hind quarter of beef. I did not particularly care for Chuck roast and other front quarter cuts. We had one bad experience with the company we bought meat from. This happened on the second or third purchase we made from them the first steak we cooked from that delivery was tasteless. In fact, it tasted like cardboard. I called the provider and told him we were very unhappy with the meat. He said do not eat any more of it. I will be there in 2 days with a new order. He was as good as his word. Two days later he brought us a full replacement order and he then explained what he thought had happened. It was winter and he said his beef came from Colorado. He said he thinks that a car with his meat was held up by snow along the way and the shipper let the meat

partially thaw out. When they hooked the car
back into a train, he said the meat was refrozen.
He said the shipper was replacing his shipment
and as he identified his customers affected, he
was replacing their orders. You could not ask for
more than that.

While discussing Beef I should mention that
when I was living in this house with my parents
the only beef that was served was pot roast or
some thin steak cut without a name that my
mother beat with a hammer kind of a thing to
tenderize it before cooking. When we started to
buy beef in quantity we learned of the very good
cuts of beef. We found recipes for preparing beef
and the use of a charcoal grill and I never ate
poor quality beef again. Good beef and other
meats were available at reasonable prices, you
just had to search for them.

Gentleman Farmer

I needed some type of tractor to cultivate my garden of 1 acre. I looked for something used to keep costs low. I found a used Troy Built rotary cultivator. This type of cultivator was just becoming popular. This model was unique. Most to the rotary cultivators had the rotor on the front and as the rotor turned in a forward motion it pulled the cultivator along. This was a simple setup, but it had limitations. If the ground was hard the rotor would sometimes pull the whole rig ahead faster than the rotor could penetrate the hard ground and you did not do a proper job of cultivating the dirt. The Troy Built was more sophisticated. It had a pair of pneumatic tires and wheels in front of the motor. These wheels were about 12 inches in diameter and 4 inches wide, with aggressive tread on the tires. The wheels were driven by a transmission and hand operated clutch. Behind the motor was a large multi tine rotor that could be engaged or disengaged with a leaver. The advantage of this setup was that you could disengage the rotor tines and drive the unit on the front wheels with the tines freewheeling. This was good for moving the rig around the yard and garden. The good thing about this setup for cultivating was the rotor tines could not push the rig any faster than you let the drive wheels operate. This allowed the rotor to properly till the ground. Whether the ground was hard or pliable. What I liked about the cultivator was that to my eyes I was looking at the beginning of a small tractor. I bought the Troy Built and then I welded an extension over the Tines in the rear and added a pair of dolly wheels under the extension to support the weight of a rider. I could now cultivate in comfort. I could also disengage the Tines and use the Troy Built as a small tractor. It looked crude but I could ride up and down the rows of potatoes, peas and green bush beans. And by removing the tines from the rotor I could cultivate between the rows. Before anything was planted, I could cultivate the complete garden. It worked well.

Back At Work

The cable trouble crews had a lot of overtime work. The problem was it was almost all 'Blood Money.' We did not 'Shoot Troubles 'in weather that had Lightning associated with it. It would have been too dangerous. But rain. wind, snow and cold did not qualify as a game changer. The worst jobs were troubles that affected large numbers of customers and the location of the cable fault was difficult to pinpoint. Once a cable fault was located it was just a matter of how fast you could replace a section of cable or repair the faulty cable. This was usually obvious too even a 2nd level manager who had 'God'(3rd level) glaring down mercilessly on him. The bad troubles were ones that clearly fell into a cable section that was buried but not in conduit, and the conductors could not be 'Broken-down' to a dead short. That would have allowed us to say 'dig here 'with confidence. The moisture might be such that it causes a lot of noise on the cable pairs and makes conversation nearly impossible but for whatever reason would not carry enough current thru the faulty insulation to melt the 2 conductors together. Sometimes we would desperately pressurize the section from each end and dig a hole in the middle and uncover the cable, open it up and attempt to go in either direction from the opening with resistant readings or gas pressure readings. Of course, this was almost always during downpours. What would happen was we would end up doing 'Binary Searches 'for the fault by digging a new hole in the middle of a section and testing. These troubles only came along once in a great while, otherwise we would have all quit. The craft were somewhat isolated from the insane part of the pressure coming down from higher managers who in many cases could have never qualified to locate and outhouse, let alone a cable trouble! The 2nd and 1 st level guys took the heat, and there was nothing we craft could do except continue to use tried and true methods that took time. It was not until I was a higher manager later in my career that I learned how to deal with these incompetent managers.

On The Lighter Side

I enjoyed the camaraderie of the Splicers and the Test Men in the central offices. We were a team. One thing we had in common was 'Pitch'. Pitch was a card game I learned from my parents. It seemed that all telephone people played Pitch and loved it. Some people call the game 'High, Low, Jack and Game'. This would refer to the 4 Game Points the player sought to accumulate. This game was played on rainy days in the sweaty confines of the Line Crew trucks, In the central offices and at the annual construction parties. Splicers would leave a job and drive 20 minuets to get to a Central Office where a continual lunchtime game was played. Someone in the central office keep a list of participants and a running score sheet showing the amount owed or the amount due you on a weekly basis. All for a penny a point. You had to be there on Friday to pay or collect. Big money, you might owe .60 cents or be paid $1.10. This passion usually resulted in lunch periods of 1.5 hours total with travel rather than 1 hour. But we never took breaks. And we worked hard when it mattered.

Chicken Coop and Shade Tree Mechanic Endeavors

On the home front I was doing a lot of work for friends on cars. I did not race anymore. But I did work on Race cars. My neighbor, Wayne Arrington was in my younger brother Donald's, high school class and as a result we did not Pal around together when we were in High School. But that sort of segregation slipped away when common interests became more important than what grade you were in at school. As a result Wayne and I worked on his cars from time to time to increase their performance. One such endeavor involved his 1959 Pontiac Tri-Power car. Wayne had previously owned a respectably quick 220 HP Chevy Bel Air hardtop. He told me that the Pontiac was 'Bogging 'coming off the line. I looked at the 3-carburetor setup on the engine and was not impressed at all with the factory provided linkage. The center carb which the car started on and ran on at light throttle was equipped with an accelerator pump. The 2 'end ' carbs did't have pumps. Their throttle was controlled with Springs, mirrors, and vacuum diaphragms. I suggested to Wayne that we design and build a mechanical, progressive linkage system. Wayne agreed and we started

scrounging up parts and scrap metal. The setup
we dreamed up was one that allowed the driver to
bring the front and back carb from a closed
butterfly position to fully open at a rate that
delivered the fuel as the motor needed it but not
so much that it 'Flooded 'the motor with fuel or
just as important it did not 'starve 'the engine of
fuel. It took some trial-and-error adjustments on
back roads to 'tweak 'the linkage, but once that
was accomplished the system was solid and
consistent.

The Blue Bird

I worked on other automotive projects as the need arose. Bob Bruce my longtime friend said he had found a nice 1953 Plymouth sedan that was cheap. The main reason was that the motor was shot. The car also needed a paint job. I told Bob that we could do both of those things if he would help with the work. Of course, he agreed. We pushed the car up on my ramp and removed the motor. We disassembled the motor and made up a parts list. We drove to Parts Wholesale, the Chrysler Corp., which included Plymouth, parts dealer in Baltimore and purchased the parts needed for the job. During the disassembly of the engine, I was working by myself, and I dropped the flywheel on my foot. It hurt like hell! I set down in the house and Arlene and I removed my shoe and sock and examined the foot. The big toe suffered the main impact and it looked bruised but there was no blood. I put ice on the foot and that was that. Rebuilding the engine which was an evening and weekend job took 2 weeks. When I was reassembling the engine, I managed to drop the flywheel on the same damm foot. This time it really hurt! I went to see Dr Gau and He Fluoroscope the foot. This was done with a machine in his office that worked somewhat like an Xray. When he looked at the image on the screen, he said there is an old break in the toe, but you did not break it today. I asked the obvious question to him, "How old does the 'old 'break look" Dr. Gau said "I would say that it was broke recently, maybe a couple weeks ago". I laughed and said Well it hurt more this time and I told him about dropping the Flywheel on the same toe twice. He suggested that I have someone help me lift heavy and awkward items to minimize injury. After the engine was running smoothly, we tackled the paint job. The body was straight. No parking lot dings. The only problem was that the paint was wore through. We decided to give the car a good sanding and mask up the trim and wait for a windless day to paint the car. We did not have a building or paint booth to paint in. We had to hope for a good wind and bug free day. We had decided to use lacquer instead of enamel, since the lacquer dries faster and would have less exposure to dirt and bugs. I had very little knowable about car painting. But I had a compressor and a paint gun and hose. I probably could have done a nice job on a house or barn, but the car paint job was less than perfect. We were able to get a nice Saturday with no breeze and few bugs. The car was wiped clean, and I sprayed it. It looked great wet. But the result is measured when the paint dries. The finish was very clean and bug free. I would label it a 10-to-15-foot paint job. The car looked fine at that distance. As you got closer the finish appeared dull. I did not find out until several years later that you were supposed to sand and rub out the paint after it dried. Well Bob was happy. The car ran well and looked much better than it did when he bought it.

Arlene's Wheels

Occasionally, I was assigned to help a different splicer in the trouble crews, and I got along well with all of them. I was not looking to any kind of a future with C&P other than promotion to splicer so I could advance to top pay for splicer. I had no aspirations of promotion to management. I was just trying to earn a decent living for my family. During the late spring of 1959 one of the splicers that I had helped when I was in Seiglers construction crew, Al Fielder approached me and said he was planning on buying a new car. Al was a good guy, very knowledgeable and pleasant. He continued his conversation about his plan to buy a Renault or some other European car. He was presently driving a 1952 Dodge Coronet 4 door sedan. Al had owned the Dodge since it was new. He had taken very good care of the vehicle. He asked me if I was interested in buying the Dodge since he did not get a good offer on trading the Dodge for the Renault. I said I was interested if the price was in my range. He said he wanted $200 for the Dodge. This car was a gift at that price. I told him I would take it. I said I needed a couple days to get the money. He agreed to give me the time to gather up the money. I knew we had around $100 stashed for emergencies, but I needed to find another $100 quickly. I turned to my parents who were always willing to help Arlene and me. They lent me $100, and we became owners of a very nice automobile. One thing that I liked about the Dodge was that it had the Gyromatic transmission. I wanted Arlene to get her driver's license, but she was having trouble with the manual transmission. Since she would be driving with 3 kids in the car, I did not want her attention focused on gear shifting more than child control while driving. The Dodge was in very clean condition and even though we had 3 kids they did not get to eat in and trash any car they were riding in. As soon as I got the Dodge, I had Arlene adjust the driver's seat and start driving around in the large field that belonged to my grandfather and bordered our lot. There were no holes to drop a wheel in, no trees or cars or buildings to run into. It was a perfect location for driving practice. The beauty of the Gyromatic was you could push in the clutch and start the engine. You could pull the gear shift on the steering column down into the 2nd and 3rd position and hold the break and let the clutch out. The engine would not stall! There was a Fluid Drive converter that let the engine run without stalling when in gear. She could release the brake step on the gas and the car would move forward. If she was on the road, after the car reached a speed of 25 or 30 MPH, she could lift her foot off of the gas and the transmission would shift into high gear. She could step on the gas and proceed. Arlene had no problem getting her driver's license. Parallel parking was another subject. The Dodge was our primary transportation for around 3 years. After we bought the Dodge, I started looking for an inexpensive beater for me to drive to work. My father was driving a 1951 Plymouth Business coupe. He liked it very much. This body style was popular in the 1940's and '50's. The car only had a front seat. Behind the seat was a large space in back to a bulkhead that extended down from the Package shelf to the floor. The trunk was massive because of the long trunk lid. These cars were built on the same wheelbase as the sedans. Salesmen and businessmen used this type of car in their line of work to carry product and samples. It was not very useful for a family since it only seated three people. Because of their limited usefulness they were less expensive to purchase than other cars. I found a 1950 Plymouth Business Coupe for $100 a few months later and purchased it for transportation to work.

I drove it for several years and we were a 2-car family!

Electric Ski Boat

The next boating adventure I remember was the Quest for a powered fishing boat for Bob Bruce to use on Liberty Lake.

Liberty Lake was built by the city of Baltimore on the North branch of the Patapsco River to hold drinking water for the city. Because of this they did not allow gasoline motors to be used on the lake. Bob told me that he would like to get an electric motor, which were acceptable, but they were expensive. So, the farmer in me came out and I told Bob we ought to make an electric motor. Bob asked how we would do that, and I told him we needed a lower unit from an outboard motor to start with. Bob said he had an old lower unit from a 2 or 3 HP motor. The unit had a shaft sticking out the top of the housing where the gas motor was previously attached. When you rotated the shaft the propeller rotated, we were in business! I thought all we needed to do was to mount an electric starter motor on the top of the housing vertically and mate the motor shaft to the lower unit shaft and you have an outboard motor. The easiest starter motor to get back then and maybe even today would be off a Ford V8. There were millions of them made and a lot of them were for sale in junk yards! We got a starter motor that looked to be in good condition, then we found a piece of 1/4 "Aluminium large enough to make a plate to cover the top of the outboard housing and larger in diameter than the starter motor. We drilled a hole in the plate large enough for the drive shaft to protrude thru then we drilled 2 holes in the plate to match the 2 threaded holes in the top of the housing. We now cut a 1/4" slot vertically down in the lower unit shaft. Then we cut the lower unit shaft off so that it was just long enough to allow 3/4 inch of the vertically mounted motor shaft to slip into the top of the outboard housing and insert in the slot we had cut in the driveshaft. Then we cut the sides of the electric motor shaft to a width that fit in the slot of the driveshaft and when it was all bolted together the starter motor would rotate and drive the shaft in the lower unit that rotated the propeller shaft. The propeller looked like it would move a decent amount of water when spinning at the speed that I thought the hefty starter motor would operate at. These starter motors were series wound and would continue to increase their rotational speed if they were not limited by the load on the shaft. The spinning propeller did not put the motor under enough load to limit the motors speed, so when the motor sounded like it was going to throw itself apart the operator had to disconnect the battery cable and let the motor slow down a bit. Then we figured out the wiring arrangement. Most cars were 6-volt positive ground back then, so we had found a 6-volt starter motor and we needed at least 2, 6-volt batteries. One battery to go out fishing and one to bring you back. We had no idea how much power this arrangement would use so it would be trial and error. We planned to pull amps from the battery until the motor slowed noticeably, then turn the boat toward the dock and switch batteries.

We felt that there was a need to blow cooling air down through the starter motor to cool it. We came up with a 4 bladed cooling fan about 5 inches in diameter, off a refrigerator. The end of the starter that would have been hanging out in the air stream when the starter was bolted to a V 8 motor now faced up. We removed that upper end cap and made some alterations to it. First, we drilled some holes in the cap from the underside. This way we avoided damaging the brushes and springs connected to the inside of the cap. Next we drilled a 1/4" inch hole in the canter of the bearing boss that protruded up from the cap surface. We drilled and tapped a 3/16" inch hole into the end of the motor shaft and then screwed a stud into the hole in the shaft. After that cap was placed back on the motor, we bolted the fan blade to the upper end of the motor shaft, and it blew air down through the plate holes on top of the motor. Great care needed to be taken so as not to get entangled in the rotating fan! To hookup the power we connected one lead from the motor housing to the positive battery terminal. The negative lead was connected to the power lug on the motor and that lead had a battery terminal that fit the negative battery terminal. To start the motor, you pushed the negative lead on to the battery terminal and let her rip. Bob had a heavy wooden rowboat that he fished from and that was our target test boat. We put the motor on the boat and put the 2 batteries in the boat and hooked up the ground side (+) of the circuit from the first battery to the motor frame. We pushed the negative lead down on the battery cable terminal then you hung on. We rowed the boat a short way from the dock then connected the battery. We were not prepared for the thrust that this motor delivered! The stern of the boat sunk down, the bow came up and we were off to the races! A couple of people around the docks thought for sure that we had a gasoline motor, from our speed they might have thought that we were preparing to Water Ski. But there was no exhaust noise. We raced away from the dock probably reaching 8 or 9 miles per hour. Great care had to be taken so no one got any clothing or body parts near the fan that was rotating on the top of the motor and blowing air down thru the inerts of the starter motor. These motors were not designed for continuous duty. After running the motor for several minutes, it was necessary to disconnect the battery cable and fish for a while letting the motor cool down. When the motor was running the boat covered a considerable distance in a short time. Bob used the motor for several years of fishing and I went on to other projects.

Life On the Homestead
And A Honeymoon

Life was moving along nicely for Arlene and I
in 1959. She was picking up a little extra money
from sewing. In addition to sewing curtains, she
did some alteration of clothes. Of course, we
were freezing vegetables from our garden. We
also bought large quantities at roadside farm
stands and froze them. Jeff was 2 years, 3
months old. He had a birth related problem with
a neck muscle that prevented him from turning
his head to one side. This was corrected by an
operation in the hospital. He had no problem
with it after the operation. He was very active
and loved playing in the yard. The twins,
Yvonne and Cheryl were 1 and year old. They
were a hand full, but well behaved. We seldom
had to smack their bottoms but would give them
an attention getter if required. We did not eat in
restaurants often, but when we did take them to a
restaurant, they conducted themselves like
grown-ups. Quite often customers at the
restaurants would approach our table and
compliment Arlene and I on the good behavior of
our children.

I made the mistake of feeding them Shrimp
when you could purchase frozen Shrimp for

$2.00/ 5 lbs. Sirloin steak was $1.00/ lb. The kids loved it. As time went on these food items kept getting more and more expensive. Once the kids had a taste for these foods, I could not tell them that they were only for grown-ups. We cut back on other items but not food. I remember that my mother always served real butter, never Oleo Margarine.   Even during the War, she was able to get home made butter from my grandfather's farm.

I told Arlene I would always find a way to purchase real butter for the table. That promise has held for 65 years. As the summer of 1959 moved along I suggested to Arlene that we ask our parents to watch the children for a week so that we could take a driving vacation. This would be a belated honeymoon. The parents split the week up and took turns watching them at our house since all their toys, clothes and paraphernalia were there. I figured that we now had a vehicle that we could drive for a long-distance trouble free. We left our home and drove to Fredrick, Maryland then across the Potomac to Harpers Ferry, West Virginia and then southeast thru the Shenandoah Valley to Tennessee. We stayed at inexpensive motels and made our way to Gatlinburg, Tennessee. I remember the motel room we stayed in at

Gatlinburg. There was a large window in the
back of the room that looked out on a stream.
There was a fur rug on the floor. There was a
fireplace in the corner. We had never stayed in
any room as nice as this in our lives.

I often wonder if the appearance of our
daughter Deanna Renee 9 months later was in
anyway related to that wonderful room in the
mountains of Tennessee. We both took our first
helicopter ride in a small sightseeing helicopter at
Gatlinburg. The town was quaint but not the
Tourist Trap it is today, sorry Dolly. That was as
far south as we drove. We then started back
north. We left Tennessee and drove into
Virginia, then into Kentucky. We drove along
the border of Kentucky and Virginia, then
crossed into West Virginia. This was true
Appalachia. There were no Interstate Highways
in that time frame. The roads were 2 lane black
top, twisting and turning. There was a lot of
poverty along the way. Houses backed up against
steep hillsides with the front porches nearly in the
road. 10 wheeled dump trucks parked beside of,
or across the road from a lot of the houses. These
were trucks that hauled coal from the mines to
railheads or other transportation junctions.
Passing these trucks loaded with coal on the
narrow roads was breathtaking. The best homes

in these little towns seemed to be the Funeral Homes. That was one business that was constant through good times and poor times. I had worked with a guy from this part of the country at the mental hospital and I remembered some of his sayings as I looked at the passing scene. You would see several dogs laying under the front porch of one of these houses and they were facing in different directions. One might be facing towards the house and his hind end would be toward the road. Others would be looking towards the road. I could picture the warm sun on the dog's butt on a cool day. Gene's saying about good and bad fortune was" The Sun don't Shine in the same dog's butt all the time". Most of these people lacked that sunshine on any day. In 1959 the part of West Virginia we drove thru must have been one of the poorest places in the US of A. But I know that these are some of the proudest people in the US of A. They split their mountains away from Virginia in 1861 and fought for the Union. They have been a sovereign state since 1863. We drove through Charleston and on to the roads leading back to Harpers Ferry and into Maryland. It was a very long and beautiful drive. The Dodge drove flawlessly for the complete trip. Cars did not get great gas mileage in the 1950s, but gas was relatively inexpensive, around .20 cents a gallon. The 230 cubic inch 6 cylinder got around 18 miles per gallon. But through the mountains we probably did not exceed 15 miles per gallon. The complete trip was no more than 2000 miles. That would have cost around $27 for gas for the trip.

We were glad to see the kids when we arrived home. We thanked our parents profusely and the kids were all over their mother. They gave me a few nods; Dads are not nearly as important as Mom. A funny thing that I think about was how we interacted as a family unit. I always referred to Arlene as 'Honey". Arlene always called me 'Honey". The kids started to call both of us Honey. The Twins were always a problem for me to identify from behind. They were not identical twins. Identical twins are created when the woman's egg is fertilized and then splits in two and the two embryos grow into two identical children. Should the woman ovulate two eggs and both become fertilized the twins are considered Fraternal twins. This type of twin is no different from 2 children from the same parents who are born 2 or 3 years apart. The fact that our fraternal twins look so much alike is just like in many families the children look very much alike. My problem was that the twins always dressed alike, were the same height and weight and their hair was the same color. I could look at their face and tell them apart, but not from behind. When they were teenagers and Renee had entered the scene, it was very frustrating. Renee was a little taller for her age and as a result she was the same height as the twins. Of course, all her other features were the same as the twins. I would walk into a room and one of the 3 girls would have her back to me and I would address her with a 'Cheryl, where is your mother? 'I would be upset when she did not answer me. I would try again, 'Yvonne, where is your mother? 'And she would turn and say She's in the back yard or whatever. I would ask her why you didn't answer me the first time I spoke. And The answer was always the same from all 3 of them, "You didn't address me". I would be ready to scream. Sometimes I would go through all 3 names before I got the correct girl.

We had a washing machine for laundry for the first 3 years we lived on Brangle Road, But Arlene did not have a clothes dryer. All wash was hung on 109 open wire lines strung between 2 poles on short cross arms in the back yard. Summer and winter, the clothes were hung and froze if it was cold, but when they thawed out, they would be dry. Doing laundry was hard work. We were fortunate to have my aunt Elaine living next door to us. Elaine was my uncle Arstelo's (Arse) wife. 3 of their children were grown, but the youngest, Debby lived at home. Debby was around 7 years old. Debby played with our kids. They had scuffles and disagreements, but it was just kids' stuff.

Aunt Elaine was a guardian angel to Arlene. She often said, "I don't know how she takes care of all those children". When I looked at Aunt Elaine, I saw the hardest working woman in my world. She 'Farmed 'a large garden, helped many of the neighbors, mowed the lawn, canned vegetables, raised chickens and took care of my often-inebriated uncle. I liked Arse, he was my hunting and outdoor buddy, but I loved Aunt Elaine for her care and concern for Arlene, the children and me. Many a bitter cold day she would enter our porch with her arms full of frozen laundry she had removed from the clothesline. She would say, these will be dry when they thaw out. And she was right, As the clothes thawed the moisture evaporated.

The Eternal Quest For A Boat

After our vacation I went back to work with Vince. We closed trouble openings that had been left with a temporary CR tape cover after a wet spot had been repaired. We dammed old "F" type cable terminals and repaired miscellaneous cracks and leaks in old lead cables. This was like trying to stop the flow of the Potomac River with a digging shovel. But one thing that always gave us a laugh was the thought that," It all paid the same". If that was what the bosses wanted us to work on, that was what we would work on. If the paycheck was equal to or higher than what it would be if we were doing work, we thought was more beneficial to the business.

I was continually looking for interesting projects to work on. Somehow Bob Bruce and I came across an external fuel tank for a jet fighter plane. It was made in 2 pieces, each half being like a half of a watermelon. The tank which we were told was from an F-80 fighter jet was about 24" in diameter at the widest point, and about 4 feet from the rounded front, the tank tapered back to about 10-inch diameter at the back. The overall length of the tank was around 10 feet. We drilled out the rivets that held the 2 halves' together and set the 2 halves on the ground with the open side facing up and the widest part of each half overlapping and decided that this looked like a catamaran! Bob and I bolted the 2 halves' together then bolted pieces of 2 by 3/4" fir across the top of the hull about 2 feet apart from front to back. We knew we would have to deck this boat over because it would not have a lot of "freeboard" that is, the distance from the deck of the boat to the surface of the water. We knew we needed more strength to hold the 2 hulls rigid, so we bolted 2X4's across the hulls at the bow and about 4 foot back from the bow and another 4 foot farther back. That aft most beam later became the point where we mounted the 3 HP gas motor we used to power the boat. We decked the boat over with canvas fixed to the gunnels by wrapping the edge of the canvas around 1/2" by 1/8" aluminum strips that we screwed to the lips of the tanks. A piece of 1" X 2" fir was arched from the 2 outer gunnels to a height of 10" at the center of the boat and supported by a 10" high 2"X 2" mounted vertically on the 2X4 across the center of the boat. All of this was covered with canvas and painted like they did airplanes in the early years of aviation. One of my aunts had an old 3 hp Sears Outboard motor that did not run, and she said that I could use it for a couple of months if I could get it running. Since I had been working on engines since I was 10 years old, I did not consider it a challenge to get that 2-cycle motor running. It was a good choice of motor for this boat because of its light weight and low fuel consumption. Bob and I had not considered any kind of computation to determine the load carrying capacity of this boat. It would be just to say," yea, looks like 2 people can set in it, probably will float them and some gas and fishing gear". One consideration that our total lack of marine knowledge let slip past us was what would happen to the water trapped between the 2 hulls as they created a funnel that became closer and closer toward the center of the boat? Well, for one thing it slowed the boat and tended to lift the bow significantly which forced the aft part of the boat down into the water and endangered the aft of the boat to take on water. We had to operate the boat at a slow speed or quickly sink the boat! The first and only sea trial of the boat in our ownership was on the Potomac River near the place where the Monocracy empties into the Potomac in Fredrick County. Bob and I loaded up the boat, life jackets, gas, motor, oars and other gear we thought would be required and drove over to the launching site with the boat. The Potomac is big water at that point and the wind was blowing about 10 ,12 MPH. There were small waves on the water, but we were not deterred. We got the boat in the water, boarded the boat and set off on a learning experience. More water found its way into the boat than we had planned on, but we keep up with it. There were no leaks, but the freeboard was minimal, so any splashing around shipped water. We spend a half hour or so on the water and decided that we needed a larger boat! I don't remember what we did with that boat, but I know that I gave the motor back to my aunt. We had invested several weekends and possibly $100 dollars in this project. That was a lot of money for Bob and I at that stage of our lives, but it seemed like the right thing to do at the time. I came away from that endeavor with a strong desire to own a proper boat. I had no idea how important boats would become in my future life. The fall of 1959 came and went. We had a great Christmas with the kids and our parents. Since these 3 children were the first grandchildren for either of our parents, they were ecstatic. Any disappointment by Arlene's parents over our marriage arrangements was never discussed. My father-in-law, Carl Burdette must have decided that his first impressions of me were not accurate, and our behavior was forgiven. It was not a subject that ever came up between them, Arlene and me. Many years later when Arlene's mother was widowed and in her 70's I apologized to her for running off with her daughter and depriving her of the opportunity to plan and attend her daughter's wedding. She accepted my apology and said not to be concerned with it.

The Final Piece of The Family Baker

As 1960 moved along Arlene was doing very well with her 3rd pregnancy and looking forward to a child in May. We visited Dr. Gau in late April and he said the baby was late. He said if it did not come in the next week or so he would have to induce labor. Well, the baby did not show any interest in joining us or the outside world, so Dr. Gau asked us what day next week did we want to have the baby? We picked a date and he said that he would advise us on the arrangements at University Hospital in Baltimore. That was the same hospital where the Twins were born. I told Arlene that I did not want to give up a vacation day to set in a waiting room at the hospital. We asked Arlene's mother to take her to the hospital and she agreed. I only received 2 weeks of vacation at that time, and we wanted to keep it for time together. Considering the general attitude of people in that era this was not as unreasonable as it might be in todays 'Touchy Feely 'environment. So, on the 4 th of May 1960, Deanna Renee Baker made her appearance, and the nucleus of the Baker family was complete. I was 24 years old at that time. Arlene was 22 years old, and Jeff was 3 years and 1 months old when Renee was born. The Twins were 1 year and 11 months old at the time of Renee's birth. The 3 older children were walking and quite ready for another plaything. Renee was mothered by Arlene and all the kids with a little help from me.

A True, Life Changing Decision

I was OK with my job at C&P but would have liked to work closer to home. I was also concerned about the limitation on my salary by not having an opportunity to advance to splicer. I was not looking for a different job or employer, but I was open to suggestions.

In late October of 1960, one of the helpers in Bob Seiglers crew asked me if I had seen the letter from AT&T asking for volunteers who would like to transfer too AT&T to work at a location they were building at Monrovia, Maryland. I said no I had not seen the letter. He said he would get a copy from his boss, Bob Seigler for me. When I saw the letter, I was a little bit pissed, but I understood what I was dealing with. The total culture at C&P was one of holding people in their jobs if they were doing a good job. This helped to assure the immediate boss that his job was secure because he had good people in all his work positions. The thought of training and developing people was the farthest thing from their mind. I talked to Vince about what I should do. I needed to get permission from our boss, Ralph Warehime to apply for a transfer. Vince said I should ask Ralph about the letter in our morning meeting so he would have to explain why he did not tell anyone in his crew about the job opportunity. We both agreed that it would corner him, and he would get even with me if I failed to be accepted by AT&T. I thought the job opportunity was worth the risk. So, the next morning I spoke out and asked Ralph if there was a letter requesting volunteers for transfer to AT&T. Ralph was clearly upset with this discussion. He quickly responded that he did not think that anyone would be interested. I pressed on and said, "You know that I live halfway between here and Monrovia and there is no immediate splicer opportunities here at C&P. I think I would like to see the letter". This was like a Death Wish. Everyone was quiet for what seemed like an hour but was less than 1 minute. Ralph opened his desk drawer and pulled out the letter and pushed it at me. I carefully accepted the letter from him and thanked him like a real gentleman. The look that accompanied the hand off the letter said everything I needed to know. If I did not get this job with AT&T my future here was Toast! As soon as the meeting was over, I slipped out of Ralph's office and went to the back of the garage where there was a phone for the Move Truck driver to call the District office from. No one was using the phone, so I called the number on the letter and almost immediately there was an Answer. "Hello, this is Art Douvaul, can I help you ?". That was the name of the guy who signed the letter. This was good. I said," Mr Douvaul, my name is Ralph Baker and I'am a splicers helper at the C&P garage in North Baltimore. I just saw you letter a few minutes ago. I am very interested in your job. Art said, "that letter was sent a month ago". He then said I'am not surprised that it was not shown to you, I have heard that from several C&P employees. He asked me about my experience, where I lived and said he would like to arrange for me to come into the AT&T office at 320 St Paul Street for an interview. I gave him the District Office phone number and my home phone number. I said if you leave a message at the District Office and do not hear from me in 2 days at the most, please call me at home in the evening.

He said he understood and would be in touch. About a week later Vince and I were working in a steam tunnel under Union Memorial Hospital in the late morning when a helper from one of Ralph's other crews walked down the tunnel and said that Ralph had sent a message to me. I was supposed to meet a "Guy" from AT&T at 320 at 1:00PM. I thanked him and Vince and I both said the same thing at the same time, "That A —hole,

Warehime" We knew that he had set on that
message until the last minute. Probably hoping
that I would miss the interview or at least I would
be going there hot and sweaty. We wrapped up
the job and Vince said, "You know what, I am
going to drive you down to 320 in the splicing
truck. "I can park in the truck space, and "I will
come into the lobby with you". You will be there
on time. We did not know that when I got there,
there would be a test in addition to an interview.
The procedure would last a couple hours. Vince
was so upset with Warehime that he did not care
if we were 6:00 PM returning to the garage. I
entered the building lobby and asked the guard
what floor Mr. Douvaul with AT&T was located
on. I showed him my C&P pass which would
allow me entry to any C&P building in the state.
C&P owned the 320 St Paul Street building and
leased different floors to AT&T's Long Lines
Department. Long Lines connected the local
customers of C&P to the world beyond C&P's
limited territory. Long Lines was a name I had
never heard until this job opportunity presented
itself. The Bell System was created in the 1880s.
Early business associates of Alexander Bell
realized that the telephone became more valuable
with every new customer. They called the
concept of providing phones for as many people

as possible "Universal Service". The Long Lines Department was created in the 1880s to interconnect the franchised companies of the Bell System to farther the usefulness of the telephone. Before the Bell System was broken up as the result of an antitrust suit in 1984, it's one million employees made it the second largest employer in the United States. Only the US Government had more employees. The Long Lines Department had around 20,000 employees. I stepped off the elevator on the floor used by Long Lines and was faced with a room with 16-foot ceilings, and equipment frames and cable neatly organized on racks. There were several desks in the middle of the equipment with suited men sitting there.

There was a long test board containing jacks to plug test cords into. In front of the boards full of jacks were test desks with Test men talking on telephone headsets and plugging and unplugging test cords as they talked with some unseen person in a distant city. I noticed that all of the Test men wore collared shirts and neck ties. I liked this place already. I walked to the closest desk and asked for Mr. Art Douvaul. The gentleman stood and introduced himself as Bob Denny, the Chief Test Board Man and said that Art was using one of his conference rooms for testing and interviews. He said he would walk me to the room, and I followed him. As we were walking, different people spoke to Mr. Denny with respect, and I realized that he was the second level manager of this complete operation. What a difference there was between this company and C&P. The second levels at C&P acted like God. This manager clearly was respected but down to earth and liked! I was introduced to Mr. Douvaul who immediately told me to call him Art. He got right down to business. He said that Long Lines was building several buildings around the US to provide a new communication system for the US government. That was all he could tell me about the work at this time. He did ask me if I had a police record, or any felonies charged against me. I was taken aback with this question, but Art cleared my surprise up quickly by saying that I would have to be issued a security clearance by the Air Force. I told him I thought I was good on that count. Art said that he was in a hurry to get the last of his work force selected because there were a lot of schools and training that they had to attend before they could accept the Central Office equipment from Western Electric, the primary installer for AT&T. He told me that the first thing he needed to do was have me take a pre employment test. After that we would talk farther. Art produced a test and pencil and set me in a corner of the large conference room and told me to start the test. But not to refer to any notes or aids. The test took me over an hour to complete. When I was finished, I gave it to Art and sat there while he checked my work and answers. Several of the questions asked me to draw common electrical circuits such as a "doorbell "circuit and a "two switch light" circuit. There was a math section with algebra and geometry, some electrical laws like Ohms law. After Art finished grading my test he said, "You got 100 on the test". "I don't see many hundreds". He asked me why I wanted this job. I said that the main reason was that I was limited in my pay grade. If I was not promoted because the economy was poor, I would not progress to top craft wages. I said I would also like to work some place closer to my home and have an easier drive, no city traffic. I said now that I've talked to you about the job, I realize that this job would provide me with educational benefits. I said C&P has only sent me to one school in 5 years, a 4-day lineman school. We wrapped up the interview on a good note. Art said he had to talk to C&P before he could make any job offers but he would get back to me in a few days. I thanked him and left. I met Vince in the lobby, and we drove back to the garage. It was after quitting time when we got back there, and we got in his car and went home. Vince and I carpooled and since I had no advance warning of the interview, I had not drove by myself that day. The best part of the whole day was screwing up Warehime's plan to make me miss the interview.

Like Starting Life All Over

Warehime found out that I was accepted by
AT&T before Art got back to me. Art had talked
to my District Manager, and he had said it would
be fine with C&P if I wanted to transfer to
AT&T. I realized later that the middle and higher
managers at C&P were intimidated by the
thought of doing anything that would upset
AT&T. There was no good reason for this
attitude except that they were thinking about how
they would act if the shoe was on the other foot!
I was called by Art a day later and officially
offered the job. I was to finish out the week with
C&P then come on AT&T's payroll on the
following Monday. Art said that all my time with
C&P would be transferred, and my seniority
would be bridged. He wanted me to start school
on Monday.

I said O.K. Where? Art said the class is in
Washington. You are to report to Mr. Denny, the
Chief Test Board man in Baltimore at the 17C
board at 8:00 AM. That was the fellow that you
met last week. Bring one week's clothing and
have someone drive you to 320. Mr. Denny will
give you an advance of $50 and you can take a
cab to Penn station and catch the next train to

Union Station in Washington. When you get to Washington, take a cab to this address, The class will already be in session, but you won't miss much. You will be staying at the Ambassador Hotel. We ask 2 men to share a room. You are allowed $5.00 a day for meals. The hotel bill is paid by the class instructors. The instructors will tell you what other expenses will be allowed. You will be there for 6 weeks, but you can come home each weekend. Take the train back to Baltimore and have someone pick you up at the station. The following week you will probably want to drive to Washington. Parking at the hotel is cheap. When I left C&P I took everything that had been issued to me. Warehime never said anything to me. I said goodbye to the guys that I was close to. They wished me well and asked that I keep them informed on my new job. I told all of them that I would stay in touch thru Vince. I took my Rain gear, my tool belt and personal tools and pole climbers, (Hooks) and my C&P pass! No one asked for it! If anyone had questioned me about the rain gear and tools, I was going to tell them that AT&T told me I would need them! I knew no one was going to say anything because the supervisors were truly afraid of AT&T. There was no reason to be, but they were. I saw the same level of concern many times over during the next 25 years.

Arlene and I had piled the kids in the car and had driven to Monrovia on the weekend before I went for the interview. I wanted to see where the site was and what it looked like. The drive was 25 miles from my house, but it was an easy traffic free drive. Most of the drive was on US route 40 a duel hi way. The site was rather inconspicuous. There was a large parking lot, some construction equipment parked here and there. And a very tall microwave tower. The tower must have been 200 feet high. It had Cornucopia antennas on the top facing in 2 directions and 2 pairs at lower locations on the tower facing in 2 different directions. There was a small building about 25-foot square in the middle of the site but closer to the road than the other side of the property. I wondered how much building was under this site and how deep was it buried? The site was just down the road from Urbana Maryland, the location of a famous local restaurant, The Peter Pan. With our reconnoitering complete we returned home.

My trip to Washington on Monday went exactly as planned. When I entered the classroom one of the 2 instructors introduced everyone and said we have been expecting you but did't think you would be able to get here as quick as you did. I said Well the train was on time, but I think I'll drive the next time. That got a few chuckles. The first week was a refresher class on mathematics called A1 class. The instructors, Burt Gunderson a tall distinguished looking man and a fellow that looked like a college professor complete with a pocket protector full of pens and other gadgets. He had unruly salt and pepper hair and it turned out that he was extremely knowledgeable of electricity, electronics, telephony, and the world in general. Bert was smart also. It turned out that these instructors were both central office supervisors from the Washington Long Lines office. My god, C&P did not have people this smart in the whole company. And these guys were just first line supervisors. Well, it turned out that most of the 15 students were Monrovia bound people. A couple of them were from the Washington test room. I found out that 5 craft were accepted as transferees to AT&T. They were all in this class. After the A1 math review week, we would have 5 weeks of Basic Electricity. We were going to get these 6 weeks in before the Christmas holidays. That would get us out of Washington by the end of the third week in December. I was to report to the Baltimore 17 C board until the end of

December and the first week of January 1961. I would then return to Washington for 5 weeks of Basic Electronics. After that Art would decide, with input from his first line supervisors, which of his craft would be assigned to Radio and Carrier and which would be assigned to # 5 Crossbar Switching. The Radio and Carrier craft would maintain high frequency carrier transmission equipment on coaxial cable and carrier on Microwave radio. There were schools for all these equipment disciplines. I was excited about the possibility of getting into Radio and Carrier. The #5 Crossbar Switching required attending a 9-month school on #5 Xbar. Location unknown!

The math review week was difficult but enlightening. I realized that several the people in the class had a distinct edge on me. Some had 2-year AA degrees. One or two had trade school degrees from schools like DeVry in Chicago. This level of math was child's play for them. I had to work to remember or learn for the first time. The instructors were excellent. They made certain that no one was left behind. They knew that some students would do well in a formal learning environment and others would excel in the trenches of the real working world. They wanted all of the diverse talents working for the

Long Lines Department. The Math class was followed by 5 weeks of Basic Electricity. The class started with the History of man's knowledge of electricity. Then we studied the theory and practical aspects of Direct and Alternating current. We learned more about magnetism than I ever thought existed. I knew that electric motors operated on magnetic fundamentals, but I had little knowledge of the full involvement of magnetism and electricity. I think that was skimmed over very quickly and lightly in my country high school. I drove to Washington early after dismissal at 5:00 pm. The time went fast. I could hardly believe how lucky I was to have gotten this job. I finally began to feel like this was to be a lifetime career. Arlene held down the home front. It was very fortuitous that she had gotten her driver's license and had a dependable car. I returned home on 12/16/1960 for the holidays. One week before Christmas I reported to work at 320 St. Paul St. with a collared white shirt and a narrow dark tie. Mr. Denny teamed me with a young man on the 17 C board. The 17C test board was at least 80 feet long. Test positions, meaning a space the width of a chair had a flat level desktop with a row of vertical key/switches along the back. Behind each switch were 2 lights in a row then a pair of cords with male jacks on the ends. The jacks and associated cords were retracted into the hole in the desktop that the jack protruded from. When you pulled the jack out of the hole the cord would extend for several feet which allowed the test man to plug the cord into any of the rows of female jacks mounted to the face of the test board. The rows of female jacks represented circuits to distant cities. A row of 10 jacks would be labeled "York" these were the circuits to York, Pennsylvania. You could plug into anyone of them and with the key on your cord pulled back to the "Monitor" position you could listen to the circuit. This was done when trouble was suspected on the circuit. If you were talking to a Technician in York on another line you could both listen and test the circuit suspected to be in trouble. You were forbidden by Federal law from ever discussing anything you heard while testing a circuit. And you were prohibited from eavesdropping on any circuits except in the continuance of your job as a trouble "Shooter". Trouble reports came to the Test Men from distant test room's, from long distance operators, and from equipment maintenance men in your office. Trouble tickets were written for each work activity and were categorized as Cleared Out. Meaning no farther action required, or

Trouble Came Clear While Testing. Which
meant you would probably see this problem
again, so you might hold that ticket for a couple
days then test the circuit again. There was a lot
of opportunity for troubles in the old "Analog"
world we lived in at that time. Since most of the
communication in today's world is "Digital"
transmission there is no chance of experiencing
many of the troubles we experienced in the
Analog world. I enjoyed the couple of weeks on
the 17C board and my time with the family. With
the coming of 1961 I was moving into a
completely different world than I had lived in
before Art Douville said you are hired

Should good health and sufficient time allow I will relate the events, adventures, good times and challenges Arlene and I experienced in the 26 years I worked at AT&T Long Lines in a future document. Arlene and I are also writing about the 25 years spent living on and operating boats for ourselves and others after my retirement from AT&T.

R Otis Baker   2021

About the Author

Ralph Otis Baker started writing short stories for friends and family after his retirement. 'Shadow of the Great Depression' was written for his children and their children and anyone else too young to realize the challenges faced in day-to-day life as late as the middle of the last century. Ralph and his wife of 65 years Arlene, live in Martin County Florida